Literature and Sincerity

YALE ROMANIC STUDIES, SECOND SERIES 9

LITERATURE

AND

SINCERITY

by Henri Peyre

NEW HAVEN AND LONDON: YALE UNIVERSITY PRESS, 1963

PARIS: PRESSES UNIVERSITAIRES DE FRANCE

Acknowledgments

The author of a book like the present one, which must embrace a vast expanse of historical, literary, and artistic knowledge, and in which the very foundations of literature and criticism are questioned, owes much to the Library (in this case, the admirable Sterling Library of Yale University) where a good deal of the reading was done; to friends with whom the subject was occasionally discussed (Douglas Bush, Stanley Burnshaw, Frederick Hilles, Georges May, Leo Schrade); and to the two persons who, with exemplary diligence and a truly "sincere" devotion, helped with the manuscript: Mrs. Lise Giraud and Miss Lois Haegert.

It is a pleasure also to acknowledge the author's considerable debt to the Director and the staff of the Yale University Press, and in particular to Mr. Benjamin Houston, who offered many a helpful correction and suggestion on the manuscript.

H. P.

Contents

to a greater sincerity. Examples drawn from Novalis, Shelley, Lamartine.

The romantic claim that their sincerity endows them with a superior aesthetic and moral merit. Chateaubriand, Musset, Wordsworth "on epitaphs," Matthew Arnold, Taine.

The heritage of the romantics: the question asked by many of their successors will be: "Can one know and tell the full truth about oneself?" A glance at Goethe and Heine.

Some reaction against romantic exhibitionism: Tennyson. Browning's monologues. Leconte de Lisle and his advocacy of impersonality in art, Flaubert.

Baudelaire and his heart laid bare. Some of his contradictory critical pronouncements. Momentary weakening of the cult of sincerity with Mallarmé, Valéry, and some other poets. The enigma of Verlaine's "sincerity."

The paradox of being sincere while writing fiction. The first person singular in the novel of the nineteenth century: differences from earlier novels of adventure or of education (*Bildung*). German and French personal novels.

Chateaubriand's mixture of probing into himself and of posing for posterity. Sénancour and his "mal du siècle": *Obermann*.

Madame de Staël's novels. Madame de Duras. Constant's *Adolphe* and his unsuccessful lifelong attempt to love himself: he has several successive or simultaneous sincerities. Extreme sentimentality and dryness of heart coexisting. His oscillations. His revealing journal.

Other personal notes by Sainte-Beuve, Balzac, Stendhal. Autobiography and fiction merge with Stendhal: his egotism, his masks, his conclusion that a work of art is ever a beautiful lie. Taine's and Renan's abortive personal novels. Fromentin's *Dominique*.

The personal novel perhaps the most original addition of the moderns to the art of fiction.

CHAPTER 7   *Autobiographies and*
             Private Diaries

Memoir writing can seldom lay claim to total sincerity:
the memorialists look back at their life of action and obstinately justify or magnify themselves. The legacy of Rousseau's *Confessions* in Britain and France. Autobiographies
recompose the past, interpret it, analyze the inner man,
instead of relating events as memoirs do. Relations between
autobiography and fiction.

Private diaries: their spread with the romantic writers:
they satisfy our fondness for fragments and for what is unfinished. Many diarists are self-centered sick men and wom-
en, inclined to melancholy, hardly concerned with the future. Novalis, Grillparzer, Hebbel, Kierkegaard, Virginia
Woolf as examples outside France.

French diarists and their search for sincerity: Maine de
Biran, Alfred de Vigny, Maurice de Guérin and his striking
originality, Delacroix. Baudelaire's *My Heart Laid Bare,*
Michelet's *Journal* posthumously published, Amiel's enor-
mous diary and his doubts about the possibility of absolute
sincerity.

The shortcomings of the genre: it is often immature and
juvenile, it requires no effort, it stresses the present moment regardless of the past and is unconcerned with any
future, it refuses to select, it dispenses with style.

CHAPTER 8   *The Age of Sincerity*

The obsession with literary sincerity becomes an all-
pervading one in the twentieth century. The inspirers:
Baudelaire, Dostoevsky, Nietzsche. Narcissism and exhibitionism mar several fanatics of sincerity.

Charles du Bos and his bulky diary. Jacques Rivière and
his writings on sincerity, perhaps the most acute of them
all. To them, sincerity to oneself must be reached only
through many a difficult ordeal. Ramon Fernandez. A
glance at Italy: Pirandello, Svevo.

Cocteau the illusionist. Duhamel and his indictment of
memoir-writing. Jules Romains derides the fashion for private diaries. Mauriac, Montherlant, and their inward

incoherence in themselves. Its danger lies in narcissism and exhibitionism of the self.

Sincerity conceived as the need to have lived one's work, as identification between the man and the artist. Its fallacies. The sincerity of the artist, devoted to the exigencies of his art, as distinguished from that of the man.

Can the notion of sincerity be banished altogether from criticism? A galaxy of examples from various critics. Looseness of our critical terminology. The danger to which the cult of sincerity exposes imaginative writing. Sincerity and imagination.

Conclusions. Sincerity in literature, as a protest against conformity and hypocrisy, as a revolt against the pressure of society and the lies of propaganda. Through their stress on sincerity, many moderns clamor for an existential attitude and for closer links between literature and life.

Introduction

SUCH A TITLE as *Literature and Sincerity* calls for some elucidation.

To begin with, the literature in question is, not exclusively but primarily, the literature of France, obviously because it is the one with which the author is most familiar, also because the word "sincerity" appears to be more current, less ambiguous, more meaningful in a French context. The same sophisticated nation in which flourished the *cours d'amour,* the utopia of chivalry, the *préciosité,* the flattery of the courtiers of the Sun King, the exquisite artificiality of eighteenth-century salons, the bravado of Napoleon and of Victor Hugo is also the country which has continuously denounced the treachery of rationalization, the perfidy of the reasons of the heart, religious hypocrisy, moral cant, social snobbery. It has cherished art above all other nations; but it has also indicted it as an idle pastime or as clownish acrobatics, unless the artist has committed himself heart and soul to his métier.

The duty of being sincere to oneself is the only one which, in their perennial revision of values, successive generations of Frenchmen have almost never questioned. Books after books are written in which, with anxious earnestness, creators and critics wonder whether the survival of literature is compatible with the pursuit of sincerity. A nation of stylists brands style as the repository of all artifices. The heirs to classicism, which had condemned the self as hateful, have, in the last hundred years, taken to confessions, diaries, indiscreet private papers, and to a debauchery of personal literature. Benevolent or nefarious, the invasion of modern letters by the urge to be sincere is one of the significant cultural phenomena of our age. Other literatures, and other arts, as will repeatedly be shown, are not immune to it.

Nevertheless, the concept of sincerity counts among the vaguest and loosest in the old curiosity shop of psychology and aesthetics. "Greatness," "profundity," "beauty" are not, to be sure, noticeably clearer; except for the last of these terms, on which barrels of ink have been spilt in vain, they have been left obstinately undefined by their users. Few artists will feel slighted if they are termed "great" or "profound." To be qualified as "sincere" however may surprise or irk them.

Some deem it an undue intrusion into their private experience; others as the statement of a blinding evidence. For which honest workman fails to work with sincerity or integrity? Need moral connotations be introduced into the aesthetic realm, which should lie undisturbed beyond good and evil? With what measure can the critic determine the degree of sincerity of a dramatist, of an epic poet, of a realistic novelist, of Piero della Francesca or Velásquez? Was Haydn less sincere than Mozart, and Mozart less than J. S. Bach? But Berlioz more than Wagner, or Tchaikovsky more than Sibelius or Prokofiev? Does Casanova fail to rank among the great because he was insincere, or a liar, or boastful, or merely erotically imaginative, while Rousseau remained faithful to his motto of sincerity above all, even when he distorted reality? Is Leonardo very surely more sincere, in his "Last Supper," than Veronese in his sumptuous one?

The very use of the word (is there a single critic who has not, at one time or another, used it?) arouses suspicions among those of us who refuse to subscribe to the sentimental criteria of the romantics and to their cult of spontaneity. Emile Zola, who had clamored for a literature as experimental as medicine and claimed to mirror reality at its most material level, nevertheless confessed, in words which his American biographer, Matthew Josephson, set as epigraph to one of his chapters: "If I have made myself heard in the turmoil of modern times, it is because I have been sincere and passionate." Many of us have derided the term and inveighed against the confusion of ideas it fosters. At the close of his essay on "The Metaphysical Poets" T. S. Eliot, alluding to the famous bidding by the Muse to Sidney to "look into [his] heart and write," sarcastically added: "But that is not looking deep enough; Racine or Donne looked into a good deal more than the heart. One must look into the cerebral cortex, the nervous system, and the digestive tracts."

However, the same American-born critic, elsewhere (*Spectator,* March 12, 1932), writing on George Herbert, asserted with cryptic finality that "the greater the elevation, the finer becomes the difference between sincerity and insincerity." He who had advocated some degree of impersonality for literature, the recourse to an objective correlative through which to universalize a particular experience, has also produced in his ripe years as sentimental and naïvely "sincere" a dedication to his *Elder Statesman* as any drama ever received.

The ancients, it is said, and it shall be reasserted here, did not as a rule proclaim the artist's duty to be himself and to have lived and suffered before he wrote a tragedy, an elegy, or a public oration. Yet Horace himself uttered the famous precept in his *Ars Poetica* (i, 102):

> Si vis me flere, dolendum est
> Primum ipsi libi.

Cicero required the orator to be burning first if he wished
to inflame others: "Ardeat qui vult incendere." The precept was echoed and expanded by Quintilian. Boileau likewise echoed Horace. He, the cool, self-controlled pedagogue
of the French classical age, as he is often caricatured, condemned outright the elegiac poet who, undertaking to
write on love, had not been in love himself. Long before
archromantics like Alfred de Musset and Henry Miller, he
proclaimed "the wisdom of the heart."

> Il faut que le coeur seul parle dans l'élégie.

Even in tragedy, the dramatist could only arouse pity and
terror if he had been sincerely affected himself:

> Pour me tirer des pleurs, il faut que vous pleuriez.
> (*Art poétique,* iii, 142)

And not only Wordsworth and Matthew Arnold, whose
relevant passages will be quoted later, but the Olympian
of the last century, Goethe himself, insisted upon sincerity
of the author's emotion as a prerequisite of success in communicating it to others. When his "famulus" Wagner in-
quires how best to recite or to preach, Faust replies: "You
will not succeed unless you feel . . . Never will you speak
from heart to heart, unless what you say stems from your
heart."

> Wenn Ihr's nicht fühlt, Ihr werdet's nicht erjagen . . .
> Doch werdet Ihr nie Herz zu Herzen schaffen,
> Wenn es Euch nicht von Herzen geht.

We may freely pour sarcasm over the notion that sincerity in the artist bestows any special merit upon the work
of art; we may advocate a more rigorous usage of our mea-
ger array of critical terms, penalize every student who laxly
drops the adjectives "sincere," "profound," "seminal," even
"romantic," "existential," and "terrific." We shall never

impose a very effective ban. We might even compile a three-hundred-page glossary of the varied and baffling uses of the word "sincere" in several languages through the last two hundred years, in the same wrathful mood in which Flaubert had planned his *Dictionary of Accepted Ideas,* confident as he pretended to be that no one would ever again dare resort to any of the platitudes he had listed in it. Our heroic undertaking would not long remain effective. The word, and what it may variously connote, is with us to stay. Why, and how, and what best to make of it had better be explored.

The Fine Arts are even more exposed than literature. Within a few months, casually glancing at the two forms of criticism which seem to be most inveterately imbedded in jargon, the criticism of painting and of music, which have both to transpose impressions received into the medium of literary (?) language, the writer jotted down a staggering number of instances of resort to "sincerity" or its equivalents. Diderot called it, among other things, "le naïf" and at times confused it with sentimentality. The Surrealist Paul Eluard subscribed to Diderot's dictum that "the *naïve* will be essential to the production of Fine Arts." Unsophisticated, unspoilt Rousseau le Douanier was at one time tried in a court of justice for having naïvely, perhaps dishonestly, had some share in a swindle at the expense of the Bank of France. Pathetically, he multiplied letters to the examining magistrate (December 1907), asserting: "In all my works, sincerity is present, which has been my goal in my actions as well as in my painting."

Yet the primary condition for being sincere is the same as for being humble: not to boast of it, and probably not even to be aware of it. Art historians will long wonder how sincere (if it matters) was El Greco when he painted his elongated ascetics and his rapt mystics. An artist, to be sure, need not be a mystic in order to paint St. Francis or

St. Dominic in ecstasy, or a drunkard in order to compose
drinking songs. But it embarrasses us if he may have been
just a mercenary complying with the orders of patrons, or a
teetotaler at the service of a group of rowdy carousers. Perugino specialized in suave religiosity. His Virgins are sometimes endowed with a touching expression of piety which
ranks the painter a close rival of Raphael. His "Deposition
from the Cross," in the Pitti Gallery, is one of the great
religious paintings of Italy, comparable to Fra Angelico's
"Christ between the two Thieves" in the San Marco con-
vent or to Titian's "Entombment" in the Louvre. Yet, if
Vasari is to be trusted, suave religious Perugino was devoid
of moral and spiritual qualities and probably of faith.

Veronese dressed up his Apostles as Venetian noblemen
attending the luxurious feast of a supper with Christ; he
was true to the spirit of his city and of his age. Was he, in
being so, any more mendacious than Leonardo, whose private morality is uncertain and whose personal faith is questionable? André Malraux calls his "Last Supper" in Milan
"a sublime romance," a break with the era when art was
subservient to faith and aimed at winning men for the service of God.

We would err if we imagined that the painters of today,
having shaken themselves free from all slavery to representation, altogether free in the presence of their canvas, scorn
the use of such an old-fashioned epithet as "sincere," or
that critics have banished that colorless term from their
sumptuous storehouse of high-sounding, metaphysical, and
geometric adjectives. Of Soutine, Chagall, and of Manessier,
the fervent painter of "The Crown of Thorns" and other
paintings with religious titles, it has been variously asserted
that their originality stemmed from their sincerity. The
same has been advanced of the stern Dutch puritan Piet
Mondrian and of the restrained Spanish artist Tapiès. Picasso and his younger rival in speed and virtuosity, Mathieu,

have paraded their facility and laughed away the notion that an artist has to delve laboriously into his deeper self and to search assiduously before finding material for his art; to those two painters the truest comes with the greatest readiness. It is doubtful whether even an acrobatic performer of critical "parades" like Cocteau would ever compose a book on "Picasso's sincerity."

Nevertheless, we have not far to look to align martyrs of sincerity who, from Stendhal to Gide, have contended that, to write well—that is to say, according to them, with sincerity and naturalness—one has to write very fast, transcribing one's impressions or the subconscious promptings of an interior monologue without organization or reflection. A distinguished painter of our age, Bazaine, in his *Notes sur la peinture d'aujourd'hui* (1948), declares that "the sincerity of an artist no doubt consists in allowing himself to be led he knows not where." One of the most scientific among today's practitioners of abstract art, Serpan, has hailed "generalized automatism, spasms of the sign, tachism, as so many returns to the deeper springs of the psyche. Never has a more radical effort been attempted by painters to transcribe on the canvas the primeval sincerity of what exists."[1] Reviewers of exhibitions of interior decoration and home furnishings abroad currently laud some of the objects displayed because "they are sincere objects." Functionalism in art and architecture has often been equated with an art freed from any fake, any deceitful superfluity of ornaments, a "sincere" art.

Critics of the cinema do not lag far behind those of other arts. At least a score of instances could be cited in which

---

1. The English language seems to lend itself less pliably than the French (or German) to those impassive assertions. The French text reads "la sincérité primordiale de l'existant" and seems to arouse no resistance in readers. It is quoted in René Huyghe, "Psychologie de l'art moderne," *La Table Ronde* (April 1961), p. 129.

the sponsors of "the new wave" in France and Italy have put their hunt for "more sincerity" forward as the secret of their reforms, sweeping away artificiality, needless luxury, Hollywood's cumbrous machinery designed to murder all true feelings. François Truffaut, one of the most glamorous captains riding the new wave, reviewing on July 10, 1957, a film in the weekly *Arts,* in Paris, decreed, in a manner typical of his friends' standards: "Nothing that is insincere can possibly matter, and this film is not a sincere film."

Music, even more than the plastic arts, would appear to be remote from the transcription of ideas, and composers might be expected to prove more addicted to silence on their intentions and emotions than many a sculptor or painter. But Berlioz and Wagner have not been sparing of their biographical or didactic prose; Debussy, Stravinsky, Boulez have not shown much reluctance to confiding to interviewers. The problem of the composer's sincerity has repeatedly been posed, often at the annoyance of the composers, who will not allow any doubt to enter the minds of impudent critics on that score. For years, in the past, music was linked with church services and inspired by religion. Did those who then composed (or compose today) a Mass or an Oratorio obey the dictum of their faith? "Where the heart is not, there could not be any music" affirmed Tchaikovsky. Yet Bach composed his *Musical Offering,* not on his own spontaneous determination, but on a theme assigned to him by one of the few sovereigns who appreciated him, Frederic II. Goethe and Valéry have often testified that great works can be the outcome of a circumstance which might appear to be exterior. Gide, who appreciated Mozart's music, dared call him "a perfect dancer à la Nietzsche." He meant that the most spontaneous of creators played at experiencing the grave religious fervor of his Masses, which he composed on order; but no one had ordered his "Jupiter Symphony," one of his noblest in C Ma-

jor, in which he freely, perhaps profanely, utilized an ec-
clesiastical motive which had already served him elsewhere.
The music critic Alfred Einstein has noted that more than
one good judge of music has characterized Mozart's Masses
as "bordering on inattention and on a worldliness which
dangerously resembles irreverence."[2]

Indeed, in our more severe twentieth century, in 1903,
the papal *Motu proprio* condemned the Church music that
was too profane: Haydn, Mozart, Schubert. But was Haydn
any less "sincere," in his interpretation of religion, than
J. S. Bach? Were the eighteenth-century Austrians insincere
when they were secular and operatic, or was Verdi necessarily so in his *Requiem* (1874), which we may find theatrical? Berlioz lived dramatically, romantically, and experienced his sorrows as "sincerely" as any man, driven almost
(but never quite) to suicide by them: whatever his beliefs
or his unbelief, he gave in "L'Enfance du Christ" a very
human interpretation of a religious theme. Brooks Atkin-
son, reviewing a performance of that piece at Town Hall
in New York *(New York Times,* December 16, 1960), made
the remark that Berlioz was an agnostic and that the flight
of the Holy Family was presented there in terms of purely
human experience. He added: "Berlioz's religious skepticism, in fact, may have been a source of strength in the
composition of this transcendent work. It left him free to
interpret a dogma-ridden story without servility. It gave
him more latitude as a creative artist than Handel had."
Examples could be adduced ad infinitum. Richard Wagner,
not certainly a religious man in the conventional sense, was
able to orchestrate the religious theme of *Parsifal* with
powerful intensity. The chalice in which Christ's blood
was supposed to have flowed, in the Grail legend, became,
with him, full to the brim with earthly passion blended

2. *Mozart, His Character, His Work* (London, Oxford University Press,
1945).

with reverence for the sacred. In our own age, few composers have been less carried away by romantic delusions than Stravinsky after he outgrew his early flamboyance; he derided the facile notion of sincerity in his *Poétique musicale,* and his successors have often lamented that he had repudiated the sincere ardor of his youth. Yet, as late as 1959, Robert Craft, the interlocutor of the master, reports, in his *Conversations with Igor Stravinsky,* the following answer to the query "What does 'sincerity' mean to you?"

> It is a sine qua non that, at the same time, guarantees nothing. Most artists are sincere anyway and most art is bad—though, of course, some insincere art (sincerely insincere) is quite good. One's belief that one is sincere is not so dangerous, however, as one's conviction that one is right.[3]

The present work has no axe to grind. It was not undertaken as an apology for sincerity in art. Even when the author felt inclined to vent his ironical impatience at the loose and contradictory uses and abuses to which the notion of sincerity has been put, he refused to be content with a mere pedantic display of men's and of critics' errors, and to indulge the paradox of a praise of lying parallel to the famous *Praise of Folly* in which Erasmus declares that one of the most enviable qualities of madmen is "their so beautiful sincerity." Rather this book endeavors to elucidate the many complexities that lurk beneath a concept that has invaded our thinking over the last two or three centuries and which apparently is with us to stay.

Insofar as the history of an idea is indispensable to the understanding of all that the collective memory of reflecting men associates with it, an account, historical and psy-

3. New York, Doubleday, 1959, p. 120.

chological, of the belated emergence of the notion of sincere literature—through Montaigne, the seventeenth-century French moralists and English divines, Rousseau, the romantics of several lands—had to be offered to the reader. It never had been undertaken before. Our inquiry, from the middle of the nineteenth century to our own time, then had to be centered on France; for it is in the country of Stendhal, Baudelaire, Gide, and of a score of poets, novelists, diarists, and autobiographers that the subject became paramount. It is (along with a few studies in German) in French that most of the books on sincerity have been written—by Dromard (1910), Belaval (1944), Gusdorf (1948), Jolivet (1951), on which more details are provided in our bibliography. A final section attempts to state the chief problems posed by a long succession of would-be sincere writers and artists and to come to grips with them. Dogmatism is, we hope, eschewed throughout; for the concept is as shifting as that of beauty, or of ugliness, or of profundity, and a writer who appeared to all eyes as "sincere" forty years ago may cease to be so to posterity, while one who, like Baudelaire, was derided as a contortionist and a masked histrion may acquire a tragic sincerity for those who will know him better and who will read him with new lenses.

At no time, we hope, will sincerity—that is, to start from a provisional and superficial description of it, a close correspondence between the man and the author, an artist's biography and his creation—be taken as a criterion of value. An artist's sincerity, as the philosopher Etienne Gilson has concluded at the end of a study of the idealized mistresses, or muses, of several great poets, is not primarily toward his love, or his loves ("sincere" lovers change sincerity, even if they are no Don Juans) but toward his art. But one conviction animates the critical thinking of this author: that art and life are not, ultimately and deeply, altogether divergent, or remote from one another, and that literature and art are far more than a mere game or a pure craftsman's skill.

One word more: "Truth" presupposes an adequacy with some objective criterion, or at least an inner coherency among our views on an exterior reality, which sincerity does not. Veracity implies our reporting the truth (facts, dates, events, even feelings) as we know or believe it to be. Frankness is taken by most of us to be a moral virtue which impels us to report our own truth as it appears to us, or even to state to others, at times with some outspoken brutality, some truths, usually bitter, which we believe they should know. Candor, a moral quality in English, when it is *candeur* in French, carries with it connotations of rather ludicrous and almost childish naïveté, for "le Français né malin" as Boileau called him. The sincerity that will be repeatedly alluded to in the following pages will be toward others, but primarily toward oneself, and toward one's art.

CHAPTER 1

From the Ancients to the Renaissance

THE ASSERTION is often made that there is no progress in literature, for genius can hardly be accounted for by its antecedents, and an original writer is more often than not hampered by the achievement of his predecessors. Indeed, he seldom can profit by his own earlier work: "every attempt is a wholly new start," as T. S. Eliot mourned, and even the technique evolved for one novel or one play is of dubious avail to an author who would not just repeat himself. Progress in that branch of literature which is called criticism is likewise uncertain; the results secured after two centuries of relativism and of freedom from rules and conventions have clearly not been commensurate with the amount of subtlety and mental agility expended by critics, a thousand times more numerous today than even in ancient Alexandria.

But, if critics cannot claim to march forward securely and to solve problems of literary appreciation which, happily, remain unsolvable, they may well take some pride in their steady sharpening of their tools, in the inventiveness with which they propose new euphemisms (at times ill-sounding and forbidding ones), and above all in the skill with which they displace old problems and direct our attention to hitherto neglected ones. Several new notions have thus come to the fore since the eighteenth century. First sensibility, then personality, originality, and imagination, respectively, became the focus of the most persistent aesthetic speculation with the German romantics, with Coleridge and Shelley, with Baudelaire in France a little later. Symbol and myth reigned supreme from the Symbolist movement down to the Freudian and Jungian interpreters of literature in the nineteen twenties. Lately, however, one word, sincerity—often linked to its twin brother authenticity and the very unclear notion thus designated—has invaded critical speculation in France. Rigorous minds have scoffed at it; analytical definers have tried to explode it; professors have ruthlessly underscored in their students' papers the easy explanation for the greatness of almost any work by its "sincerity"; moralists have even denounced the peril of assuming too readily that sincerity is necessarily a virtue. The word will long haunt the moderns. The concept of sincerity has become the most potent idée-force in the literature and psychology of our age.

The view that sincerity is a literary virtue or even a merit is a relatively recent one. For the ancients, the most praiseworthy qualities of literature lay in the polish of descriptions, in the elegance of diction, in the terseness of sentential style, such as Seneca cultivated, even in the abrupt condensation of Thucydides and of Tacitus. Rhetoric was indispensable in civilizations steeped in oratory and where the gift of suasion could be richly rewarded in public life. Even with writers relatively untouched by rhetoric, like Plato, ease, naturalness, a winning nonchalance that violated rigid grammarians' rules, and occasionally the force that the Greeks called *tonos* and the Romans *robur* were singled out for praise: the exigency that the author be one with the man or that the man live his experiences before recording them hardly ever entered the minds of ancient theorists of literature. The most thorough historian of autobiography in antiquity, the German Georg Misch, had to conclude after ransacking ten centuries of Greek and Latin letters, that the Greeks, being primarily concerned with art and its purifying process, had taken little interest in the raw material of life or in any slavish adherence of art to lived experience. Wilamowitz rightly remarked that "the Hellenes . . . were unable to conceive an individual man in the full reality of his existence."[1] They would indeed have been astonished and dismayed by the preference granted by many moderns to the document over the artistic narrative, to the brutal transcription of one's experience over a generalized and objective presentation of it, to memory over imagination. Even the philosopher whose motto was "Know thyself" never stressed such knowledge as acquired through the truthful recording of all one's past deeds and thoughts. The lack of self-awareness among the Greeks contributed to the freshness which, more than perhaps any other single quality, draws us to their creations. Self-knowledge was stressed by them far more than in the Orient, where the individual counted but little in politics and in art; but it had to be merged into the relationship of man to the city or transcended into a vaster and higher entity than the individual. "Ascende per te ipsum supra te ipsum"—thus Georg Misch sums up Platonic dialectic. Plato's long and very personal seventh Epistle throws little insight into the philosopher's moods or upon his "sincere" experiences during his stay with Dion of Sicily. Thucydides characteristically omits from his famous history any mention of his feelings when he was exiled from Athens for twenty years for having failed, as a military commander, to save a city from the Spartans. Few modern generals or statesmen have imitated such an example of

1. Quoted in Georg Misch, *A History of Autobiography in Antiquity* (English translation, 2 vols. Cambridge, Harvard University Press, 1951), *1*, 193.

objectivity in relating events in which they participated.

The Romans boasted that elegy was, along with satire, their own discovery and their domain. There is indeed in their elegists a sense for half-shades and for psychological complexities which has attracted many moderns from Du Bellay to Baudelaire to their amorous and plaintive distichs. Yet even in their most direct moments, when they abjectly confessed their love for an unworthy Lesbia or Cynthia, those Latin poets did not claim that they were being sincere toward themselves. They did not go very far in the analysis of their own character. Catullus cried out his love and hatred indissolubly blended; both were caused by Lesbia's behavior. But the poet did not relish the analysis of his own contradictions as would a modern, who would be bent upon reaching the utmost sincerity in studying the exact proportion in which such feelings were mixed in himself. Propertius once urged one of his friends, Lynceus, to confide his love to verse, instead of coveting Cynthia (in the last elegy of his second Book). He even attempted a humorous portrayal of his youth and career and a playful horoscope of his future, placed in the mouth of an imaginary soothsayer, in the long elegy which opens his last Book. Ovid, likewise, in the concluding elegy of the fourth Book of his *Tristia,* related his own childhood and youth, all devoted to poetry, his three marriages, his exile, and craved for pity through displaying his self-pity. But Ovid, pathetic as he may become at times in his wailing at his enforced residence on the Black Sea, seldom gives modern readers the impression that he reached that exact correspondence between his poetry and his feelings which we call sincerity in literature.

The ablest commentator on the Roman elegists from our point of view, Archibald W. Allen,[2] rightly concluded that,

2. In " 'Sincerity' and the Roman Elegists," *Classical Philology, 45* (1950), 145–60.

to an ancient, literary sincerity, insofar as he was aware of it, only amounted to "a relation between the artist and the public." The author had to make his audience believe what he wrote; hence the stylistic devices that ancient oratory was fond of analyzing. No critic before Quintilian seems to have complained that Callimachus or Tibullus was not wholly sincere, or that Ovid in his *Amores* was even less so; or to have hinted that Virgil's superiority in his *Eclogues* sprang from a greater degree of sincerity. Literature was then considered as a finished work offered to readers to please them; readers and critics were less concerned with the process through which it had originated in the writer. Its appeal was often all the greater for some conventionality in the theme itself, which had been consecrated by Homer, Apollonius of Rhodes, or Theocritus: a young poet vied with the elegance of the older ones in describing once again the shield of Achilles, Ariadne on her rock island, or the wedding of Thetis and Peleus.

There is more intimacy in Cicero's letters, an abundant store of episodic and familiar details, and some inkling of the contradictions which may simultaneously coexist in human character. Yet neither in his manner of writing nor in his revelations on his moods can Cicero be called a model of sincerity. Horace praised his predecessor among satirists, Lucilius, for having laid his whole life bare and clear "as if painted on a votive tablet"; but, in spite of a few playful glimpses of himself which he allows us, Horace cannot be said to have aimed at any naked exposition of the good and the bad in him. Neither probably had Lucilius, who had written about his everyday affairs without attempting to search into his own character. A more tragic sense of the inner division in man entered into the world with Christianity. Saint Paul confessed in a famous passage his inability to effect the good which he wanted to pursue, and he appealed to "every man to be fully persuaded in his own mind," in the fourteenth chapter of the Epistle to the Romans. Gregory Nazianzen, in the fourth century, keenly felt, and tried to express in poems, his inner duality. A few years later, Saint Augustine undertook to make himself true ("verum facere se ipsum"); he described the stages of his spiritual growth and the enigma that he was to himself, but with an inordinate amount of exclamation and even of declamation, which smacks of pathetic appeal to emotions rather than of naked analytical sincerity.

It was to Saint Augustine, almost a thousand years later, that Petrarch, one of the dozen men who have been hailed as "the first of the moderns" turned for spiritual comfort in the imaginary dialogue with the African Saint called his *Secret (Il mio Segreto,* also known, for it is in Latin, as *De Contemptu mundi).* Far more than in his somewhat stilted epistles to posterity, Petrarch confessed himself in that treatise. Stung by the upbraiding of Saint Augustine, who had confessed and denounced in an unforgettable sentence the quest for love in one who is in love with love, the singer of Laura attempted a defense of his passion as spiritual and religious, only to yield to Augustine's reproaches in the end. For he acknowledged seeking the beautiful instead of the true, and admitted that the Saint rightly discerned insincerity in him. But the accent of a heartfelt confession is more contagious in some of the gravest of Petrarch's canzone, especially the one which was used to open the second part of his poems in the older editions: *I'vo piangendo i miei passati tempi.* Anguish fills the poet's soul at the thought of death and drives him to repent and to analyze the self-torturings tearing his soul. Elsewhere in his poetry, however, the modern reader must confess to experiencing a feeling of remoteness which makes it well-nigh impossible for him to admire Petrarch as he was admired in Europe for two centuries after his death. Even the kind of revival that has restored John Donne, Maurice Scève, and Gongora to the pinnacle of fame seems unlikely to take place for the bard of the *Canzoniere*. He lacked a certain irony toward himself, probably also a certain relentlessness in the introspective analysis of his deeper self. A prose treatise like his *De Vita solitaria,* expounding through many a rhetorical device the wretchedness of the busy man and the happiness enjoyed by the contemplative and solitary man, is tainted by the complacence and—the word must be added—the insincerity of many a humanist.

A century ago, bold historians like Michelet, Burckhardt, and Taine ventured generalizations on the Renaissance; they confidently stressed the invasion of life, the eagerness to copy nature and to find in nature the teacher of a new ethics, the cult of the individual as some of the features of that sixteenth century which Michelet dubbed "a hero." Subsequent research has stressed the vagueness of the very concept of Renaissance and disintegrated it into a series of renaissances which began with Giotto and Joachim de Flora, even with Abelard and as early as the year 1000. There lurks a peril for our perspective of the past in excessive knowledge: for we are certain, if we look for them intently enough, to discover predecessors to every innovator and sources or preformations for every idea. History becomes a succession of insensitive transitions, and the so-called originality of an age or of a period vanishes in the process. Everything is already said and probably has been for centuries; but, at certain times, it is said anew with a fresh accent, and the implications of what was said earlier and had not been heeded suddenly loom revolutionary. Scholars focusing their magnifying glass on unacknowledged figures called precursors or intermediaries assume that man's intellectual history is cumulative in the sense that nothing is ever lost that was uttered or printed, however obscurely; that artists and writers must have been well read and, if not, must have mysteriously breathed what, as we laxly put it, was "in the air." Alas! even in our own age, when media of information are more plentiful than ever before, anyone who has ever conversed with artists or with authors living in the midst of a great city must have been struck with surprise at the number of things in the air which they seem not to breathe or to scent. They may have had predecessors, but, unless they need them as a shield for their own innovations, they hardly pay attention to them.

The uniqueness of the Renaissance is doubtless a myth, as is the uniqueness of the Romantic movement. Yet several traits that were found only in exceptional men before 1450 or 1550 became more general in the fifteenth century in Italy, in the sixteenth century in France and England. They also were integrated into a more organic whole, becoming part and parcel of what deserves to be called the spirit of the Renaissance. Three such features contributed to a new emphasis of the sincerity of the artist, if we may use such a word anachronistically but conveniently: the closer link between art and life and the new merit granted to a creator's lived experience; the eagerness to make a clean sweep of conventions and of medieval allegories and a sudden and joyful concern with the future; and the worship by the individual of his own individuality, his greed for the unbridled expansion of his age and for his personal glory.

The question of sincerity is of course hardly relevant for a great deal of literature; it does not apply to the drama (except for the expressionist drama of Strindberg and the "ich-drama" of his German followers), or to history, to fiction like that of Rabelais or Cervantes, or even to memoirs, which are often, in the Renaissance, a boastful record of deeds accomplished or picturesque gossip about men of importance and ladies of gallantry. But in Italy and in England even more than in France, the Renaissance is also the age of lyricism. Songs, lyrics, odes, and sonnets proliferated, in which the poets often prided themselves on their independence from their models (the Roman elegists, Petrarch and his followers) and on their ability to translate directly the emotions of their hearts into verse. They hardly ever used the word sincerity. But the student of their works cannot escape asking the ever-recurring question: were Du Bellay, Ronsard, Desportes, or Surrey, Sidney, Spenser sincere in their personal lyricism, and does it make any difference to the beauty or to the appeal of their poems to us?

The answer can hardly be an unqualified yes or no, and it hangs upon our definition of a sincere poet. Clearly, no amount of sincerity, that is, of direct experience and even of intense suffering by the singer, ever sufficed to make a song worthy of mention. A poet must be an artist before anything else. But he must also be enough of an artist to convey the impression that he is sincere and not just an entertainer. All artists have been obsessed with the desire to repudiate artistry and even art itself. Rightly or wrongly, the reader and even the critic of today, other things being equal, will prefer a sonnet sequence in which they can descry the lineaments of an actual experience in the presence of nature, of woman, of the sorrows and joys of life. In sixteenth-century France, Louise Labé possessed that directness of tone and that pathetic intensity of feeling which were lacking in Petrarch's followers. No woman poet since Sappho had yet found such accents to convey the throes of passion. Her Lyonese compatriot, Maurice Scève, is a more refined artist and was long neglected for having cultivated obscurity. Only since 1920 or thereabout have generations attuned to Mallarmé's and to Valéry's poetry turned to him with a jealous enthusiasm, claiming for him more psychological complexity and more magic of imagery than the leaders of the "Pléiade" had possessed.

Not many of the ten live decasyllabic poems of Scève's *Délie* deserve such a claim; but the few which do embody an experience of the fear of mortality, of the faith in love's triumph over death, of metaphysical anguish, and of refined sensuousness which stand alone in sixteenth-century France. The author's jealousy of his mistress' husband, in particular, when he imagines her (in his poem No. 161) naked in the arms of him who legally possesses her, unfaithful to the law of love while bowing, not ungrudgingly perhaps, to the human law of marriage, has hardly been conveyed with such power, before or since, by any poet. Was Scève sincere or merely echoing Tibullus' elegies over his Delia? Was his Délie only an anagram of *l'idée* and a Platonic abstraction?

V. L. Saulnier, who wrote in 1948 the most exhaustive work on Scève, collected all the sources and allusions to Tibullus, Virgil, and others in *Délie* and scanned all the interpretations of the heroine as Hecate or Diana. With no partisanship whatever, he wisely concluded that Délie had been, at the start, an authentic woman, a poet of talent, Pernette du Guillet, whom Scève had known as early as 1535–36. She married after having, for a brief while, accepted Scève's love. The poet, like most poets, added many an intricacy to her delineation; he probably merged in her image those of women sung in Latin or Italian by earlier bards; he treated his model as a painter does his, eliciting her essential features and far transcending the scant reality before him. But, in the very imitation of literary predecessors, sincerity can and does flourish. For a gifted artist selects what he will imitate, espouses the feelings expressed by the foreign or ancient poet, distorts his literary models. "Literary fidelity does not exclude the sincerity of the experience," Saulnier concludes.[3]

Men of letters who lived when the revival of ancient learning was in full bloom strove hard to mold for them-

3. Verdun L. Saulnier, *Maurice Scève* (2 vols. Paris, Klincksieck, 1948). See Chapter 8 on "The Loves of a Poet."

selves a sensibility akin to that of their models. They succeeded in the attempt, and it became natural for them to perceive nature through Greek mythology and to love their mistresses most truly when they could picture them to their readers, and to themselves, as younger sisters of Lesbia, Delia, Cynthia, or Amaryllis. Proust's heroes likewise were sincerest when they transfigured ancillary loves or a Parisian *cocotte* into Botticelli's or Bellini's women: life for them had to imitate art, and women's ungrateful part was to serve as pretexts for men's mendaciously sincere idealization. No Renaissance poet in France was more pugnacious in his rejection of ancient and foreign models than was J. Du Bellay, although he plundered the writings of a Paduan humanist in order to defend the French language against the prestige of transalpine fashions. Yet when he wished to record an apparently lived and ardently felt passion for a married woman encountered in Rome in 1553, Du Bellay resorted to the Latin language and, forgetting his earlier manifesto, confessed that the French muse was his legitimate wife but the Latin one a mistress whom he courted amorously. His Latin elegies, *Faustina,* have much charm and conjure up a dramatic love adventure with an attempt at characterization. His earlier *Olive* had been a colder and more conventional sonnet sequence in the Italian tradition. His *Regrets,* composed in Rome simultaneously with his Latin poems, in spite of the promise held out in the early sonnets, are an entertaining and often satirical diary of his Roman sojourn but omit any direct portrayal of the Angevin exile's heart.[4] The poet's regret for his native land and his yearning for a more homely life than that of Roman intrigues, however deeply felt, becomes a pre-

4. J. Du Bellay's Latin poems have been reprinted, with a French translation by Thierry Sandre, as *Les Amours de Faustine* (Amiens, Malfère, 1923). At the beginning of his *Regrets,* the poet characteristically called his verse "the surest secretaries of his heart" and announced that, eschewing

text for somewhat long-drawn strings of vignettes inter-
spersed with complaints.

Ronsard's poetical output of high quality stands second
only to that of Victor Hugo in the French language; the
range and the originality of his love poems was hardly to
be equaled, even by the romantics. It is well nigh impossible
for us today to judge Ronsard's poetry by other standards
than those which the romantics bequeathed to us. We forget, or passively take it for granted, that imitation was not,
in the sixteenth century, a device of facility or the mark of
a deficient personality. A whole tradition had to be im-
ported and assimilated before a poet could even dream of
revealing himself in his verse. In its better moments, the
imitation practised by Ronsard or Sidney was not only
original but creative. However hard the literary historian
may try to broaden our taste and our enjoyment of earlier
literature through replacing it in its historical framework,
we are likely to be irked by the lack of dramatic force in
those ingenious catalogues of the charms of a lady and in
the repetitious assertions of the lover's alternate or simultaneous burning and freezing. We insist upon the poet's
having suffered actual pangs of love and, according to our
own moods of wishful thinking or of quixotic championing
of ladies' virtue, we like his belle to have either rewarded
him or driven him to utter despair.

An actual experience is often clothed by a youthful poet
in the conventional garb of the fashion then prevailing.
Such may well have been the case for Ronsard's early love
sonnets, although a more playful and pagan side of his nature had been expressed in some of his lighter odes. But

---

polish and adornment, he would make them mere diaries or commentaries.
Discarding Greek, Latin, and Italian models he would, he says, simply write
"ce que la passion simplement me fait dire." The romantics will make a
similar claim for their verse.

Ronsard's sensuous temperament soon fretted under the constricting armor of Petrarchan convention. He admitted unambiguously that he loved two women at the same time, an admission that always intimidates at first the one who dares make it, as if true love could only be true to one person alone. "Je suis amoureux en deux lieux." Marie, the very young peasant girl and the more mysterious Sinope then shared his heart. To sing of Marie in sonnets which move modern readers by their freshness and their tragic revolt against death, Ronsard resorted to the imitation of a Latin poet of the time, Marullus. Once again the use of such a prop gave heart to a poet trying to unfurl his wings. He was attempting to be an artist above all else: he had been intensely shaken by his own loves. As Ronsard's most expert student, the late Paul Laumonier, put it, "of all the poets who sang of love in the sixteenth century . . . none suffered more sincerely from the resistance of authentic mistresses nor enjoyed with keener pleasure the favors, even the slight ones, which they granted him. . . . He was not being insincere because he imitated other poets. Did not his personal adventures necessarily resemble theirs? Were not the causes and the effects of their love also the causes and effects of his own? The emotions caused by his mistresses were very close indeed to those which they had experienced and described."[5]

Sincerity cannot ensure the quality of the work of art. But it can coexist with the use of bookish reminiscences in

5. Paul Laumonier, *Ronsard poète lyrique* (Paris, Hachette, 1923, new ed.). The first edition was dated 1908. Pp. 472–76 touch on the question of Ronsard's sincerity, and the very apt quotation from Émile Faguet is given on page 476. Laumonier also remarks that poets are no less sincere when they change the address to which their love songs were sent and use for one mistress, Ronsard's Marie or Lamartine's Elvire, what was originally written and felt for Cassandre or for Graziella. Proust will later observe that many men have only one way of falling in love just as they have one way of catching a cold.

a poet steeped in the classics, who will mourn his dead beloved with tearful lines borrowed from Latin poets exactly
as a pious person will pray to his god or lament a bereavement with sentences borrowed from the Scriptures. Émile
Faguet had sensibly observed it, and Laumonier could but
quote him with approval. After all, the number of ways in
which a man may love, the number of wishes he wants fulfilled by his lady, the number of rapturous or grateful
thanks he can offer in return have always been woefully
limited. Love is perhaps, even after seven or eight centuries of literature woven around it since the Troubadours
and the bard of *Tristan and Isolde,* the most monotonous
of our feelings. Artificiality often lies in the attempting to
feel differently from others for the sake of originality or in
the unnatural forgetting of the expression given by admired
predecessors to passions which they experienced and cultivated before us.

The tendency of a modern reader is to believe that a
poet of past ages was more fully and frankly himself when
he expressed the sensuous aspect of his love than when he
idealized his feeling and purified it of all fleshly greed. It
is true that the French poets of the Renaissance often
fretted under the Petrarchist and the Platonic conventions
proposed by their models, and that Platonism, in French
poetry, seldom struck such a correspondence between its
idealistic worship of an essential Beauty and the genuine
mood of the lover as it did in Italian, and even more in
Spenser or in Shelley. Ronsard, like Du Bellay, soon turned
against the followers of Petrarch. He could not conceal his
true temperament, bent as he was on Epicurean enjoyment
and on the joyful acceptance of his own inconstancy. Nowhere, however, does his poetry strike such a vibration in
us as in the two books of sonnets to Helen which he wrote
after his forty-fifth year. As an older man he failed to meet
with the prompt response he had received from the ladies

to whom, in his greener years, he had offered his tribute. The ghost of decay and of death hovered before him. He had acquired a full mastery over his technique and wielded the sonnet form with variety and dramatic power. He still played with mythological names, toyed with enumerations and hyperboles, personified the god of Love, tempered the expression of his suffering with humor. But, in the celebrated sonnets where he owned to Helen that he had gambled his heart at dice and lost it, or where he asked her to draw from his own heart the ashes with which she would mark her brow on Ash Wednesday, and in the oft-quoted masterpiece which Yeats transposed—sincerely— into "When you are old and grey and full of sleep," we are bound to admit that the poet conveyed the impression of having been more than a skillful artist: he was a man ardently and sorrowfully in love.

There is perhaps even more artifice in the English sonneteers of the second half of the sixteenth century than among the French. They came last in Western Europe and had therefore one more set of models, the French, to waylay their imitative zeal; their delight in strings of metaphors and in conceits outdid that of their predecessors. With every one of them, the question of their sincerity has been asked with some relevance; they themselves had pointed to it. Giles Fletcher could impudently contend, in his *Licia*, that one need not be or have been in love in order to write on love. But the majority of poets preferred to suggest that, in a woman as in a poet, truth enhanced beauty. "O let me, true in love, but truly write," exclaimed Shakespeare in concluding his twenty-first sonnet; and elsewhere, multiplying comparisons with roses and thorns, he praised the loved one in the well-known lines:

> O how much more doth beauty beauteous seem
> By that sweet ornament which truth doth give!

We know too little about Shakespeare to hazard a guess as to the degree of his sincerity in the *Sonnets,* which differ markedly from the Italian and French ones by their lesser degree of personal experience directly recorded and by their dramatic character: the drama is enacted among three protagonists, the poet, the friend whom he loves, and the lady who is the mistress of both. It is a struggle against time and death, both vanquished by the power of love which can forgive and by the eternity of poetry.[6] Shakespeare's genius was too universal and too plastic in experiencing imaginatively the most diverse feelings to abide the question of the sincerity of the man behind the masks of a supreme artist.

Even the most prudent commentators of Spenser have been tempted to discriminate among his works and to bestow their highest praise on those which seem to impart a lived and sincere experience: the *Epithalamion,* for example, or the *Amoretti.* The latter are a mosaic of borrowings, chiefly from Tasso. But, like Ronsard, Spenser fused his borrowings into a new and highly personal whole. It takes modesty in a young poet not to labor under the illusion that none ever loved like him before, and to resort to those who had already felt, and written, on an experience that he could only repeat. Émile Legouis did not hesitate to suggest, in his 1923 volume on Spenser: "Spenser's sonnets [*Amoretti*], dedicated to her who was going to be his fiancée, then his wife, are among the most sincere." But he did not mistake sincerity for greatness and was careful to indicate that sixteenth-century minds were not disturbed by their own contradictions and seldom, if ever, attempted to reach a unity or even a harmony out of their antithetic Christian and pagan features.

6. The recent interpretation of Shakespeare's *Sonnets* proposed by J. W. Lever in *The Elizabethan Love Sonnet* (London, Methuen, 1956), is more plausible than most.

The most often quoted text in Elizabethan poetry in which the sincerity of the artist is loudly claimed is by the greatest English lyricist of the age next to Spenser and Shakespeare, Sir Philip Sidney. In the opening sonnet of his *Astrophel and Stella,* which was published in 1591, five years after the knight-poet's untimely death at thirty-two, but which had been read by several people in manuscript in the author's lifetime, Sidney proclaimed as his motto the advice given to him by the muse: "Fool, said the muse to me, look in thy heart and write." Elsewhere in the same sonnet sequence (No. LXXIV), he asserted that he was not one of those who pillage other writers: "I am no pickpurse of another's wit." And, in conversational language, answering his own question as to why his verse pleased and expressed his thoughts easily and smoothly, he added:

> Guesse we the cause? What, is it this? fie no.
> Or so? Much lesse. How then? Sure thus it is:
> My lips are sure inspired with Stella's kisse.

The claim was bold, but hardly original. Indeed, next to "I love you," there is no phrase in literature more trite and yet more convincing than "I am sincere and nakedly my own self in loving you." Or again, forty-fourth sonnet, Sidney asserted that his language was the faithful interpreter of his mind: "My words I know do well set forth my mind," and, in the ninetieth, that he was only transcribing the bidding of love: "And love doth hold my hand, and makes me write."

Indeed, no other Elizabethan sonnet sequence, perhaps not even Shakespeare's, appeals to us so forcefully as *Astrophel and Stella.* The light Song,

> In a grove most rich of shade,
> Where birds wanton music made,

relating how Stella refused her suitor's demand with such

tenderness that her repulse constituted a full avowal, is unequaled in Shakespeare and in Donne for its directness, its portrayal of the woman's personality, and its tragic intensity. Borrow, Sidney did of course, from Petrarch and from Tasso and from the French. At the very moment when he declares that Love is holding his hand, he may be aware of Petrarch's lines in which the Italian poet had said that "in the fair eyes of Love he was little by little reading when he spoke and wrote of Love." But would he have been more sincere in banishing memory altogether from his invention?

Sidney's biographers have, as usual, fought battles over the unsolvable and therefore tantalizing question: is the poet singing a pure or Platonic love, playing variations on an effete theme, or is he remembering an actual experience? Among those supporting the former view are those who are irked by the discrepancy between the known details of a writer's life and the portrayal of his mistress and of himself in his work, and who judge such inaccuracy to be a sin. They prefer to place literature in a world apart, above life and obeying its own laws, but also outside life. Among those supporting the poet's remembrance of an actual experience are scholars like the late Abel Lefranc who champion the thesis that literature rests on reality and is inspired by actual events and an actual experience. They know so much that they soon discover under every word written by the writer of old, allusions, clear to them alone, to incidents of which they assume the author to have been aware and to secrets ingeniously, at times anagrammatically, disguised. Others, at a loss to define why certain poems strike us as greater than others, fall back upon the criterion which few care to question: that the most felicitous and most moving pieces are also the most sincere. John Drinkwater's statement in the Sidney edition in the Muses' Library is typical: "*Astrophel and Stella* being a love poem, the first thing to be done when it is submitted to our judgment is to enquire whether it be sincere. If in this it be found wanting, I for one can see no purpose in urging anything further in its defence, for, lacking that one vital quality, it lacks everything. . . . The sign of poetic truth is written large over the pages of *Astrophel and Stella*."

But Drinkwater failed to make clear what he understood by such sincerity. Sidney had enough imaginative power to identify himself with the lover in the poem; he was enough of an artist to break with several conventions of his predecessors and to portray the birth of love with originality. He fretted under the traditional necessity of celebrating the intellectual virtues of the lady of his heart and, after a few exercises on the familiar theme, he did not conceal that his love was total and did not exclude desire. Had Sidney loved, in actual life, Penelope Devereux, the probable inspirer of his sonnet sequence, as ardently and as generously as he did in verse? The question is a childish one. The noble knight and first English gentleman had evinced only very tepid enthusiasm for marrying Penelope when her dowry seemed unattractive. He had to live according to the demands of courtly life. He later married another lady, Frances Walsingham, while Penelope was wedded to Lord Rich in an unhappy marriage, the laws of which she did not observe too strictly. Accuracy to details of actual experience is not required from poets, whose truth is other and higher than that of history. Sidney's sincerity, if the word may be used where he is concerned, is one of feeling and more particularly of psychological analysis of feeling. He was not a great poet merely because he allowed love to hold his hand and make him write, but he did probe into the secrets of a heart more searchingly than any Elizabethan lyricist had done before him.

Sidney had placed his sonnet sequence under the aegis of faithfulness to the dictates of his heart. John Donne, early in the seventeenth century, strikes us today as much closer to us, because he takes himself much less seriously and boldly dramatizes in his songs and sonnets what T. S. Eliot has called "an awareness of the apparent irrelevance and unrelatedness of things." Donne brushed aside a great mass of ornamentation and of idealization of woman which had encumbered Elizabethan poetry. He cultivated argumentative paradox, ingenious dialectics, and wit. In so doing, he gave a new sincerity to poetry, and he appeals to those, numerous in our age, who read more sincerity in wit than in pathos, in impudence than in adoration. The sincerity of Donne, modeled after that of Ovid's youthful *Amores,* does not imply that the poet had actually lived what he expressed in his insolent declarations of inconstancy in love, in his brutal chiding of a woman who forgets to "hold [her] tongue and let [him] love," not even in the sophistry of the mock-Platonic "Ecstasie." It is all too clear that many of those songs and elegies of the future Dean of St. Paul's are brilliant exercises in the art of shocking the traditional reader of the day, calculated to please a small coterie of intellectuals and probably not to displease women readers who had been surfeited with idealizations of their spiritual beauty.

> I can love both fair and brown . . .
> I can love her, and her, and you and you,
> I can love any, so she be not true.

It is rather a tearing of many veils and a humorous and brutal admission that the pursuit of a prey half-consenting to be won and the renewal of desire through variety cannot be eliminated from love, even in poetry. Donne did not have to heed the dictates of his heart. Indeed, he had never seen the girl whose death he lamented unforgettably in the first of the two Anniversaries, but he was eager to enjoy the patronage of her father, the powerful Sir Robert Drury. Donne the man was doubtless a nexus of contradictions and he was truer than most men in juxtaposing them. He ardently longed for serenity and for a refuge against the passing of time and the onslaught of melancholy, at the very same moment when he was playfully boasting that he and his lady were vicariously married by the flea which had bitten both of them or bidding the "busy old fool," the sun, let his mistress and him enjoy their bed in the morning (borrowing an insolence from Ovid).

Yet commentators of Donne have been unwilling to surrender the claim for a basis in actual experience in his best poems. Even Sir Herbert Grierson, who did much to provide all students and lovers of Donne with the essential tools for their study, wished to believe that Donne, when he was tender and tragic instead of cynical, composed verse which "bore the imprint of some actual experience." Another highly competent student of Donne, Joan Bennett, was inclined to ascribe the more fervent love poems of Donne to the inspiration provided by his wife, Ann Moore, to whom Donne indeed wrote with tender fidelity thirteen years after their marriage. Sincerity rests on something far more complex than an actual experience and the mere recording or transposing of autobiographical data. Donne had at least two souls inhabiting his breast. His dramatic cynicism, which strikes a responsive chord in our serious and often humorless critics worshipful of wit, cannot be explained away as the mood of one period, which the poet would have outgrown to become a tragic lover haunted by death in "The Funeral," "The Relique," "The Anniversarie." Conflicting moods coexisted in him. He drew upon one of the sources of his inspiration when he railed at woman's inconstancy and tore up the effete conventions inherited from Spenser and Petrarch and threw himself into the personage with zest and playful passion. He tapped another parallel source when he composed graver and more solemn pieces addressed to the Countess of Bedford or to Mrs. Herbert or perhaps to his wife. Some of us will, in the last resort, believe that Donne's greatness rests upon his more "romantic" poems ("The Anniversarie," "Twickenham Garden," "The Message," "The Funeral," for example) or on those in which the argumentative intellect is blended with passion and with pathos, like "Lovers' Infiniteness" or "The Ecstasie." Intensity is the virtue of such poems, rather than the elusive merit of sincerity. The poet is not indulging witty exaggerations or cerebral metaphors. He moves as much as he delights. His experience, imaginative or actual, vibrates long in the reader. Baudelaire alone has probed deeper.[7]

The poetry of the confessional, as it might be called, is a sizable province of the seventeenth-century poetry to which our own century has been drawn with fascination ever since T. S. Eliot pointed out the similarities between that age and our own. Eliot's assertions, made at a time when the complete texts of Donne, Herbert, Traherne, Crashaw were, when accessible, known only to a few specialists, will be contradicted, or at least tempered, as time goes on. "A thought to Donne was an experience; it modifies his sensibility," Eliot imperatively advanced in 1921. Not a unique case surely among thinkers and among poets! Of Milton, Shakespeare, Dante, and even of Ronsard and Scève the same assertion could be made; nor is it self-evident that the "dissociation of sensibility, from which we have never recovered," which struck the creator of "Prufrock," began with Donne and was recovered in the twentieth century. The disintegration began with the Renaissance, and with the waning of the Middle Ages which made the Renaissance inevitable; it existed, like a worm in the fruit, in the very

---

7. From the immense literature of the last two decades devoted to Donne, only Joan Bennett's *Four Metaphysical Poets* (2d ed. Cambridge University Press, 1953) and J. B. Leishman's *The Monarch of Wit* (London, Hutchinson House, 1951) need be mentioned here.

flowering of the Middle Ages to which we fondly like to attribute a unity of belief and a lack of disquietude which may well be mythical projections of our own longings.

Be it as it may, gravity and fervor in the analysis of the self, which may be taken to be constituent elements of what is usually called sincerity, increased in a few of the poems of Lord Herbert of Cherbury, of George Herbert and Richard Crashaw. The rise of Puritanism was a potent influence and led to a stern soul-searching. A few Catholics, accustomed to confession, did likewise. George Herbert may be said to have been more intent than many of his contemporaries upon the laying bare of his heart, in "Confession" for instance:

> Within my heart I made
> Closets; and in them many a chest;
> And, like a master in my trade,
> In those chests, boxes; in each box, a till;
> Yet grief knows all, and enters when he will.

In the first and the second of the "Jordan" poems, Herbert protests against the convention that leads other poets to say that only fictions and "false hair" become poetry. "Is there in truth no beautie?" he questions. And he disavows his own past, when he seeks luster, "quaint words and trim invention." He would now rather be unadorned and true.

> There is in love a sweetness readie penn'd,
> Copie out only that, and save expense

is his own advice to himself. Only by opening the heart fully through confession and letting the Lord in everywhere as a welcome invader does the Christian make his heart safe. Sincerity, in seventeenth- and eighteenth-century England, and even later, will, far more than in France, retain a religious connotation.

But, as a mockery to the historian prone to believe that ages of the past had an organic unity of their own, Robert Herrick, a clergyman, lived and wrote precisely when Donne was forsaking poetry and Herbert was composing his. He included in his *Hesperides* no fewer than twenty-seven pieces entitled "On Himself" and described his life in many others. Yet there is neither confession nor self-revelation in Herrick's graceful lyrics, little of the acerbity of tone which Donne put into his wit, none of the solemnity of Herbert. The amiable poet recaptured in English the polish and the urbane quietude of Horace and of Tibullus. He sang variety in love, and the petticoats of several Julias, for he found several ladies safer than one, the playful teasing of love less perilous to his nonchalance than passion. Rather than look in his heart, rather even than repeat, after Sidney and Drayton, that his verse was the true image of his mind, the Devonshire parson chose to flutter at the surface of life and of himself. Sincere he is, if sincere means freshly and spontaneously naïve, ingenious portrayer of his own superficiality, disarmingly naïve. But sincerity with him hardly reaches greatness.

Late in the sixteenth century, one man, Montaigne, made it his central and sole purpose to study himself nakedly. He did not plan to rival earlier autobiographies, such as Saint Augustine's, nor, in his own age and language, the vivid *Commentaries* of Montluc, another Gascon who died three years before the first edition of Montaigne's *Essays* appeared. The facts of his life interested him less than his own moods and reactions to outward events. Much of his career indeed remains shrouded in darkness: his youth and slow growth and his adolescent dreams, his loves, his ambitions, his disappointments. Much, probably far too much, has been made by many a scholar, following Pierre Villey's remarkable study, of the evolution of the essay as practised with growing mastery by Montaigne and of the sinuous continuity of Montaigne's thought. Life seldom submits to such a neatly organized pattern. Neither Montaigne nor Nietzsche went through harmoniously progressive periods, sloughing off one system to evolve another one and discarding earlier beliefs as they espoused more mature ones. Both were multifarious personalities from the start; according to the demands of circumstances or to the caprices of inspiration, they gave expression to one another of their simultaneous moods, tapping one or another of the superimposed strata of their deeper selves. In Montaigne as in many a complex human being, there always coexisted a destroyer and a preserver. He was an ironical dissector of all global notions and of all prejudices, who cherished some dilettantism and the anarchy of a born doubter. He could also prove a consistent pursuer of wisdom and of spiritual balance, who amorously polished his own statue after having appeared to hammer all its pieces asunder.

No one before Montaigne had been endowed with such a piercing gift for the analysis of man's inner life. Insolently, he proclaimed from the outset that he was the chief, and even the sole, object of his rambling disquisitions. With seeming nonchalance, he reported a number of inconsequential and trivial details about his own behavior: how and what he liked to eat or drink, how he rode on horseback or otherwise traveled, what he read, what he thought when serious, and what fanciful dreams or impudent desires crossed his mind. Some of his more disorderly and most revealing essays, such as the famous capricious development hung on a few lines of Virgil (Book III, v), praised folly as even Erasmus had not done. In them, he aimed at a genuine self-portrayal through keeping within bounds wisdom, whose excesses are as perilous as those of folly, and through casting intellectual order and moral restraint to the winds. Throughout his work, Montaigne distrusted the most consistent foe of sincerity: the desire to discover an underlying unity behind our contradictions and to portray one's life as a harmonious unfolding of an expanding personality. He never fell a prey to the bourgeois complacence or to the Olympian and occasionally self-righteous attitudes which even the greater genius of Goethe, or the would-be heir to Montaigne and Goethe, André Gide, did not eschew in their old age. He was probably fortunate in not living into the most perfidious years of any great career: those which spread from the age of sixty to that of four score years and over, at which age both Goethe and Gide met with a patriarch's end.

One of the most momentous discoveries of mankind, first anticipated by Heraclitus and driven to its fullest consequences by Diderot and the German romantics, may be credited in its modern formulation to Montaigne: the rejection of being in favor of becoming, of *l'être* in order to delineate what changes, *le passage*. Montaigne's own ego, and, more generally, man, whom he imagines to have many features in common with Michel de Montaigne, is to be seized as he changes and in the very process of his changing. All is flux in nature. Only a person who is aware of being carried down the stream can fully espouse and render the perpetual fluidity of a world of which, Shakespeare will say in immortal lines, time takes survey.

The psychologist of the *Essays* was thus aware of the dialectical process of thought which his hero, Socrates, had wielded with such dexterity. He realized that some passiveness was required from him who claimed to study himself in his becoming, or else too much activity, too conscious a use of will power would transform and deform the object observed by the subject. At the same time, Montaigne understood that a searching self-analysis is a corroding agent, whittling away many illusions and delusions. He strove for some equilibrium, and he justified his desire for sincerity through his purpose as a moralist. The dilemma was for him whether to stress all that in him was mediocre or base, so as to be easily content with his own, and man's, imperfections, or to depict himself as somewhat nobler than he was, so as to attempt aiming higher and thus to improve others. But one can only improve others if one is first determined to improve oneself. The most penetrating student of moral life as envisaged by Montaigne, Gustave Lanson, praised the blending of modest idealism and of half-ironical humility in the *Essays* and congratulated the author for keeping shy of the hypocrisy of much ethics, in which duty is merely "what we require from others."

Montaigne took naïve pride in his undertaking, "a thorny undertaking" as he calls it in Book II, sixth essay. "No description," he added, "equals in difficulty or in usefulness the full portrayal of oneself. . . . I depict chiefly myself bare and whole." He was, however, not unmindful of the unpleasantness with which any intensive pursuit of oneself and of sincerity is tainted: exhibitionism. Almost as much as Rousseau, albeit with keener humor, he considered himself as unique and took pride in it. Unweariedly he recurred to the strangeness that he detected in himself and to the puzzle that, to others as well as to himself, he was bound to constitute. Stressing that strange uniqueness, however, can come perilously close to boastfulness. Montaigne was not immune from some consciousness of his superiority to his countrymen in an age in which deceit and fanaticism were rife, as is shown in the first chapter of his third book, "De l'utile et de l'honnête." In the essay in which he most vehemently announced his hatred of lying as the worst of vices and therefore his cherishing sincerity as a pre-eminent virtue, "De la présomption" (II, xvii), Montaigne did not ignore the fact that a fervent self-explorer can fall in love with his own mirrored image. Like Narcissus, "he relishes himself, he wallows in himself." But such narcissism implies some straining after effect and too ready an acceptance of his own polished image on the part of the gazer.

How far did Montaigne's sincerity reach? Modern French interpreters, and not a few of his Anglo-Saxon admirers—whose name, from the seventeenth century in England down to Emerson and a number of moderns, has been legion—have often contended that Montaigne's amiable frankness has disarmed all potential fault-finders. One Frenchified Englishman at least balked at Montaigne—Horace Walpole, who on October 27, 1766, while reading the *Essays* at Bath, vented his boredom to Madame du Deffand: "Truly the doting of a pedant, a rhapsody of commonplaces . . . His Seneca and he make every endeavor to learn how to die—the one thing in the world which we are most certain to do without having learned it." His correspondent retorted that Montaigne was no more vain than other men, and less so than those who appear modest. "The 'I' and the 'me' recur on every page, but what knowledge can be had, if not through the 'I' and the 'me'?"

In the previous century, the metaphysician Malebranche had taken Montaigne to task far more sternly in his *Recherche de la vérité* (II, v) and warned his readers against the nonchalant air of naturalness and the affectation of cavalier frankness of the moralist. Malebranche was an Oratorian priest, deeply impressed by Descartes, himself in several respects a scion of Montaigne and a man of the world throughout his scientific and philosophical career. Pascal, the Jansenist, had been even more averse to Montaigne, from whom he had nevertheless absorbed the larger part of whatever history and philosophy he ever knew. In the influential treatise of logic compiled by Arnauld and Nicole under the title *Logique de Port-Royal* (Book III, chapter XX, paragraph vi) appeared the first determined onslaught against Montaigne's claim to being sincere. He was charged with slyly omitting all that might have harmed him in the eyes of posterity. Rousseau followed suit and, in a little-known text which was revealed by Sainte-Beuve, he bluntly called him "a falsely sincere man who wants to deceive through telling the truth; he shows himself with some faults, but he only grants himself amiable ones: every man has hateful faults too" (project for a preface to the *Confessions*).

It is true that Montaigne accused himself of many peccadilloes, and of only very few serious deficiencies, physical, intellectual, or moral. On the subject of his ancestry, he sinned by omission. Throughout his travel diary in Italy, he posed for a man who, concerned with his disease of the stone or for better motives, observed prudent rules of continence and visited honest women exclusively. His biographers, bearing in mind his earlier revelations on the ardor of his temperament and some indulgence in debauchery of which he may have been guilty in his youth, have good reason to doubt his word. Elsewhere he boasted of having displayed warlike courage in allusions, none too specific, to battles which he probably never fought. In his chapter on physiognomy (III, xii), he related how, having been captured by enemy partisans during the religious wars, he had saved his life and recovered a casket in which he kept his money, merely through his unperturbed behavior and imposing mien. But the account is contradicted by none other than Montaigne himself. In a letter to Monsieur de Matignon, written on February 15, 1588, he had with greater humility owned to having been robbed of his casket beyond recovery—nobleness of mien notwithstanding.

Such lies are trivial, and sincerity can hardly imply that every sentence we jot down be factually accurate. Even a little boastfulness in claiming the deportment of a nobleman or descent from a long line of ancestors of high birth is a venial sin. But there were worse pitfalls besetting Montaigne's attempt at self-portrayal, and he was aware of

them. Contradiction with oneself is inevitable, if a fixed
and probably constricting pattern is to be avoided. The
father of all essayists, long before Rousseau, Emerson, or
Whitman, knew how to justify his versatility: "To hold
oneself tied and necessarily obligated to one way only is perhaps existing, it is not living. The most beautiful souls are
those which have the greatest variety and suppleness" (III,
iii). A second peril threatens a conscientious analyst of his
own qualities and faults: he tends to like himself overmuch
and he forgets his need for self-improvement. "To be
amused by oneself . . . is also to find oneself to one's liking
. . . and to love oneself to an excess." Elsewhere, he admits:
"I adorn myself ceaselessly, for I describe myself ceaselessly."

The most persistent confession of our faults is, indeed,
more than half-consciously, an attempt to anticipate, and
perhaps to disarm or to silence, criticism. A sizable dose of
coquetry slips into any narrative of our lives or into any
analysis of our inner and outer selves. Montaigne, like Gide,
and many other males, soon became an aged coquette posing before multiple mirrors. He played at hide-and-seek
with himself, but he never took the game quite seriously
enough to be caught in it altogether. He believed that a
man ought to bring genuine love and an earnest desire to
participate with far more than words, to our relationship
with women, the third and most complex of the three "commerces" ("Des trois commerces," III, iii). But he deemed
it madness to bind all our thoughts to such a "commerce"
and to commit ourselves to it with a furious and indiscreet
affection. As Pascal might have said, and doubtless did
think of his predecessor, he remained nonchalantly unconcerned with salvation and eluded the wager or the Kierke-
gaardian choice between either and or. Is such dilettantism
a truer form of sincerity to oneself than the more fanatical
self-involvment of those martyrs—the only ones to whom
Pascal would grant his credence—who are ready to stand

up and be slaughtered? Montaigne, like Renan, would probably answer affirmatively.

Dimly, at the dawn of an age of criticism and of self-analysis, unsystematically as was his custom, never very searchingly since he shunned too rigorous a mode of thinking, Montaigne perceived the moral dilemmas of him who pursues sincerity. The man who confesses becomes prone to accepting all of himself; he thus turns complacent; he even cherishes his confession as an exorcism of whatever is evil in him. A fault may appear as far less objectionable once it has been revealed to others and thus shared with them. Or else the self-portrayer, through describing every mole and wart on his own face, ingratiates with his audience and rests content with the display of his minor and rather attractive vices, and fails to climb higher. Montaigne's sincerity was not of an heroic kind. Yet, in the most libertine of his essays (III, v), he spoke gravely in tones such as had not yet been heard in the West, disclaiming the moral facility which may go with superficial sincerity and deriving from his bold self-portrayal a lesson of bold and honest behavior.

> Besides, I have made it a rule to dare say all that I dare do, and I take no pleasure in thoughts which cannot be published. The worst of my deeds and conditions seems to me less ugly than the ugliness and cowardice I find in not having the courage to confess it. Everyone is discreet in confessing; one should be discreet in the deed; boldness in one's failings is in no way compensated and held in check by the boldness to confess them. He who would bind himself to say everything would bind himself to do nothing that one is forced to bury in silence. . . . One must see one's vice and study it in order to describe it. Those who conceal it from others ordinarily conceal it from themselves. . . . Is

there any ugliness in sinning which frees us from having to confess it?[8]

8. On the subject of Montaigne's sincerity, the following references will be found relevant and most enlightening: Gustave Lanson, "La vie morale selon les *Essais*," *Revue des Deux Mondes*, 94th year (February 1 and 15, 1924), 603–25 and 836–58; Alexandre Micha, "Montaigne le joueur," *Cahiers du Sud*, No. 269 (January-February 1945), 53–63; Micha, "Montaigne et le drame de l'intellect," *Mercure de France*, No. 1019 (July 1, 1948), 453–62; Paul Ballaguy, "La Sincérité de Montaigne," *Mercure de France*, No. 843 (August 1, 1933), 547–75; Hugo Friedrich, *Montaigne* (Bern, Francke, 1949); Francis Jeanson, *Montaigne par lui-même* (Paris, Editions du Seuil, 1951), whose thoughtful introductory essay first appeared in *Esprit* (September 1951), 321–42. The attack on Montaigne's exhibitionism by the men of Port-Royal is to be found in *The Port-Royal Logic*, translated by Thomas Spencer Baynes (Edinburgh and London, Blackwood), Part III, Chap. xx, pp. 274–76.

CHAPTER 2

From Montaigne to Diderot

THE FERVID and often jealous affection the French
have almost always lavished on their seventeenth-century
literature has been a source of surprise to observers of their
country. Foreigners have remained unconvinced by the
earnestness with which French educators unraveled in the
dramatists and moralists of the century philosophical secrets and ethical messages second to none—not even to
those that other nations preferred to read in the ancient
writers, in Shakespeare, or in the Bible. Yet the nourishment of the French on their own "classics" survived political upheavals, revolutions in taste, and the onslaughts of
the Romantics, the Symbolists, and more recent iconoclasts.
Proust, Valéry, Gide, Mauriac, Camus—all have repeatedly
longed for the values that lay implicit in French classical
literature.

A tradition of clinging to a glorious past, nostalgia for
the age of French predominance, an insistence upon reason
as a curb upon imagination and intelligence as an antidote
to sensibility may be among the so-called "national traits"
of the French character, and explain the pre-eminent place

still held by the age of Louis XIV. Above all else, however, the French have admired in their seventeenth century a deeper probing into the mind and the heart, an illumination of the secrets of the man within, more effulgent than at any other period of their literary life. The Renaissance, up to Montaigne, had ransacked outlying treasures, waged impetuous battles, unleashed instincts and urges hitherto held in check by religion. It had glorified youth, beauty, and energy. The dramatists, the moralists, the religious thinkers, and the scientists of the age that followed the Renaissance set out to learn more about man in himself and in society, and man in relation to God and to nature. They cherished beauty, but preferred it, on the whole, stripped of ornamental wreaths and of fanciful imagery. More perhaps than any age since, they equated beauty with truth, and they unweariedly chided authors and artists who did not follow nature. Truth and nature were never very deeply elucidated in their multifarious and contradictory meanings; nor were their humbler or younger relatives, sincerity, originality, or genius. Those words probably can never be satisfactorily defined, and those who ask with Pilate what any one of them means will not, and need not, wait for an answer. A pursuit of truth and naturalness is among the two or three features most French classical writers had in common. What we would term sincerity today (sincerity to others in an age of politeness and of etiquette, sincerity to oneself in an age when the flattery of courtiers was rife) entered into the seventeenth-century ideal.

Generalizations about that mythical entity we call a century are ill-advised, and never more so perhaps than about the span of a hundred years from 1600 to 1699. For even in France, where those hundred years were not marked by the same turbulence that prevailed in England or by the havoc wrought by the foreign wars that afflicted Germany, unity was sought but seldom achieved; divergent forces were

curbed but not long repressed; a common ideal was proposed by thinkers, preachers, writers, and by courtiers, but
not often adhered to; successive ministers failed to pursue
the work of their predecessors with any continuity of views.
By common consent, the classical period proper has been
shrunk by historians to the twenty-five years from 1660 to
1685, and even then conformity was certainly not the rule.
Louis XIII reigned over a very different France from that
of the Sun King, and the last decade and a half of the century has been conveniently lopped off by scholars and assigned to the following one, since it failed to live up to the
standards of classicism. Not only chronologically but also
in its character, the seventeenth century must be considered
as heterogeneous. Zealots of that latest literary idol, the
baroque, have shown that simplicity and restraint were not
always to be found in seventeenth-century prose, and that
garish rhetoric, willful extravagance, turbidity, tawdriness
also marred the prose of many a writer of that age—such
faults being caricatural excesses of baroque virtues. It is
nevertheless correct to present the classical ideal in style as
one in which an effort toward artistic sincerity prevailed.

Such sincerity entailed the discarding of Ciceronian
mannerisms which had been usefully learned by Du Vair
and Jean Louis Guez de Balzac, early in the century, but
which had to be outgrown once French prose writers felt
they had mastered the secrets of rhythm and were in danger of being seduced by too much symmetry. Traces of
préciosité linger in La Rochefoucauld; La Bruyère is not
immune from some striving for witticisms and for striking
surprise and contrast effects. But the elimination of superfluous adornments and the abhorrence of all that sounded
meretricious or false characterizes the French classical style
illustrated by Pascal, Saint-Evremond, Bossuet, even by the
authors of memoirs and of letters of 1660–1685. Simplicity
and restraint for the first time in modern letters were ad-

vocated by theorists and practitioners of prose, as against
the self-conscious display of pomp and of scholarship that
had marred the work of French and Italian humanists. Clarity in writing was deliberately and gradually imposed upon
schoolboys and writers until it became a national ideal, and
clarity owed its value to the double purpose that it was
meant to fulfill: courtesy to the reader, who is spared un-
necessary labor and whom art should "please," and sincerity, that is, the direct conveying of the unveiled meaning
intended by the author. The stylistic ideal concisely formulated by Pascal in what is usually presented as the first section of his *Pensées,* pursued by Pascal himself in his *Provin-
ciales* and by most prose writers between 1655 and 1685,
rests upon adequacy between content and form, the idea
or the feeling to be communicated and the vesture which
will most exactly mold itself on it. "Beauty is fitness expressed": that formula by a modern British writer on art,
Sir Walter Armstrong, best exemplifies the artistic ideal of
the French seventeenth century.

Do not the words "artistic" and "sincerity" jar when
matched? The question will be asked later in this book
whether sincerity can coexist with style and with literature,
insofar as literature designates the awareness of an aim
which is the production of an emotion of beauty, and the
conscious use of devices calculated to move thus, through
pleasing, soothing, striking, overwhelming the reader. The
best known among the commentators of the *Pensées,* Léon
Brunschvicg, states in his edition that "the transparency of
style is, in Pascal, the immediate effect and the reflection of
his absolute sincerity." He adds elsewhere that "the concern for style [which marks the moralist of his age] is not
to be found in Pascal to the same extent as in others. . . . All
is sincere in Pascal." Pascal himself, enigmatically, asserted
in one of his thoughts, No. 590 in the Brunschvicg edition:
"For religions, one must be sincere." ("Pour les religions,

il faut être sincère," which may mean "In the realm of religions" as well as "in their favor" or "to serve them.") Yet Paul Valéry, in a brilliant attack on Pascal, charged him not with insincerity but at least with charlatanry and with an unhealthy and unscientific appeal to emotions, in particular to the emotion of fear. He denounced his polishing his style, his labored search for rhythm and for metaphors, his eagerness to frighten the unbeliever out of his nonchalant quietude which recoils before no argument, marshals every device of rhetoric. In truth, no classical writer in France ever contended that art was incompatible with truth, not even Descartes, a less emotional prose writer than his fellow mathematician, Pascal. Sincerity, if it were ever driven to such a Jansenist excess as to foreclose all intent to move or to attract the reader, would devour literature itself.

Seventeenth-century sincerity, to be appraised aright, must be placed in its historical context. It grew out of a revulsion against a twofold peril encountered by that age: that of politeness turned into social falsehood and grimaced masquerading and that of heroic tension and of rigid sclerosis of the whole being through an exalted will power. The latter has usually been linked with the name of Corneille. The founder of French tragedy was indeed fond of portraying man's will power struggling against passions or ennobling them through forcing them to rise against mediocrity and indulgence. He has been distorted, in traditional textbooks, into the monstrous delineator of a duel between love and duty, or between love and the assertions of an ego bent upon preferring self-love to pity, to tenderness and the promptings of the heart. Such a caricature of Cornelian psychology, which is in fact subtle and rich in complexities, has lately been rejected by French critics. No French author has been so successfully vindicated and so freshly reappraised as Corneille has been by the scholarship of

1920–50. Corneille's women, if they seldom condescend to
the exquisite tenderness of Shakespeare's heroines, if they
reject the vacillations of capricious passion and seem to
ignore the urge of the senses, unlike Racine's feminine
characters, are true women nevertheless, perhaps truer to
average life than Desdemona or Cordelia, than Roxane or
Phèdre. Few speeches can match, for noble and candid self-
portrayal, the "sincere" declarations made by Pauline, in
the second act of *Polyeucte,* to Sévère, the man whom she
once loved or was near loving. Everything is implied, even
the tumult of her senses, if it is toned down in expression
and if regrets and emotions are filtered through an analytical
intellect. Self-control and passion enhance each other, but
passion is far from being annihilated.

Lack of humility may legitimately be deplored in Corneille. He was doubtless more pious than either Shakespeare or Racine, and yet he has portrayed, even less than
they, the qualities of humility, charity, and mercy that we
associate with Christianity. André Gide has contrasted his
psychology with that of Dostoevsky, and deplored the fact
that the French, swayed by the examples of Corneille and
Balzac, should have depicted characters who think they are
as they want to be, and who ignore or understress their own
contradictions or their weaknesses. The Russian novelist
discovered, if he did not always plumb them to their depths,
abysses of shame in man and woman, from which he cata-
pulted his heroes to summits of saintly remorse and of
angelic humility. Corneille's characters slur over their moments of weariness, discourse with grandiloquence about
the person they wish to pass for in the eyes of others and in
their own, and do not equate sincerity (which they fail to
mention) with the laying bare of what might be weakest
in them. They do, however, rejoice in their masterly knowledge of themselves. Truth is difficult, but they will face it

unflinchingly rather than dupe themselves with subter-fuges.[1]

The formulation of an ideal of politeness which was soon to spread to Western Europe as a whole was, along with Cartesian philosophy and Corneille's tragedy, one of the significant achievements of the third decade of the French seventeenth century. Like clarity, that ideal had to be pain-fully acquired by the French: more than clarity, it was a foreign import, from Spain and chiefly from Italy. The ac-ceptance of rules of courtesy and of *bienséances* by the aristocracy and the middle class constituted a victory of women over the brutal unruliness of males, of graceful arti-ficiality over instinct. Such a victory entailed sacrifices, that of candid speech in particular. The literature of the classi-cal age, with Boileau, La Fontaine, Molière, and later La Bruyère, railed at the hypocrisy that had become the rule in Paris, Versailles, and Chantilly. It held up frankness as an ideal too seldom revered. La Fontaine's *Fables* are never more bitter than against mendacious flatterers. Molière's misanthropist wages war against the circumlocutions that coat the bitter pills to be administered to worldly poets, coquettish superannuated ladies concealing the ravages of time, and foppish noblemen. Sincerity does not consist in brutality and in the parading of their greed by imperious males, but the refinement of language, of manners, and of

---

1. Instances of the proud courage of Corneille's characters seeking the full truth about themselves and rejecting emotional delusions are numer-ous. Even when one of those characters remarks, "Hélas! pour me tromper je fais ce que je puis," he is deploring but admitting the necessity to confess the full truth. In one of the lesser plays of Corneille, *Héraclius,* a hero who thought he was guilty of incest says:

> Ah! s'il m'était permis de ne me pas connaître,
> Qu'un si charmant abus serait à préférer
> A l'âpre vérité qui vient de m'éclairer.

"Abus" is of course self-deception.

the ritual of love by the Précieuses had turned society life
into an elaborate lie. This ritual caused an overstepping of
the tenuous line that separates civilized restraint of one's
passions from the unhealthy stressing of the imagination
and the transference of sex to the brain, as D. H. Lawrence
was later to call it. Molière's nature was probably impetuous and sensuous; he knew himself to be doomed to a
short and exhaustive life, and he had little time and even
less patience for some of the ingenious fences raised by the
Précieuses between desire and fulfillment. But, above all,
he found a rich source of comic situations in upholding
the claims of common sense and in deflating pretentious-
ness and falsehood.

Comedies and tragedies are hardly likely to make much
of the duty of sincerity to oneself, which moralists and introspective psychologists liked to advocate, under other
names, in the age of La Rochefoucauld and Bossuet. Tragic
characters such as those of Racine are fond of investing
with an orderly expression the passionate vacillations of
their hearts; they look into themselves with a lucid eye,
but do so in order to justify their surrender to passion or
to strengthen their love through posing upon it the sacrifice of their sanity and of their reasoning power. Comic
personages do not indulge abstract analysis of their motives; they must be presented in action, and must appear
ridiculous or humorous in their outward behavior or in
the contrast between the ambitions which they pursue and
their lower but truer selves.

But sincerity to others constitutes one of the great themes
of Molière's comedies. The three important plays of his
mature years, *Tartuffe, Don Juan,* and *Le Misanthrope,* all
composed between 1664 and 1666, revolve around that subject. Ever since the Greeks, whose actors used to play under

a mask, dramatists have been haunted by the power of masks. The taste for African art and for the circus, widely spread among poets and philosophers in our century, has revived the interest in masks as a symbol of art considered both as an artifice and as a means of revelation. Shackles recently imposed upon free political and social thinking by several tyrannies have cornered many authors into refuges where ambiguity and veiled suggestiveness had to be turned into effective weapons. The enigmatic avowal of young Descartes, "larvatus prodeo" ("under a mask do I go forward"), has caused much ink to be spilt. Molière as an actor had, for several years, appeared on the stage under one of the masks that helped the Italian comedians provoke the laughter of their audience. He shook free of the device after his early plays. But he had soon observed that not only histrionic puppets but most men also wear masks.

In a bold move, he undertook to portray men and women who attempt to dupe others through appearing to be what they are not. They are taken in by their own game of deceit, like Don Juan and like Tartuffe himself. Those who seek to redress the universal evil of sham pretense, as does Alceste, become enmeshed in their inner contradictions; the champions of truth shrink in anguish from the truth in themselves. One of the most astute commentators on Molière, the Englishman W. G. Moore, showed how the tragic comedy of *Tartuffe,* even more strikingly than the other great plays of Molière, gravitates around the brief moments when the impostor is driven to the lifting of the mask. Self-controlled and calculating as the protagonist is, there comes a moment when, impelled by desire, perhaps by passion, yearning for pity, wearied of his aloneness, he becomes at once hypocritical and sincere. He even coincides with the projection of himself which he offers to Elmire, the wife of his host and dupe, as he promises her, "De l'amour sans scandale et du plaisir sans peur." This saintliness added to his discretion ensured both security and the easing of remorse to his accomplice: "Et ce n'est pas pécher que pécher en silence."

Tartuffe is an object of ridicule and hatred because he has perfidiously aped all the outward features of true piety and made a mockery of every Christian virtue. The blending of a little sincerity with his dark plotting makes him more dangerous to society. The hero of *Don Juan* is a more appealing character: he is not pursuing any material interest; he is capable of generosity; his vices, impiety, avoiding the payments of his debts, and seducing gullible or half-willing feminine victims, are those to which men and women prove most lenient. He fails to tell the truth, and yet one wonders whether he does not become sincere in his flights of eloquence and in his love declarations, when he, too, removes his mask or ceases to be identified with the superficial mask he put on.

The word sincere recurs more frequently in *Le Misanthrope*. "Sincère Eliante" admires Alceste's outspokenness. "Etre franc et sincère est mon plus grand talent," boasts Alceste at the end of the play after having, in the first act, ranted against conventions, pretenses, and exaggerations. Alceste wants at all costs to unmask the bitter and even the gentle lying which is the condition of life in society when politeness has transformed outward behavior but envenomed the heart. He sets up his own pugnacious and youthful frankness against universal corruption. The play, once again, seems to rest upon a conflict between truth and the fallacious mirrors that distort it. Alceste, like Cléante, the reasoning character in *Tartuffe* and Molière's mouthpiece, if there be one in that play, firmly intends to expose and chastise those who dare

> Egaler l'artifice à la sincérité,
> Confondre l'apparence avec la vérité.

But it is uncertain where Molière takes his stand in *Le Misanthrope*. For there was in him at least as much of Philinte, the resigned and mundane friend of all mankind, the diplomatist skilled in compromise, as there was of Alceste, the impetuous advocate of frankness driven to the point of tactlessness. The harmless drawing-room poet Oronte, even the foppish noblemen and the old, or not so young, coquettes who adorn their appearances and disguise their wrinkles or their imperfections are, after all, hardly more than windmills stormed by the quixotic misanthropist.

Molière went deeper than in his other comedies when he outlined the character of Alceste—too deep, indeed, for the safe working of the comic devices and too deep for his public, which he was attacking frontally. For men will refuse to recognize themselves in the religious hypocrite or in the seducer, or even in the miser and the would-be gentleman; but few men could dissociate themselves from the polite skeptic Philinte, and few women could feel spared by the barbs aimed at young Célimène. Alceste, who insists upon men being logical, is himself guilty of blatant illogic. He vents the anger of his black bile (Molière had originally entitled his play "L'Atrabilaire amoureux") on others, but he never asks himself whether his wrath against the fashionable poet and the other marquis is not due to his own impatience of those rivals and to the disturbed state into which his ardent and frustrated love has thrown him. Sincere to, or against, others, Alceste never really attempts to reach full sincerity to himself. He lures himself into hoping that he can change Célimène through loving her; he even makes himself believe that he is loved by her, when he is hardly more than esteemed and liked, and expertly toyed with. And, when spite gets the better of his patience, he goes so far as to transfer his affection to Eliante, who is the sincere character in the play, but also a colorless one and one with whom Alceste should sense that he never

would be happy. The play is a study of the difficulties that
prevent a man who is passionate and irritable from reaching sincerity.

The modern reader may well be disappointed by the
poets, the novelists, and the historians of the French seventeenth century, who all failed to observe human nature, in
others and within themselves, with enough boldness to
render it free from the conventionalities then prevailing.
The novel had to wait for *La Princesse de Clèves* before it
could match the drama in psychological truth to life, and
even then its technique was unripe. Another hundred years
were to elapse before historians became critical of their
sources, objective in their narratives, and relativistic in
their perspective of one nation or culture replaced among
others in time and space. Lyrical poets, after the original
minores of the late sixteenth and early seventeenth centuries whom we have lately rediscovered (Lacépède, Chaste-
net, Jean de Sponde), did not, in France, reach the intensity
of Donne, Crashaw, Marvell, or the towering greatness of
Milton. The moralists were the original contribution of
France to a close psychological analysis of man, along with
her philosophers and her religious preachers.

With them, the notion of sincerity slowly progressed, and
it is clear that they perceived more nuances, and more dramatic contradictions, in human nature than imaginative
writers were as yet able to embody in their creations. The
same André Gide who upbraided the French for being too
slavish adherents of a view of man resting upon self-respect,
pride, and the will to appear other than one secretly is did
not fail to note that he, and Dostoevsky, had nevertheless
had predecessors among the French moralists. "Man is at
times as different from himself as he is from others," wrote
La Rochefoucauld in his maxim No. 135. Saint-Evremond
similarly reproached Plutarch with not perceiving that man

"is very different from himself; wicked, virtuous, just, un-just, humane and cruel. Plutarch prefers to ascribe to alien causes what, in man, seems to jar." The same Saint-Evre-mond, who survived the generation of Corneille's admirers to grow old and mellow in exile, scattered in his nonchalant letters and sundry writings clear-sighted remarks on the complexity of human nature. But he refused to dramatize his, or man's, contradictions, as Pascal and other converters of unbelievers had been prone to do. Unafraid of death and determined to enjoy life urbanely unto the last, he con-fessed to le Maréchal de Créqui that he had never experi-enced within himself the struggle between passion and reason: "Reason in me willingly agreed to what I felt like doing, through a feeling of pleasure."

The French classical age, when closely scrutinized, fails to answer the definition, often forced upon it in the past, of an "age of reason." Reason was everywhere distrusted, or circumscribed to a modest province of life, and one of its first duties was to admit that passion and taste and im-agination and faith escape its sway, indeed must trample it under their feet. In a curious text which echoes a con-versation with Pascal (quoted by Faugère and subsequently by Brunschvicg in connection with No. 276 of the *Pensées*), Pascal's friend, Domat, wrote: "We do not act from reason but from love, because the heart governs in us, and not the mind, and all the deference which the heart feels for the mind consists in this, that, if it does not act from reason, at least it makes us believe that it does." Bossuet, after some early fascination with Cartesian rationalism, protested against its tenets and, like many persons in his century, re-fused to worship at the altar of clear and distinct ideas. "Be-sides such ideas," he wrote to M. D'Allemans, "there are general and confused ones which nevertheless enclose such essential truths that to deny them would be to overthrow such truths." Indeed it could plausibly be argued that the

fallacy through which we have long mistaken the French
seventeenth century for the golden age of rationalism is to
be explained by the deceptive vocabulary which men then
had at their disposal. Words that served for the analysis and
expression of intellectual matters or of social behavior (such
as distinguish, discriminate, delicacy, and untranslatable
terms like *ménagements, bienséances, finesse*) then sprang
up on all sides as society became more attentive to nuances.
But affective moods and the mysteries lurking beneath the
clear consciousness of self-analytical individuals were not
then adequately rendered by that vocabulary. The unconscious was dimly perceived and feared, but could not be
probed. Generic words like "the heart" or "passion," and
even conventional metaphorical turns like "transports" and
"flames" were resorted to. The "je ne sais quoi" sufficed
to allude to all that was feared, and respectfully kept at a
safe remove, in human nature.

La Rochefoucauld is in many respects the most relentless
analyst of the forces in us that defeat our attempts at sincerity. He hunted down all our subtle ways of practising
self-deception. Sincerity as an opening of the heart, as the
felicitous French phrase *ouverture de coeur* calls it, is very
rare (he asserts in his maxim 62) and we often mistake for
it a subtle dissembling which is calculated to draw the confidence of others. Or else, he hints in his *Sundry Reflections,*
v, we conceal under a show of sincerity a desire to repay
ourselves for our faults and to diminish their seriousness
through gaining the merit of confessing them. We are all
so eager to talk about ourselves and to present our faults
with the slant with which we wish them to be viewed that
such an eagerness makes up the better half of sincerity.
Lovers and mistresses, he notes in the same volume, insist
with each other that they must "sincerely" and mutually
declare the waning of their feelings when it comes; but
they do not in truth want to be told when they are no longer

loved. They wish rather to be assured that, as long as they are not told otherwise, they are loved indeed.

The favorite target of La Rochefoucauld's arrows is the weakness of most human beings and their readiness to welcome self-deception. "Weak persons cannot be sincere," he justly points out in maxim 316, and the obstacle to sincerity is less a desire to tell lies than it is a strange inability to be true. Dissembling is less perilous than such powerlessness to know the truth about ourselves ("Treatise on the False" in *Sundry Reflections*, XIII). La Rochefoucauld, a seventeenth-century Nietzsche, after a fashion, and an agnostic, inclined toward a materialistic explanation of men's motives; Pascal, a Jansenist mystic, the severe gentleman of Port-Royal; Bossuet, the exponent of orthodox Catholicism—all might have agreed on one message which they unweariedly offered to their readers and to educators: rationalizing, listening to the insidious "reasons of the heart," and letting imagination (envisaged in its deceptive aspect and not in its creative one) rule us and the world, usurping the role of reason—these constitute the most formidable obstacles to clear-sightedness and to wisdom as well as to saintliness.

But does telling ourselves, and others, the truth bring about inner peace and satisfaction to those with whom we live? The seventeenth century was tormented by the question, and it has left us a remarkable work, the first modern psychological novel, in which the consequences of sincerity are forcibly presented. The heroine of *La Princesse de Clèves* married a husband whom she liked, respected, and admired, but whom she loved only with moderation. She was resigned to a life of splendor and of dignity and subconsciously admitted that passion, such as one hears and reads about, was not for her. But everyone around her, at the court of the sixteenth-century king where the scene is laid, talked of love and seemed to indulge in entrancing affairs of the heart. She was attracted to the Duke of Nemours and he was drawn to her, preferring her to the most brilliant marriage prospects. Her mother died, after having warned her of the perils of extramarital love. She had no children. Religion seemed to play no part whatever in her life, except as a refuge at the end. Her only recourse lay in her passion for truth.

In a famous scene, the Princess confesses to her husband that she must absent herself from the court with him and that he must provide her with the moral fortitude needed to crush her nascent affection for another man. Her husband is touched by her confidence at first, then poisoned by the realization that he is not loved, that someone else has inspired his wife with the ardent feeling that she never seemed to experience for him. He endeavors to prove worthy of her frankness and of her nobleness of soul. But he is bitten by jealousy and soon dies. She obstinately refuses to marry M. de Nemours, fearful as she is of love and of the ephemeral nature of most attachments, oppressed by her responsibility in having unwittingly caused her husband's misfortune, anxious to preserve her dignity and to remain "queen of her griefs." No morality is offered by the author who had probably herself experienced a similar anguish in her inability to love Monsieur de la Fayette, her husband, with any degree of fullness and who portrayed in her three novels the situation of a husband made jealous by the disaffection and the proud love for truth of his wife. The heroine was sincere to herself and to her husband. She discreetly gave her unusual avowal as evidence of her sincerity and hinted that such a noble confession should content him. But she merely succeeded in ruining two and perhaps three lives, deriving some sadistic satisfaction from the suffering she thus inflicted upon her husband, subconsciously resented as an obstacle. Anatole France, who prefaced an edition of *La Princesse de Clèves* in his youth, recalled to his readers the way in which life imitates literature. Madame Roland, during the Revolutionary days, confessed to her husband, who was noticeably older than herself, that she loved another deputy, Buzot, but would not yield to her love. She only brought unhappiness to Buzot and to herself, and jealousy and bitterness to her husband. Sincerity in matters of sentiment can work worse evil than omission and even perhaps than pious, or uxorial, lies.

It would be idle to presume that a sketch of the progress of literary sincerity could ever show a regular growth or the cumulative impact of earlier volumes upon those that succeed them and touch upon similar themes. Nature does not make leaps, old-fashioned science used to repeat, but the inventiveness of man and his discovery of his own mysteries do proceed by leaps and bounds. A strong current of ideas may be reduced to a trickle, take refuge underground, then reappear and swell into an irresistible river. In several respects, the moralists of the eighteenth century proved more timid analysts of the labyrinthine caves in which men hide their self-deception than their predecessors of the classical age. Comic writers kept shy of the royal road on which Molière had triumphantly galloped; their satire of social types and conditions seems shallow in comparison with the great comedies of 1660–73. No follower of Racine dared pierce through the deceptive reasons through which passionate creatures justify their yielding to sentiment. No theologian was as harsh as the Jansenists in denouncing the insidious refinements of self-love which corrupt introspection and lure it into complacency. *Manon Lescaut* is in many respects a more successful work of art than *La Princesse de Clèves;* its characters are more alive, in part because their contradictions are not theorized upon or wondered at but merely laid before us. Their struggle against their instincts is foredoomed from the start, and half-hearted. They evince little anxiety to see pitilessly into themselves.

One of the main concerns of the age was to act upon the behavior of men in society even more than on their minds and to reform faulty and illogical institutions. Those for whom "the soul's joy lies in doing" usually waste little time on the dispassionate analysis of their motives. The indefatigable Voltaire is the prototype of such men; even Diderot, more contradictory, more complex, more addicted to the self-revelation which is the soul of love letters, has kept surprisingly silent on the question of sincerity. René Pomeau, the author of a little book, *Voltaire par lui-même* —published in a series in which French writers are supposed to appear to their readers as they saw, or depicted, themselves—could not conceal his embarrassment; for the author of the bulkiest and of the greatest *Correspondence* left behind by any literary man, hardly ever wrote intimately about himself.[2] Repeatedly he entertained the project of memoirs, but they soon turned into the vilification of alienated friends (such as the king of Prussia) or they became pseudo-memoirs attributed to Wagnière or some other person; they never touched upon his own inner life. He was repelled by Rousseau's display of feeling and by Diderot's advocacy of passion. He lacked neither passion nor feeling himself and he was not spared suffering, although cruel posterity may wish he had been inflicted far more. But he did not choose to translate his own experience directly into his literary works. He did not wish the man and the author to be one, and he mischievously concealed his personality and even his identity under masks or in borrowed characters. Even Montesquieu, the sedate magistrate and student of constitutional law, revealed himself more freely than Voltaire, in the detached thoughts which have been posthumously published as his *Carnets*.

2. René Pomeau, *Voltaire par lui-même* (Editions du Seuil, 1955).

One great writer—great for the French if not always equally appreciated outside his native country—in the first half of the eighteenth century, Marivaux, appears to have been persistently haunted by some of the questions with which we are here concerned: Can truth to oneself and to others coexist with love and its subtle calculations and deceptions? Is it possible to remain truthful in the art of writing, which more than any other seems to imply adornment and fallacies? Marivaux has long suffered in the eyes of posterity by having his name serve, under the form of the substantive *marivaudage* to denote a way of love that hardly concerns the heart and keeps passion at a distance, while all the resources of a calculating brain are called into play. In Marivaux's works each of the would-be partners assumes a disguise to hide his feelings as well as his social rank, to force the other one to the avowal of his nascent attachment, and to enhance the price of his own final surrender when both reason and sensibility, desire and tenderness are satisfied that no disappointment will ensue. Marivaudage, as Edmond Jaloux remarked, has thus become synonymous with insincerity itself.

Lately, however, several of the most perspicacious philosophers and the most acute critics in France have set out to rehabilitate Marivaux. His plays, even minor ones, have been staged superbly and to the point of satiety in several theaters. His novels have been promoted to the forefront of French fiction of the pre-Balzac era. Marivaux has been one of the most substantial gainers in the tide of taste that has sent young Frenchmen, between 1930 and 1960, back to the eighteenth century, in defiance of the verbal inflation and of the glorification of unrestrained feeling which have then been branded as the disease of the romantics. The French have not quite succeeded as yet in imposing their cult of Marivaux abroad; but, as in the cases of Racine and Stendhal, they are likely to win eventually over the resistance of the less vocal Anglo-Saxon critics and of the Germanic ones, who are prone to distrust lucidity as antithetic to profundity.

Marivaux's comedies and his lesser known but extremely keen essays and journalistic fragments might well be construed as an attempt to dislodge insincerity from the domain which is usually reserved for self-deception and for a coquettish game of half lying to others: the province of love. Marivaux has explored no other realm but that one. Long before his spiritual offspring, Alfred de Musset, and the romantics in general, he was convinced that love alone gives zest to living, a "polish" to the most boorish clowns, esprit and finesse to young men and women. "Without the sting of love and of pleasure, the heart of man is a paralytic," says a character in *La Surprise de l'amour.* Love is the chief affair for those contemporaries of Watteau and Lancret, even for the underprivileged among them, servants or managers of the estates of the rich. They yearn to love long before they actually experience the devoutly wished-for revelation; they thus bring about the feeling about which they have heard so much, almost through an act of will power. Much later, Balzac (in *Beatrix*) and Proust were to stress more forcibly the immense role that the will to love fulfills at a critical moment in the birth of a feeling traditionally described as blind and sent by destiny. Marivaux is undoubtedly the pioneer in uncharted lands when he focuses the searching light of his subtlest disquisitions on the beginnings of love. Nero in Racine, Phèdre herself, Romeo and Othello, Eneas and Dido had all loved at first sight. How and why Chimène and Pauline, Hermione and Roxane had begun to love and to admit it to themselves did not concern Corneille, Racine, and their audiences. The feeling was taken for granted, full grown and already exasperated by obstacles and unfulfillment.

Marivaux's characters cannot, like Racine's, be compared

to wild beasts in their cages. They have senses, to be sure, although the sensual manifestations of their passion are seldom alluded to, except for some occasional blushing or stammering. Marivaux was well aware of all that can be connoted, and concealed, by the word "desire" and of the animal substratum of most attractions. "Every day indeed, in matters of love, one does very coarse things very delicately." But one of his most persistent contentions is that desire, which can be the source of the most radiant poetry or a form of hideous greed, must be balanced by tenderness. His heroines are not naïve or prudish in this respect. "What a nasty lover indeed," they say, "is the man who desires you more than he loves you: not that a certain amount of desire is absent from even the most delicate lover, but in him, at least, the feelings of the heart are blended with the senses." The whole strategy of women courted by the males is, in fact, to take the stings off the desire or, at any rate, to insist that another phrase should be substituted for the direct one:

> Go and tell a woman whom you find lovable and for whom you feel love: "Madam, I desire you very much, you would do me great pleasure if you granted me your favors"; you will insult her, she will call you brutal. But tell her tenderly: "I love you, Madam, you have a thousand charms for me"; she listens to you, you fill her with joy, you speak like a gentleman. Yet you are saying exactly the same thing and paying precisely the same compliment. Only the phrasing differs, and she knows it well. Every woman understands that she is being desired when she is told "I love you," and she is grateful for the compliment only because it means "I desire you." But it means that politely.

Marivaux's feminine characters stand out with originality among eighteenth-century women because they never behave, speak, or feel like children. They "see clearly into

their hearts," as Silvia declares with relief at the end of
Le Jeu de l'amour et du hasard. They see no less clearly
into the heart of the man who desires and loves them. They
do not have to forsake chastity or restraint in words. But
they know as well as their partners that the love about
which they reason with subtlety is physical in its essence.
They know equally well that only tenderness and esprit in
its broader sense of spirituality, as well as clever intellectual-
ity, can make that love civilized, refined, and lasting. Marivaux has ingeniously remarked that passion is often strong-
est in intelligent and moral persons and in virtuous women,
for it grows richer and gains density, as it were, through all
the qualities of the mind which go to the strengthening of
the feeling, once it has been admitted as valid. He says of
one of those ladies who have first offered some resistance
to love: "All that she had felt for virtue accrues to the profit
of her passion."

But lucidity, the most eminent quality of Marivaux's
characters, never forsakes them. They consider lack of sincerity as the root of all further cheating. For, "we endeavor
to deceive ourselves first, in love, in order then to deceive
others without any scruple." In *L'Heureux Stratagème*
Marivaux even seems to hint that infidelity is preferable
to an enforced fidelity in marriage, which is tantamount
to a constant lie. True to the eighteenth-century spirit, he
pointed out the drawbacks of marriage in which "we are
forced to act exactly as if we loved each other, even after
we have ceased to do so." For sincerity can hardly withstand
the wear and tear of once-fresh feelings, which familiarity
entails. One of Marivaux's last comedies, first performed in
1739 and seldom given since, is entitled *Les Sincères*. The
adjective sincere recurs often in the play and the question
asked by the heroine is: Is one ever sincere? She upbraids
her suitor for expressing his feelings with too much warmth,
for exaggerating in his language. But their striving for com-

plete sincerity in their feelings and in their expression of their feelings destroys their love in the end. For sincerity must remain instinct with tenderness and prone to mercy to one's partner; it must be a gradual progress toward what the philosopher Gabriel Marcel, who is also a dramatist, has called "an inner clarity, a transparency of oneself to oneself, and of oneself to the other one."

Credit must also be given Marivaux for having meditated on the relationship between style and sincerity harder than any other man of his age. A gifted scholar, Frederic Deloffre, underlined in 1955, in a lengthy study of the dramatist's art of writing, the originality of his views on style. Marivaux was long and bitterly taken to task by his contemporaries for his obscurity and his lack of smoothness, even of naturalness. Boileau, La Bruyère, and a score of classical critics had, in the preceding fifty years, set up *la clarté* and *le naturel* as the two requirements of all good writing. Marivaux was irked by the charge of obscurity and, as early as 1719, he published in the *Mercure* a brief but pregnant essay entitled "Pensées sur la clarté du discours." He retorted to his critics that clearness in writing must not be secured at the cost of the full force and the meaningfulness of the thought to be expressed. For if, in order to be clear, hence polite to his audience, the writer impairs his own originality, represses the more audacious thoughts which his mind harbors, banishes an unusual image, then he has proved untrue to himself. Long before Mallarmé, the eighteenth-century apostle of a modest share of obscurity seemed to sense the value of suggestion in style. In another article, in *Le Spectateur* of August–September 1723, the dramatist ingeniously refuted those who charged him with being deficient in naturalness. He who is subtle and complex in his ideas or in his sensibility should, in order to remain sincere, express his own nature just as it is. Naturalness consists, he maintains, in "staying within the singular-

ity which was given us" and in "resembling oneself alone."
Style is primarily a correspondence, as adequate as possible,
between content and form. Words can wield immense power and crystallize a subconscious and almost nonexistent
feeling into an acknowledged and dangerous one, merely
because that feeling will have been honored with the word
of "love." Marivaux's characters sedulously shun inflating
words and resort to the fashionable language of *galanterie*
of their age and of the previous one, that of *préciosité* and
of heroic novels. His heroes and heroines alike want to feel
in the person whom they are ready to love, as the protagonist of *La Double Inconstance* says it of Silvia, that in him
or her, "c'est un coeur tout pur qui me parle," that no
screen of words obfuscates the sincerity of feelings.[3]

None of the eighteenth-century moralists appears to have
reflected as consistently on the question of sincerity as either
La Rochefoucauld or Marivaux. None of the novelists has
attempted to treat that rather undramatic theme in imaginative and concrete form. The noblest character of the age
and the truest heir to the classical tradition was Vauvenargues, who died at thirty-two in 1747. The most significant
part of what might be, too ambitiously, called his philosophy is his eulogy of passions, written long before Rousseau
and Diderot were to sing the same tune and initiate romantic attitudes. "Passions have taught men reason." "A life
without passions is very similar to death." "Genius depends
in great part on our passions." The recognition of passion
as the main source of men's creative originality and as the

3. On Marivaux, see the excellent scholarly study by Frederic Deloffre
on *Marivaux et le marivaudage* (Belles-lettres, 1955, series of Annales de
l'Université de Lyon) and Gabriel Marcel's short preface to three plays of
Marivaux in the Edition des Loisirs, 1947. Several of the quotations used
here have been borrowed from the convenient and suggestive little book
by Paul Gazagne, *Marivaux par lui-même* (Editions du Seuil, 1954); the
quotation on page 65 appears on page 94 of Gazagne's book.

essence of life itself was to lead to the plumbing of new depths in men's attempts to be wholly sincere. But Vauvenargues, as Saint-Beuve noted, dug no abysses. His maxims lack pointedness of form and arresting depth. The young army officer was too inclined to didacticism and to generalities, and dwelling in generalities is probably the pitfall of all maxim-coiners and the reason for the inferiority of that seductive but disappointing literary genre. In another respect Vauvenargues almost touched upon one of the paths through which Rousseau and the moderns would try to reach a greater degree of sincerity: he accepted and, on one occasion at least, justified his own contradictions, stating that "If anyone finds that I contradict myself, I answer: because I have once been mistaken, I do not intend to be always mistaken." But Vauvenargues remained an unoriginal psychologist and, even in his letters to his friend Mirabeau, who came from the same region of Aix-en-Provence where he himself (as well as Sade and D'Argens) had been born, he failed to reveal his personality with any depth.

Chamfort, much less likable as a character, proved more piercing, and his epigrammatic aphorisms, which enchanted Schopenhauer, are among the most felicitous ever coined. He enjoyed the advantage of being a misanthropist and a misogynist, two positions that a truly intelligent man cannot hold very long but which add venom and sting to his arrows. Chamfort's entertaining attacks against love, fame, ambition, foolishness, and stupidity (the French word *sottise* denotes both of the last two, and more) are most efficacious against men in society: they do not entitle that arch-pessimist to an enviable rank among those who analyzed man in general, or themselves in particular, with an unusual degree of sincerity.

Equal disappointment meets a search for sincerity in the novel of the second half of the eighteenth century. The most popular of those novels with the moderns, *Les Liaisons dangereuses,* does not go far enough into the introspective analysis of the characters by themselves, though the epistolary device used could have lent itself to it. The seducer and his accomplice might have admitted to themselves that a good deal of sincerity entered into their naïvely diabolical schemes. Only once does Valmont, in letter cxxv, relating the fall of La Présidente, confess that he came out of her embrace "only to fall at her knees and swear to her an eternal love; and it must be owned, I meant what I was saying." Others combined memoirs and fiction with varying degrees of originality and loudly contended they were saying the whole truth and nothing but the truth. Such was the Marquis d'Argens, whose memoirs (1755), after the author's announcement that nothing could deter him from reporting the truth without disguise, invented most impossible adventures set in France, Spain, Algiers, and Tunis.

Notorious and curious Rétif de la Bretonne provides students of eroticism with more substantial fare. His fecundity as a novelist and, if we can trust him, as a progenitor (he listed the twenty "natural" children he had when still young) is astounding. The quality of his writing and of his psychology is not equally admirable. There are, however, insights into the mechanism of love and even fresh descriptions of feelings in his best known work, *Monsieur Nicolas.* The book is offered to the "friend of truth" who will not be disappointed, for the author loudly proclaims his love of truth in its purity. In the fifth section or "Epoch," he repeats it: "I prefer truth to the fine morality of the imagination, for truth alone is moral [la morale]. . . . My aim is to present life as it was, without any reservations or any mask. . . . I must be sincere: I tell everything." But Rétif's place is rather among the realists, among the inventive and entertaining storytellers of amorous prowess, of whom Casanova is the most famous, than among the moralists who laid the human heart bare.

A suspicion soon creeps into the reader's mind when an author loudly proclaims his sincerity or his humility. Too much self-consciousness does not match unaffected self-revelation too happily. English predecessors of Rousseau, and even of Richardson, who never applied the adjective sincere to themselves, reached in fact closer than any of their French counterparts to an unreserved rendering of the smallest facts of their lives. We have in mind the two diarists whose names are usually associated, who were loyal friends, who both wrote around 1660–70 and who were only revealed in 1818–22: John Evelyn and Samuel Pepys. They are indeed very dissimilar. Evelyn has been less leniently treated by posterity, for he showed himself as too pious and a trifle self-righteous, and not too acute in his thinking or rather too close to Dryden's characterization of his countrymen as "true-born Britons who never think at all." His capacity for ingurgitating countless sermons fills us with awe, but we do not find that his religion led him to scan the mysteries of his heart as relentlessly as it did some Puritans in seventeenth-century England. Bunyan, in the same decade, had reached higher flights of poetry and made an impassioned attempt not to allow "his ways to be hid from his Lord" in his *Grace Abounding* (1666).

Pepys, Evelyn's fellow Anglican, went as far as any man has before our own age in recording his faults or his foibles, and the most trivial details of his uneventful but entertaining life. He, unlike other diarists, never cherished the illusion that he was different from all other men. He did not even like to think he was worse than the average and, while there was some silliness in him and an almost total lack of irony, those traits never reached the degree at which they might become a mark of originality. We learn from him how he took medicine; how he had to resist drinking wine; how he could not stand barelegged, not even while changing his stockings, without risking catching cold; how he

indulged ancillary loves and tried to hide his deviations
from uxorial rectitude from his jealous wife; what he wore
and what he ate. But Pepys was more concerned with details of his work with the Navy and with exterior incidents
or inconsequential little facts than with his own inner life.
His famous diary, amusing up to a point, shows him to
have been egocentric in a very prosaic fashion, untouched
by anything poetical or imaginative, unaware of any contradictions within himself, and hopelessly superficial. Such
diaries are not devoid of historical instruction and even of
enlightenment on human nature in its rather mediocre
specimens. But the kind of sincerity of which we are trying
to find lineaments before the romantic age hardly appears
in them.

Neither does it in Boswell, the naïvely astute visitor of
Rousseau in his Swiss retreat, whose *London Journal* contains some of the most undisguised confessions of the age.
The young Scotsman did embark upon his author's career
with a firm resolve to know himself according to the Delphic precept, and he added, dryly: "A man cannot know
himself better than by attending to the feelings of his heart
and to his external actions, from which he may with tolerable certainty judge what 'manner of person he is'." He
thus undertook to record his actions and his sentiments in
a diary. He suffered from graver internal conflicts than
either Evelyn or Pepys, for there were two men in him and
one often disapproved of the other. He feared himself to
be a prey to severe hypochondria and found a cure in indulging the weaknesses of the flesh. He even sensed that
there might be a perilous closeness between his desire for
religious fervor and his proneness to sexual passion. But
he did not, unlike nineteenth-century "sincere" men, delight in his duality or in the contemplation of his contradictions. Pathetically, he endeavored to set for himself rules
of good conduct; as he continued to lapse from his ideal of

abstinence, he half justified his behavior as a legitimate pleasure to be snatched by a man afflicted with a gloomy disposition. He knew that he was an able writer, but he did not claim to be, and indeed was not, an especially acute portrayer of souls—not even his own.

If we cross the Channel back into France, the name of Diderot should detain us before we dwell on the ancestor of the nineteenth- and twentieth-century addicts to confession, self-reprobation, and exaltation of their ego, Rousseau. Diderot's popularity with our contemporaries has lately eclipsed that of all other Frenchmen of his age. There is originality in his philosophical intuitions, depth and force in his analysis of men, of art, of science, and an intensity in the passion with which he lived his ideas which rightly endear him to us today. There is also in him that variety of faces which adds mystery to the portrayal that successive biographers draw of him. His capacity for loving was boundless, and emotional warmth overflowed in him at all times. He praised passion as the hallmark of greatness as rapturously as any romantic ever was to do, and he well knew that the sway of passion entailed susceptibility to conflicting impressions and a chameleon-like capacity for metamorphoses. He warned his children that the picture of him painted by Van Loo was faithful to him only to a point. "I warn you, my children, that picture is not I. In a single day I had a hundred different countenances according to the thing by which I was affected."

Diderot seems to have been surprisingly little concerned with the question of sincerity in life or art. He is one of the most spontaneous extroverts on record and too generous to indulge for any length of time the minute self-analysis that consciously sincere men will undertake. He was generous to the point of living in and for others more than himself. Even his candid and certainly unrestrained letters to

Sophie Volland, but for one exception,[4] fail to show him
pausing to examine to what extent his love was sincere, an
affair of the senses or of the heart or of habit, or what conflicts his infidelity to his wife caused in him. Yet Diderot
left behind him a work, *Paradoxe sur le comédien,* whose
fortune, ever since that dialogue appeared in 1830, has been
as great as that of anything else he penned, probably disproportionate to the real value the author attached to the
work. The problem of the sincerity in the actor is put there
in a striking way. And a man of letters, as Diderot was
aware, is also an actor after a fashion.

The argument of Diderot's dialogue is well known, and
it has irked many a professional actor who has tried to refute it ever since. The comedian's profession is a disturbing one, indeed, a "monstrous" one, as Hamlet calls it, consisting in "forcing one's soul to one's own conceit." He is
a perpetual liar. He must simulate emotions and feelings
he does not experience. If he did experience them and
were thus "sincere" on the stage, he could never, Diderot
contends, be capable of progressing in the mastery of his
art, for he would necessarily experience those affective
moods less keenly after the tenth rehearsal or after the
hundredth performance and could not possibly become an
expert actor. Besides, the actor, being by definition an in-

4. My friend Georges May directed my attention to a very curious passage on the subject of sincerity in letter writing contained in Diderot's letter
to Sophie Volland of July 14, 1762. Diderot asserted in it that his letters to
his mistress were a faithful portrayal of his life, and that self-knowledge
thus attained was more vital than the observation of distant stars by the
astronomer. But he added: "Much courage would be needed if nothing
were to remain hidden. A man would more willingly accuse himself of the
project of a big crime than of a small, obscure, and vile feeling. It would
probably hurt him less to note down 'I have desired the throne at the cost
of the life of him who occupies it' than to write: 'One day, as I was bathing
among a great number of young men, I noticed one of surprising beauty
and I could not restrain myself from going close to him.' That sort of self-
examination would prove beneficial to the person doing it."

terpreter, must adopt the tune and the airs, as well as the inner nature, which are appropriate to each of the parts he will impersonate. He thus must curb the spontaneous promptings of his own nature. Before he can do so, he must observe the character whose mask he will assume, and observation is best if it is cool and dispassionate. It does not preclude feeling. But it does not match well an oversensitive nature. "It is one thing to be sensitive," says Diderot—using the French adjective, *sensible,* which would be better rendered by the phrase "a man of feeling"—"it is another thing to feel. One is an affair of the soul, the other a matter of judgment." Sensibility, he repeats, is the mark of kind persons and a virtue in most people, but a sign of mediocrity in a genius. It took some courage, he adds, to pronounce such an avowal, "for if ever nature kneaded a sensitive soul, that soul is mine." The actor is not, and cannot be, sincere, that is to say, he cannot experience a true emotion and take himself, even temporarily, for the character whose part he is playing. His task is to produce an illusion, but not to produce it in himself. If he must cry, let it be "like a seducer at the feet of a woman whom he does not love, but whom he wants to deceive."

The importance of that brief dialogue is considerable, for it involves not only the comedian but the orator, the lecturer, the writer, and many of us in real life. Diderot clearly chastised himself in the book, for he knew what a pliable personality his was and what a comedian lurked in him in his moments of most exalted sensibility. Yet it must not be overlooked that the book was a paradox, and not immune from the delight in one's own subtlety and from the permissible sophistry that marks brilliant reasonings used to deflate conventional ideas. Diderot, whose nature was rich enough to embrace many contradictions, forgot, when composing his lively dialogue, the warning which he had uttered in another inspired page of his writings, *Ré-*

flexions sur le livre "De l'Esprit" par Helvétius: "There is
nothing which must be proved with less affectation, which
must be more hidden, less clumsily displayed than a paradox. . . . A paradoxical author should not storm the soul of
his reader, but enter into it stealthily."

The man whom Diderot's paradox chagrined most deeply
was the great reformer of the French stage in the years
1913–25, Jacques Copeau. The avowed purpose of that very
earnest, at times solemn and oversensitive actor was to re-
instate sincerity at every stage of the training and performance of the actor, whose business it is to pretend, or at least
to mold himself on others. In an acute preface to a new
edition (1929) of Diderot's *Paradoxe sur le comédien*
Copeau says: "He applies his monstrous sincerity to trying
to be what he is not . . . to experience what is fictitious.
. . . He exposes himself to losing his face and to losing his
soul." Excessive impressionability may indeed constitute
a peril for the comedian. Diderot did not err when he
blamed a well-known actress, Mme. Riccoboni, for not being able to rise above her own sensibility and falling a victim of it. He rightly warned another one, Mlle. Jodin, that
judgment alone makes a cold actor and that unrestrained
sensibility and verve make a bad one, but that sense and
warmth may be united and that the secret is to render the
feeling experienced, actually or imaginatively, with a "just"
artistry.

In the paradox itself, Diderot—who elsewhere never
wearied of advocating naturalness and simplicity, the brush-
ing aside of all the teaching received in art academies, and
the imitation of nature and of a few masters faithful to nature—made the mistake of opposing the training painstak-
ingly acquired through observation and repetition. Jacques
Copeau, in his preface to the *Paradoxe,* objected to such an
artificial opposition. He maintained that the comedian is
never constrained to express what he does not feel but has

to undergo intensely a vicarious or imagined experience. The privilege of feeling thus is granted those who strive for it. The best actors are not those who espouse the character to be interpreted most readily but those who have to resist before they are conquered by their part. The process is often a threefold one. The impersonator of a part is at first attracted or challenged by it. Then he studies the part, and a loss of freshness is entailed by the slow learning by heart and the wearisome familiarity with the text. But further study creates a new and, as it were, an acquired freshness, a mastery of the actor's emotions which allows a keener insight into the secrets of the part. The comedian's sincerity is thus an acquired one. His spontaneity has first to seek itself. "The essence of his trade is to succeed in giving himself. To give himself, he must first possess himself."[5]

The function of a paradox is to stimulate duller minds. In this, Diderot has succeeded, and it would be pedantic to refute his assertions systematically. The use of the adjective "great" or "good," applied to comedians or to any other men, is as facile as it is unavoidable. Some have been great thanks to consummate art and impeccable self-mastery, exclusive of passion. Others have proved able to recreate in themselves at will the passions and emotions of a character. Diderot was at times a comedian, like most men who address themselves to a public. When he had made up a moving story, he used it repeatedly, as any writer will. Herbert Dieckmann has recorded the anecdote of a friend's visit to Diderot.[6] The friend found the philosopher in tears and saying: "I am in distress on account of a tale which I am telling myself." But the anecdote, as Dieckmann dis-

5. Diderot, *Paradoxe sur le comédien*, Présentation de Jacques Copeau (Plon, 1929). See also Yvon Belaval, *L'Esthétique sans paradoxe de Diderot* (Gallimard, 1950).

6. *Diderot Studies* (University of Syracuse Press, 1952), 2, 28–29. Dieckmann's article is on "The 'Préface annexe' de *La Religieuse*."

covered, originated in fact with Diderot himself, who inserted it in the original preface to his novel *La Religieuse,* the tale, of his own invention and narration, which thus moved him to "sincerely" histrionic tears. He knew that a rare power to communicate emotions and to electrify others with his own dynamic élan was his special gift, and he did not endeavor to curb the use of such a gift through restraint and discretion. The courage to be wholly sincere was not what he lacked, but rather the patience to weigh every motive of his actions and the selfishness which a minute watch upon oneself entails. A far more original and intuitive thinker than Rousseau, a deeper and nobler nature than Voltaire, Diderot never quite achieved the quality both these men displayed in their masterpieces, and his influence upon the world has proved less vast than theirs.

CHAPTER 3

Rousseau, Sincerity, and Truth

WITH ROUSSEAU, Goethe once solemnly declared, opposing him to Voltaire, a new world begins. Many a thinker, from Kant to Lord Acton, many a writer, from Tolstoi to our modern apostles of a return to nature, and many critics of western civilization have testified to the influence of that man who, said Lord Acton, accomplished more with his pen than any other man who ever lived. Historians will long argue as to Rousseau's actual impact on the French Revolution and on other revolutionary movements elsewhere: such an action can hardly be weighed accurately, for it was felt in depth, and therefore assimilated, by inflammable and dynamic personalities. Philosophers may grudge him a place among those whom they like to regard as the only genuine philosophers: the creators of a system logically evolved and consistently maintained. Fastidious critics may denounce the considerable amount of rhetoric that entered into his art as a writer of prose and the speciousness of much of his reasoning. Nevertheless, Rousseau, even more than Montaigne and Pascal, more than his rival Voltaire, more than his descendants Chateaubriand and Michelet, has remained alive and passionately read among us.

Not a small share of credit for that extraordinary survival of a man of letters through two centuries must be given to Rousseau's struggle for sincerity. The word (not always clearly distinguished from the word "truth") recurs a number of times in his autobiographical writings and in his letters. The notion itself is central in his life and in his thinking. No man before him, and only a few since, have given such a personal slant to all their meditations or have referred everything to themselves. The boastful proclamation that opens the *Confessions* was in a sense justified. Rousseau may not have been so pure in heart and unsullied in his intents as he tried to believe and to make believe; but his undertaking in confessing how he had become himself and in providing posterity with a rare and valuable psychological document was as unique as he claimed. To this day, no other revelation by the legion of self-confessed, self-incriminating egotists in love with sincerity who followed Rousseau has surpassed the *Confessions*, the *Rêveries*, and the *Dialogues* in originality. To Rousseau must be traced back the worship by many moderns of sincerity as a test of greatness or as a substitute for almost any other quality, moral or aesthetic.

The story of his life, which has been told a hundred times and, in its essence if not literally, never more truly than in his impassioned *Confessions*, need not be related here. But it is clear that none of Rousseau's several bodies of ideas, on society, on the state, on education, on the theater, on man, can ever be divorced from the manner in which the thinker reached and lived those ideas or from the events of his life and the impressions received from them. Such is probably the case for a good many writers and even for a good many philosophers. The "personal heresy" which austere reformers would like to banish from criticism may indeed remain in abeyance when Aristotle, Shakespeare, Velásquez, Spinoza, Bach, Kant are studied. But other geniuses or talents,

Rembrandt, Rousseau, Goethe, Byron, Wagner, Tolstoi, Nietzsche were human, all too human. The truth or the beauty which they revealed may have lost something in objectivity, even perhaps in universality. Yet a truth that has to be experienced first and that has to reach generality only after having been an affective and an individual truth is not necessarily to be ruled out. Rousseau was probably not wrong when he maintained that any truth must be felt as such by us and that its usefulness is one of the criteria of its validity.

The stress laid by Rousseau on sincerity may be accounted for by several reasons: sickness contributed to making him an introvert and to directing him to the acceptance of himself as a sample and as a model for mankind. Volumes have been written on the nature of the physical ill with which he seems to have been born, none of them conclusive. The crux of the matter, as always, lies in the effect exercised by the somatic element upon the mental one, and, on the extent of such an effect, Rousseau's word may be trusted. André Gide remarked in one of his *Feuillets* that "disease proposes to man a new disquietude which must be legitimatized. That is the source of Rousseau's value. Without his sickness, he would have been only a flat and unbearable rhetorician, someone like Cicero." The exaggeration is patent and the speculation on what Rousseau, if differently constituted, might have been, is idle. But it seems clear that he was born with some peculiarity affecting his sex organs, that he acquired habits of masturbation which instilled dread and remorse into his conscience, and that psychological and other impediments prevented his unreserved enjoyment of physical love, except, as he relates, during his short-lived trip down the Rhône valley with Madame de Larnage. Later on, as his disease became a serious one, affecting his kidneys and urinary organs and entailing acute and prolonged pain and an unpleasant and ineffective treatment, Rousseau's idiosyncrasies became more marked. He appears to have been no longer eager or able to engage in physical intercourse with his wife, and we know from a very noble letter he wrote her (*Correspondance générale*, No. 3835) how they became estranged in consequence. Indeed, Rousseau's liaison with Thérèse, who was neither virtuous nor bright and ceased early to have any feminine charm, is doubtless to be explained in part by Rousseau's physical ailment and by a fear, which haunted him, of proving unsatisfactory as a lover or as a husband whenever he was at all intimidated. Other great men, Heine and Baudelaire, to name two, have married "beneath their level," as we say, for selfish or sordid reasons, and have submitted, with a meekness that astounds us, to a conjugal or para-conjugal life that was an inferno. But few have ever behaved as gentlemen more consistently than the plebeian Genevan brought up with little schooling and with even less morality. Not once in his autobiographical writings does he mention Thérèse Levasseur and her worst foibles otherwise than with affection and delicacy. His gratitude to her withstood many a sad ordeal. Even in his letter of August 12, 1769, which he sent her when she was planning to leave him, Rousseau treated her with fairness and respect, lucidly analyzing his own faults as well as hers, and preferring to stress the links that had long bound them to each other. Instances of such clearsightedness, in matters where few men remain self-possessed, are rare indeed.

Significant also was the fact that Rousseau was a self-made man who, painfully, belatedly, had had to acquire the elements of a normal education without a teacher, translating Tacitus and Seneca, discovering the elements of music, of grammar, of philosophy through slow and devious paths, learning about human nature the hard way. His native gifts were so remarkable that he proved able to spell (in an age when French spelling was amateurish to a point we can hardly conceive), to wield all the cadences of French prose, to develop an argument cogently, to organize the most cumbersome mass of ideas in a manner unsurpassed in his century. Wit he lacked and humor occasionally, when he was reduced to impotence by shyness or moved to anger or passion. The acid irony of Voltaire, the jocular verve of Diderot were not his gifts. He could not easily divorce himself from himself, and leave off his endeavor to be true and sincere, hence he was self-conscious and often sanctimonious in his preaching to others. But only a self-made man like Rousseau could be filled, as he was, with a sense of wonder at his achievement, obtained entirely through his own deserts and strivings, and be impelled to set himself up as an example of that rarity: a man who to himself was true.

Rousseau was also an ill-adapted creature at a time when rebels were scarce and when it occurred to a very few persons to question the social order in which they were born and the mundane values that prevailed in the only society in which a man of letters could hope to find his audience: that of the aristocracy and of the cultured middle class of Paris and of the provinces. Success, in that society—which was more open than most of us fancy and which welcomed a gifted and ambitious upstart with no title and no money, were he Law the Scot, Galiani or Casanova, the Italians, Rousseau the Swiss—came promptly to Jean-Jacques. He might well have been wrecked by it, had he been less stubborn in preserving the integrity of his self. He wrapped himself up, after the stir aroused by his First Discourse indicting the arts and culture, in an attitude of aloofness from the enticements of society and assumed the mantle of a prophet and of a reformer.

There was pose in his behavior and some insincerity in the way in which he intoxicated himself with his declamations. Controversies have raged as to the conflicting versions given by Rousseau and Diderot of the former's visit

to the latter, imprisoned at Vincennes. They do credit to
the ingeniousness of scholars rather than to their sense of
psychological reality. For even if, as is likely, Diderot
prompted his visitor to uphold the negative in the famous
debate on whether the development of arts and letters had
made man better or happier, the speed and the ardor with
which Rousseau made such a thesis his own are proof that
it fitted his innermost aspirations. Diderot assisted him in
becoming himself. Such is the only beneficial way in which
an influence can act upon any of us. Moreover, as any writer
should know, the process of writing is a process of self-dis-
covery at least as much as it is one of communication of our
ideas to others. Rousseau could hardly be charged with insincerity because it dawned on him, while he composed the
First and the Second Discourses, that those views which he
was warmly expressing had convinced him first of all that
they were like the new truth a neophyte hails as his private
treasure and delight. Sincerity seldom springs from a cold
and scientific mood. One may submit to a factual and objective truth in a coldly self-possessed manner, but sincerity
implies an élan which shakes the whole being and an exaltation of sensibility. Indeed, with Rousseau and the romantics, it was most often a passionate tension, and with
those who, in the tradition of Benjamin Constant, tried to
be dispassionate and cool, it remained even then an exaltation *à froid,* a grim determination not to be taken in by the
forces of sentiment.

In his *Confessions* and, much more curiously, in a preface
to his comedy *Narcisse,* written in 1735 when he was twenty-
three but acted and published in 1752, Rousseau tried to
refute the charge of having been insincere in his First Discourse. He maintained that the views expressed there were
his own indeed, though he failed to state when they had
thus become his. He also contended that the cultivation of
the arts and the publication by him of a musical drama did

not constitute an abandonment of his thesis that man would have been better if an excess of civilization had not corrupted him. He had not advocated returning to a state of ignorance, still less of innocence, which, once lost, cannot be recaptured. He remained convinced that reflection can only increase man's sorrow, through making him regret the joys experienced earlier and preventing him from relishing the present ones. But the arts could be cultivated in such a way as to foster the metamorphosis of man into as natural a man as he well could be in an age already far advanced on the road to corruption.

There lurks some embarrassment in that preface to *Narcisse* and, as is often the case, some sophistry in Rousseau's argument. But it may be admitted that the clamorous success that made him fashionable after his two Discourses failed to render him more mundane or over-prolific, or at all subservient to the fashions prevailing in the circles where he was acclaimed. Jean-Jacques was and remained temperamentally ill-adapted to society, the foe of that dispersion of oneself that social success favors. Happily for him, he had little gift of ready repartee; witty remarks, scathing retorts, or winning compliments never occurred to him when they were called for. His wit was slow, "l'esprit d'escalier," and only on his way home would he think of the bright sayings he might have uttered to win the applause of a gathering. Posterity has been the gainer, for brilliant conversationalists usually rob their writings of what might have made them deep or strong. They nourish, instead, the passing moments during which they shine out among their friends. Rousseau evolved his very plausible theory of the relative being (the social ego, forced or led by society to be other than he really is) and the absolute being. The latter does not exist relatively, that is, by comparison to others and through the constant jumping over artificially erected obstacles; he yields to absolute feelings unreservedly. His ques-

tion is the one put in the first of the *Rêveries d'un promeneur solitaire:* "Detached from them and from everything,
what am I myself?" Only through concentrating on those
absolute and "natural" feelings and eliminating the social
ego did Rousseau reach, after many an ordeal undergone by
his morbidly oversensitive nature, a state of invulnerability.

Even more than Montaigne, with more indulgent self-
acceptance than La Rochefoucauld or Pascal might ever
have consented, Rousseau, who at times was fiercely logical,
admitted the contradictions inherent in his nature, and in
human nature in general. Casually, at the end of the third
book of his *Confessions,* he mentioned that "there are times
when he is so little like himself that he might well be taken
for another man of a wholly different character." Much
earlier, in 1746 probably, in the revealing fragment, *Le
Persifleur,* of a paper Diderot and he had projected to write,
alternating with each other,[1] Rousseau laid his complexities
bare, with the complacency of a very young man in awe
before the contradictory riches of his mind, but also with
that incisiveness which he often brought to his self-analysis:

> Nothing is more dissimilar from myself than I am my-
> self; therefore it would be useless to try to define me
> otherwise than by that singular variety; it is such in my
> mind, that it occasionally affects even my feelings. At
> times I am a hard and ferocious misanthropist; at other
> moments, I wax ecstatic amid the charms of society and
> the delights of love. Now I am austere and devout . . .
> but I soon become an arrant libertine. . . . In a word,
> a Proteus, a chameleon, a woman are less changeable
> creatures than I am.

Like many of us, Rousseau erected his own temperament
into a general rule; or rather he took advantage of such

1. *Le Persifleur* (The Banterer) is to be found in *Mélanges, 10,* 63, in
the Musset-Pathay edition of Rousseau (Paris, Dupont, 1824).

mutability in his desires, feelings and ideas to stimulate his own growth into a richer creature. Some of those contradictions are mere whims and should not be overstressed. Behind them, as he remarked in the ninth book of the *Confessions* when he described his work on the manuscripts of the Abbé de Saint-Pierre, lie deeper reasons which a searching mind may discover and upon which he may act. Rousseau then projected a treatise on *La Morale sensitive* in which, in his usual pragmatic way, he aimed at modifying the role played in us by memory and the impressions produced by the outside world. An education of nature *à la Wordsworth* seems to have been his object then, and the turning of all exterior impressions and of our contradictory moods to good account, in the interest of virtue.

But contradictions went deeper in Jean-Jacques. Like his spiritual son, André Gide, and most of us moderns, he was "a being of dialogue." Indeed his *Dialogues,* which are the work of a tormented man and of a distraught brain, composed in the midst of what Byron called a "long war with self-fought foes," are one of the most complex and arresting revelations ever attempted. Rousseau wished to preserve many of his differences with his own self, instead of slurring over them as we are prone to do or of drowning them in the smooth river of a uniform and polished prose. Repeatedly, in his letters and in a crucial passage excised from his works, the first preface to the *Confessions*,[2] Rousseau admitted that he dreaded the weakening influence of style, which tends to make everything monotonous and artificial. He wanted to respect and preserve spontaneity in writing: "I shall not waste time in making the style uniform; I shall

2. The original preface to the *Confessions,* an awkward piece of some twelve pages for which the famous first paragraph was substituted, composed in December 1764, is to be found in *Annales de la Société Jean-Jacques Rousseau, 4* (Geneva, Jullien, and Paris, Champion, 1908). The second preface to *La Nouvelle Héloïse,* alluded to further down in our text, is included in standard editions of Rousseau's complete works.

have always whichever style comes to me, I shall change it according to my moods, I shall say each thing as I feel it, as I see it."

As to even deeper contradictions in him and in every man, they should not be superficially reconciled for the sake of that "hobgoblin of little minds," Emerson's "foolish consistency." They are for him, as they were for Pascal, the sign of opposite aspirations in our nature, or of the paradox inseparable from man's fate. It seems best, certainly more sincere, to oscillate from one pole to another and to outgrow such antinomies dialectically through a fecund synthesis. Kant, the philosopher of antinomies, and Hegel, the founder of nineteenth-century dialectics, were, as is well known, admirers of Rousseau. Toward the end of the second preface to *La Nouvelle Héloïse,* composed in the form of an imaginary dialogue, Rousseau wisely answered his interlocutor: "You want man to be always consistent. I doubt that to be possible to him. But one thing to him is possible, to be always true. That is what I want to try to be." True to facts? True to a higher truth, that of feelings, underlying the facts? True to others? True to himself, or to one of his selves? Rousseau fails to specify, and he probably would have branded as sophistry any attempt thus to discriminate, or to quibble. The task of appraising his sincerity, or his services to truth, has fallen to his biographers and critics. And disagreement is rife among them, for Rousseau's ideas, and the impetus given them by his personal accent, seem suited to divide otherwise objective scholars along partisan lines. Two excellent students of his thought have reconstituted the underlying unity of Rousseau's diverse views with a magnificent rigor: Gustave Lanson and Ernest Hunter Wright. They probably have credited Jean-Jacques with more systematic logic than he would ever have claimed, or coveted, himself. We believe it wiser to admit that Rousseau's case lay in his attempt to reach a wholly sincere philosophy which would be his own primarily and satisfy his sensitive and even his sensuous self as well as his brain. He could reason with cogency and appear to deduce arguments from one another with a rigor akin to that of Spinoza: in his *Contrat social,* in parts of *Emile,* in his letters to M. de Malesherbes (probably written with a view to publication), even in letters of advice on religious and moral matters such as he wrote late in his life (*Correspondance générale, 20,* Nos. 3781 to M. de Franquières and, in December 1769 and January 1770, to Madame de Berthier). But the very strain of his style in such pieces and the stress on exterior consistency betray a painful effort on the part of the author to mask his painful quandary. A close scrutiny of the celebrated and beautiful *Profession de foi du Vicaire Savoyard* or of the *Contrat social* soon reveals flaws in the reasoning and non sequiturs in the links of a seductive chain. Behind the author's apparently implacable progress toward his conclusions, it is easy to discern comings and goings, a sinuous recurrence of themes and of fixed ideas, the distrust of a cramping and inflexible rational method. Rousseau, indeed, confessed his abhorrence of order and strict logic in a letter to the Benedictine scholar Dom Deschamps on September 12, 1761. The attitude of Rousseau the man was harmonious rather than logical, and the thinker in him should not diverge from the man. His claim to be true was not necessarily to the kind of truth that a rational thinker reaches and clings to.

While he was completing his explosive *Lettre à D'Alembert sur les Spectacles,* in 1758, soon after his violent passion for Madame d'Houdetot, which rocked his sentimental life to its foundations and almost cost him his reason, Rousseau adopted as his motto three Latin words: "vitam impendere vero." He even proudly had them engraved as his seal, as much out of boastfulness as out of a desire to keep those words ever near him lest he lapse from his ideal. He had

hit upon the phrase in the fourth Satire of Juvenal, alluded
to as the Satire on Domitian's turbot. A huge fish had been
caught in the Adriatic and presented to the Roman emperor; a ludicrous council was then held to decide what
was to be done with the turbot. Crispus, a weak old man,
was called in among others. Of him Juvenal scathingly remarked that he never had bent his energies to resist a tor-
rent and lacked the courage to free his soul in his words
and "vitam impendere vero," to sacrifice his life to truth.

How close did Rousseau come to such an ambitious ideal?
His life, especially after 1756–57, became that of a pathetically sick man, afflicted with a persecution mania and
alienating those who might have assisted him in retaining
his sanity and in behaving with prudence and even with
slyness in an age when other authors of dangerous books
published them anonymously. The scales of justice have, in
our opinion, to be weighed in favor of Diderot and of
Hume, even of Grimm and Madame d'Epinay in the "infernal affairs" which opposed them, against their will, to
Rousseau. Yet if Rousseau had not thus revolted against
his friends and denounced as conspiracies what were mere
discourtesies or slight ironies on their part, we would be
the poorer for having lost the *Confessions* and the *Rêveries,*
and probably others of Rousseau's works of a more impersonal character. Men like him have to be loved far too much
to be loved enough, and to be dealt with tactfully and mercifully. He did not meet with the angelic woman whose
patience and semi-maternal tenderness might have soothed
him; she alone might have brought about the reconciliation
wiith the friends he had hurt, which he was yearning for.
Twice, on March 17 and 26, 1757, he appealed to Madame
d'Épinay:

> Diderot knows my bad temper and the sensitiveness
> of my soul . . . one word, only one word of gentleness,

would have caused my pen to drop from my hands,
tears to drop from my eyes and I would have been at
my friend's feet. . . . *(Correspondance, 3,* No. 349)

Let him first appease me, which surely will not take
long; for never was there any conflagration within my
heart which could not be put out with one tear. *(3,* No.
356)

Madame d'Épinay was not generous or intelligent enough
to take the hint, or to answer the plea. Rousseau's rancor
soon turned against her. Her sister-in-law, Madame d'Houdetot, owes the fascination she exercises over posterity to
Rousseau's pages in the *Confessions* and to the inspiration
she gave to the novelist of *La Nouvelle Héloïse.* She was
not especially pretty, not any more than Madame de Warens
or the other women who played a part in Rousseau's love
life. A woman stands in no need of physical beauty with an
imaginative man, if she has personality, spontaneousness,
charm, and wit as she did. "Let us leave pretty women to
men who have no imagination," remarked Proust. She was
twenty-six when Rousseau, at forty-four, met her. She had
two children and a husband who allowed her complete
freedom, as he had a liaison with another married lady to
whom he remained faithful for forty-eight years. She had
a lover, Saint-Lambert, an officer and a poet, who admired
Rousseau and had enjoyed some fame for having been the
lover of Madame du Châtelet, Voltaire's mistress, and for
having been responsible for the pregnancy from which she
died, with Voltaire and, of course, her husband grieving at
her bedside.

Madame d'Houdetot grew extremely fond of Rousseau,
visited him often, went for long walks with him, allowed
him far more intimacy than a mere friend usually receives
and a morning kiss every day which set the middle-aged
man's combustible temperament aflame.

    the memorable kiss
Which every morn his fever'd lip would greet,
From hers, who but with friendship his would meet;
But to that gentle touch, through brain and breast
Flash'd the thrill'd spirit's love-devouring heat,
In that absorbing sigh perchance more blest
Than vulgar minds may be with all they seek possest.

Thus Byron versified the pathetic tale of the ninth book of
the *Confessions* in the third canto of *Childe Harold* (Stanza
LXXIX).

But Madame d'Houdetot was determined to remain
faithful to her lover, Saint-Lambert, then waging war somewhere with his regiment, and Rousseau, who appreciated
Saint-Lambert and almost loved him for being loved by her
whom he adored, admired her fidelity. He went into raptures of burning desire when close to her, perilously close
if his letters to her are to be trusted. But he was, according
to the standards of his century, and perhaps because of ill
health and worry, an old, or an aging, man at forty-five. And
he was in love with virtue. Saint-Lambert heard of their
intimacy, was hurt, received Rousseau's apologies, accepted
them with generosity, and answered with delicacy the philosopher's strange request that he, her lover, persuade Madame d'Houdetot to establish among the three of them a
firm friendship.

The conversation between Rousseau and the young and
aristocratic lady seems to have stopped at no barrier in their
pursuit of frankness. She was lively, fond of pleasure,
touched by the worship of an interesting and famous man,
imprudent probably. He was beside himself with passion
and frustrated desire. He was proud of the appeal he had
for a woman twenty years his junior, and he complacently
recalled in a letter which he preserved but did not send her
how he elicited indiscreet compliments from her:

That invisible flame, from which I received a second life more precious than the first, restored all the vigor of youth to my soul and to my senses. . . . From those entrancing moments when you made me experience all the pleasure ever derived from a love received with sympathy, though not reciprocated, you became so dear to me that I have never dared to wish to be happy at your expense. . . . (*3*, No. 380)

But he will not forget how, in the grove near the waterfall, she often declared to him: "You are the most tender lover whom I could imagine; no, never did a man love me as you do." He retained copies of the inflamed love letters he was sending her. She burnt all of hers, which Rousseau had returned to her at her request, and it is thus difficult to evaluate Rousseau's good faith in that lamentable affair. He probably would have broken all his good resolutions if she herself had yielded unreservedly. Since she did not, he reasoned eloquently about the moral superiority of that rare being, a man deliriously in love whose highest joy was to hear his beloved talk of the other man who was her absent lover.

My ill-fated passion is known to you; no passion ever matched it . . . it can make me forget all, even my duty, but not yours. . . . But you belong to him [Saint-Lambert]. If you are mine, I lose, though possessing you, her whom I honor or I ravish you from him whom you love. No, Sophie, I may die from my mad ardor, but I shall not debase you. . . . The crime is already committed a hundred times by my will. If it is in yours, I accomplish it, and I become the most traitorous and the happiest of men; but I cannot corrupt the woman whom I idolize.

Thus he wrote in the spring of 1757 (letter No. 374). Thérèse, for all practical purposes his common-law wife, was then in his home, waiting for him to return from his amorous walks, though he fails ever to mention her in those letters. A little later, he penned that heart-rendering epistle (No. 380) which he refrained from delivering to Madame d'Houdetot, but sedulously preserved in his papers.

> You know it, you [the more intimate second person singular "tu" is used here] who saw my aberrations if, even then, your person remained sacred for me! Never have my ardent desires, my tender pleas dared for one moment beg for the ultimate bliss, without my feeling being detained by the inner cries of a soul aghast. . . . I would have given the universe away for one minute of bliss; but to debase you, Sophie! Ah! no, that is impossible and, even if it were in my power to make the decision, I love you too much ever to possess you.

There was an element of sincerity in those pathetic declarations. The conviction that a love proves more lasting and reaches more deeply if it remains physically incomplete, however close one may have risen, or descended, to the ultimate completion, was a strong one with him. A number of men, not all of them idealists, have shared it, and a current French saying has it that "the women with whom a man does not go to bed are the truly dangerous ones." Claire, in *La Nouvelle Héloïse,* gravely explains to Saint-Preux that since desire in love grows from encountering obstacles, it is best for it not to be countered and thus not to fear extinction. Rousseau, who is credited with creating the modern myth of the natural man, untainted by the sense of sin, may well have secretly harbored the fear that sex might be sin after all; or, more probably, he may have been daunted by the dread that he might fail at the supreme moment, as he did in the presence of fair and easy Zulietta, the Venetian courtesan, who declared him more fit for mathematics than for love. Even Rousseau's unconventional behavior in writing to Saint-Lambert on September 5, 1757, to explain how he and Madame d'Houdetot spoke tenderly of him and how he yearned for a three-cornered friendship, then complained to her lover of Madame d'Houdetot's hardening, revolting as it may seem to an orthodox moralist, may not have been insincere. Jean-Jacques was not altogether worthy of his motto then; he lied by omission, to say the least. Yet the dream of a domestic and harmonious triangle in which he would be the chief purveyor of feelings was an old one with him. He had felt little, if any, jealousy for the first or even for the second of the credited lovers of Madame de Warens, who shared her favors with him. Jealousy is, with many men, an acquired or even an assumed feeling, a "relative" one, Rousseau might have called it, caused by our behaving as society expects us to, and he was not susceptible to it. Perhaps, also, Rousseau sensed that the most attractive among women can become exasperating if too constantly with us, and that polyandry is a suitable guarantee against such a disillusion.

One is tempted, however, to be less forgiving to Rousseau when, after Madame d'Houdetot turned cooler and kept him at a distance, writing to him noncommittally "mon cher citoyen" (Rousseau transcribed those letters with his own pen), he proffered lessons of sincerity to her. On July 13, 1757 (No. 383), he wrote her:

> Whoever has the courage always to appear as he is will sooner or later become what he must be, but nothing can be expected from those who assume a parading character. . . . Let us be frank, Sophie! Frankness alone raises the soul and, through affording self-esteem, gives us a right to be esteemed by others.

And, four months later (No. 424), he challenged the world to point to a better man than he, "a soul more loving, more sensitive, more enamoured of the charms of friendship, more touched by honesty and beauty."

The crisis of 1757, with the "midday demon" tormenting the philosopher, is the most lamentable in his life, in the eyes of the dispassionate observer of Rousseau. Yet to it he owed the last sentimental exaltations he was destined to experience. The link between such erotic exaltations and literary creation is a mysterious one; but it seems plausible to surmise that Rousseau's prodigious fecundity in the years 1758–60, when the *Lettre à D'Alembert, Emile, Le Contrat social, La Nouvelle Héloïse* poured from his pen in quick succession was connected with the fire which then stirred his senses and his imagination. On his conduct to his wife, to Saint-Lambert, to Madame d'Houdetot whose petulance and spontaneity were not totally devoid of co-quetry, few of us will make bold to pass moral judgment. Let the unhappy and wise men who, when their hair greyed and their youthful arrogance receded as they climbed to the summit of their life and giddily surveyed the descending slope in front of them, fought temptation better than he, throw the first stone at the pathetic lover that he was. The wisdom of passiveness was then not yet discovered by Rousseau; he had to be love's martyr, and an even more woeful martyr to his own delusions, before he could grow into a serene botanist and solitary dreamer.

That Rousseau deluded himself in that love affair is undeniable. A colder and more analytic philosopher might have been more lucid; a more experienced connoisseur of women would have been more wary. A man less infected by the bug of literature would have written less prolifically and would not have retained drafts of his love letters. A more conquering Don Juan would have been less profuse in declarations of respect for his lady friend's technical chastity and less insistent on "appealing to her sincerity" as he did in the unsent letter No. 380 or on begging her to show "a rustic sincerity" as we hear he did from his friend's letter, No. 463. There is self-deception, though no hypocrisy, in Rousseau and probably, as his biographer and admirer Jean Guehénno charged, some inability or unwillingness to distinguish between truth and sincerity, between truth as we owe it to others and to facts and the fervent exaltation of our soul passionately expressed.

Our purpose, however, is not to check the confessions of a sickly man bent on self-justification against the events of his life as they happened and to rejoice whenever we take a great man in the act of distorting or contradicting the factual truth. Rousseau repeatedly warned his reader that the truth he was aiming at was his, that is to say, the truth of his feelings and his reflections as he lived the events of his life, not necessarily that of an accurate and continuous narrative of the events themselves. If he occupies a central place in any historical sketch and analytical consideration of sincerity in literature, it is because Rousseau, blending delusions with clearsightedness, conciliating lies with truth,[3] struck new paths in psychology and proposed a new formulation of philosophical problems. In his Herculean labor he was sustained by the proud conviction that he remained closer to his own deeper truth than most thinkers had been before him. How and why?

First, he placed the center of a man's inner life in his sensibility. "I felt before I thought," as he declares in the opening pages of his *Confessions*. Such, of course, has been the case of most men and women since Adam, but few had made so much of that commonplace truth; fewer still had taken pride in it. For the Cartesian formula, Rousseau substituted his "Sentio, ergo sum." Every one of his self-ex-

---

3. Diderot, in one of those genial flashes of his, declared: "The great man is not the one who produces an impression of truth, it is he who best knows how to conciliate lies with truth." *Oeuvres complètes, 11,* 254, "Salon of 1767."

aminations will recur to the same assertions of the primacy, chronological and logical, of affective existence over intellectual life. "To exist is to feel," he says in *Emile*. In the remarkable *Second Dialogue*, Rousseau again asserts, with some courage, that he had to be moved to love or hatred first, before an object or an idea could acquire meaning for him. "I can only see inasmuch as I am moved," he will again explain to the Maréchal de Luxembourg. A tension of his whole being toward the thing to be observed, impelled by a strong affective interest, was thus the prerequisite to his observation. Imagination preceded perception; love came before understanding; partiality overruled objectivity. Rousseau was not alone in that respect, but he was among the first to accept himself as he was and to question the superiority of rational knowledge.

He was even more original in the legitimacy, even in the dignity, which he granted sensuous life. His phrasing, like that of his age, is confused. Psychological terms were then few, and used very loosely. Rousseau did not hestitate to describe himself as "un sensuel" and as "endowed with physical sensibility to a rather high degree" *(Second Dialogue)*. Unlike many of his predecessors and contemporaries, he refused to intellectualize sensations. He accepted them as they were. With him, and a few colder observers of human nature such as Rétif de la Bretonne and Casanova, a new era opened in literature in which sensations became accepted as valid and their evidence weighed, often victoriously, against the spiritual and moral aspects of man. In his *Journal* for October 23, 1946, Charles du Bos, a man fundamentally different from Rousseau, indeed incapable of living through his senses, shrewdly noted:

> With Rousseau, we witness the beginning of the study of the inner man effected on and in that man himself. Until he came, there always remained a certain space,

a distance between the observer and the object observed, even when in fact the observer and the person observed were one and the same. The deeper reason for the change is that, with Rousseau, sensation is first granted full franchise. Before him, no dignity was granted inner moods until they had undergone the cleansing, as it were, of a certain intellectualization.

Indeed, the violence of his sensations filled Rousseau with dread as well as with a secret delight. From the outset, the *Confessions* laid stress on the spanking administered to him, when he was just ten years old, by Mademoiselle Lambercier. The genteel old maid never again resorted to that mode of punishment, after she noticed what a strange thrill the innocuous flagellation sparked in the boy. Rousseau's sincerity in recording complex impressions, scarcely noted in writing before him, constitutes the great value of the early books of the *Confessions* as psychological documents: his extreme susceptibility to being loved or scolded, his "convulsive trembling" and his "burning blood," his shyness which caused him to cherish his own sensations more dearly, his impulse to obey and worship a woman, and his need for a "mother-substitute." Then he acquired that strangely pre-Proustian notion that to possess a woman, even—or especially—a willing one like Madame de Warens, is also to debase her. Students of the psychology of sex (Havelock Ellis read Rousseau closely and wrote on him) and psychoanalysts who have rediscovered the "polymorphous perversity" of the child could well draw many a lesson from Jean-Jacques' sincere analysis of his own sexuality. Where Montaigne, and of course Saint Augustine, had sinned by omission or excessive discretion, Rousseau broke all conventional barriers, without ever lapsing into indecency. For the first time, sex was granted an eminent part in the portrayal a serious writer offered of himself.

Rousseau also perceived that the anarchic and potentially destructive force which sensuality was in him was offset by a strong "moral sensibility." His declamatory recourse to conscience's voice and his appeals to virtue were more than lip service or rhetoric. He needed all the fervor of his feelings to curb the urges of his senses. But sensuality becomes a real peril only when overheated by a quick and rich imagination. If romanticism can rightly be characterized, as it customarily is, by the primacy of sensibility and of imagination (we should add: of sensuousness, also) over reason, Rousseau was indeed the first romantic on the continent. Desire, which paints pleasure in rosy hues, longing for the pleasure once experienced, expectation which precipitates a feverish man toward the idealized person, counted far more for Rousseau than mere fulfillment of a physical urge. He may not have proved an adequate lover of Zulietta in Venice, and the frigid temperament he ascribed to Madame de Warens, in more delicate terms than most men use when they thus make their favorite remark about women, may have been a divided responsibility; but he realized that love reduced to its mere mechanics is what in us differs least from animals, and that imagination alone, firing the potential lover with desire, makes it a challenge for him who needs obstacles to rise above his own mediocrity, and turns it into a source of poetry.

In that, again, Rousseau analyzed himself with more perspicacity than any one had done before. "If he cherishes the fulfillment of love, it must for him have been preceded by desire," he wrote of himself in the second of the *Dialogues*. Repeatedly, in the *Confessions*, he described his peculiarity, later to be called "bovarysme" (for Madame Bovary certainly was one of the innumerable children of Jean-Jacques), which consisted in a discrepancy between the actual fulfillment of a desire and the inflamed aspirations which first depicted it as more ardent than it could ever prove. After his Venetian adventure (*Confessions,* VII) he concluded: "No, nature has not framed me for sensual delight. It poured into my wretched head the poison of that ineffable happiness, the appetite for which it instilled in my heart." A similar avowal occurs in Book IX, when Rousseau lucidly dissects the compensation mechanism through which, finding it impossible to have his aspirations fulfilled by real beings, he let his delirious imagination populate his private universe with fictitious ones closer to his heart. Anticipating Proust once again, but less systematically and discouragingly than he, Jean-Jacques had more than one inkling of the fundamental subjectivity of love. The origin and the core of it often lay in erotic reveries or in an insidious working of the brain and of imagination which then conjured up a creature painted in all the glowing colors lent by the lover ready for love. A very little known, brief but pregnant, musical drama composed by Rousseau at Motiers, *Pygmalion,* which was performed in Lyons and later in Paris, is most revealing. There, in accents not unworthy of Goethe, the sculptor vents his indignation at the senselessness of nature which fails to answer his appeal and resists his creative force which would absorb it. He concludes, addressing his Galatea, who has taken on life from her molder and lover: "I gave thee all my being; I shall now live through thee alone."

Lastly, Rousseau also appears as a precursor in his original allusions to the power lurking in memory. It may be submitted that, with Baudelaire, then with Proust and several moderns, memory ceased to be regarded as a handmaid to intelligence and a storehouse for the imagination; it usurped some of the functions of imagination and claimed to be creative. Rousseau's memory may not have been accurate as to details. His was not a voluntary memory, straining itself to bring back to the surface facts and dates and the actual haphazard sequence of events in a life. It was

not the sudden flooding of consciousness by sensations recaptured or unleashed by some minor impression on the
senses, which Proust magnified into a mystical revelation.
One always and only remembers oneself, as an old saying
has it. Rousseau perceived and understood past events and
moods best when he summoned them up "to the sessions of
sweet silent thought."

In the third Book of his *Confessions,* he laid bare, with
far more frankness than most autobiographers, the extreme
difficulty he encountered in writing and in thinking. He
added:

> I can see nothing of what I see; I can only see clearly
> what I remember, and I am bright only in my mem-
> ories. Of all that is said, done in my presence, I feel
> nothing, I penetrate into nothing. I am only struck
> by the outward sign. But later, it all comes back to me;
> I recall the place, the time, the tone, the look, the
> gesture, the circumstance; nothing escapes me.

Elsewhere, in concluding Book IV of the same work, he
formulated the problem of truth in an autobiography with
remarkable clarity. Facts he considered he owed to the
reader; for it was up to the reader to deduce and to recon-
struct, from them, the character of the author. But memory
stored them up with unequal solicitude. Very early impressions were liable to be more vivid than later ones; memory
had effected its alchemy on them for a longer period of
time; later impressions became transformed by the early
ones with which they blended, for memories are not just
stacked up like books or objects on a series of shelves. Modestly, for once, Rousseau explained his purpose:

> I should like, as it were, to render my soul transparent
> to the reader's eyes; to do that, I try to show it to him
> from all points of view, to throw light on it from all

sides, to let him see every slightest motion in it, so that he may be enabled to judge by himself the principle from which all in me originates.

Sensations, feelings, imagination, memory: those are the four cornerstones of Rousseau's temple of sincerity. His search for sincerity went much beyond his record of his own life, novel as that was in his time, even beyond that description of indiscreet moments of his existence when he was guilty of petty larcenies, of inexcusable lies, of sensual aberrations, of inability to control his temper and his mania of suspicion. It became the basis of his philosophical and religious attitude. A dozen men, from Pascal to Kierkegaard and Nietzsche, have already had bestowed upon them the doubtful honor of having been the father of Existentialism. None deserves it more than Rousseau. To him, philosophy is worthless if it consists of a system that claims to embrace all knowledge and to account for the universe. For most French thinkers, Descartes, Pascal, Claude Bernard, Taine, a method enabling the mind to reach some degree of truth is the true pursuit of the philosopher, not the erecting of a comprehensive but flimsy structure christened a system. In his *Profession de foi du Vicaire Savoyard*, Rousseau formulated his conviction: "General and abstract ideas are the source of men's biggest errors; never has the jargon of metaphysics brought about the discovery of one single truth." Much later, almost on his deathbed, he composed that admirably reasoned and moving piece, the third Promenade of the solitary dreamer. In it, he serenely explained the origin of his break with the philosophers of the Encyclopedia and his dissatisfaction with the sort of exterior truth, often merely negative, which those men reached.

He, Jean-Jacques, had to answer the torment of his unquiet soul; misery, solitude, struggle, uncertainty had been his lot from childhood; his speculation aimed at affording him a degree of serenity and reasons for living. Others knew far more than he did, but their philosophy seemed to be alien to them.

> They studied human nature so as to dissert about it with learning, not in order to know themselves; they labored in order to teach others, not to enlighten themselves from inside. Several of them only wished to do a book, any book, provided it could meet with success. . . . Shall I eternally allow myself to be tossed about by the sophistry of those who are more eloquent than I, when I am not even sure that the opinions which they preach . . . are truly theirs? . . . Their philosophy is for others; I needed one which was for me. (Third *Promenade*)

As he became tortured by sickness and imaginary foes, he formulated his hostility to rationalism with some exaggeration. His mind was exhausted by the strain of writing too much too feverishly during his "annus mirabilis." On July 20, 1764, from Motiers, he confessed to a Genevan correspondent (letter 2147) his need for a purely physical life with nature. "Reason kills me; I should like to be mad so as to be healthy." Too much can be made of such passing moods and of the exasperated tone of a man who wrote letters with reluctance and difficulty. Indeed, much of the abstract reasoning contained in *Emile* and *Le Contrat social* is the most cogent and the most solid done in his age. Montesquieu himself appears like a disconnected writer and an inconsistent philosopher when compared to Rousseau. The moral advice Rousseau dispensed to correspondents who consulted him as a teacher of wisdom is remarkably lucid and shows him as a lay confessor equal in tact and firmness to the most skilled Jesuits. His insight into the hearts of lonely and misunderstood women deploring to him the vacuity of their lives and asking for the secret of happiness (Henriette de Maugin in 1764–65, Madame de Berthier in 1769–70) is that of an acute psychologist. In spite of his occasional contradictions, there are some points on which Rousseau did not waver. His philosophy had to be an *Erlebnis,* a lived and concrete experience: it had to be existential. It also had to help him, and possibly others, live: utility and fecundity were among the criteria of truth for him. To a young disciple who requested advice, he answered in 1758 in a very Goethean manner: "Man is not made to meditate, but to act."

Above all, it had to be his own, and not a borrowed garb. "How many men between God and me!" exclaims the Vicaire Savoyard, rejecting churches and priests in order to come closer to God. Too many books also stood between Rousseau and life, and he swept them aside. Theory and practice, thought and life, the abstract and the concrete should not, for him, be divorced. He could only understand ideas through his own self, and explain his own self genetically, through its history. He ushered in the new spirit of the age that followed his, when the genetic method invaded science, when biography became a prerequisite to criticism, and when history, in Renan's terms, became the true philosophy.

Yet Rousseau did not remain the captive of his own self, condemned to solipsism and naïvely contemplating his own singularity. He was convinced of his uniqueness and anxious to point it out to others. "I would rather be forgotten by the whole of mankind than be looked upon as an ordinary man," he owned in a curious fragment, "Mon Portrait," written probably in 1761 and only published posthumously in the fourth volume of the *Annales de la Société Jean-Jacques Rousseau.* Remorse and the need to atone for his faults through confessing them and thus to be absolved by posterity were in him inseparable from his reminiscence of the past. He magnified several of his faults in order to be

granted an even more dramatic absolution. Deep in his
soul, he remained convinced that, if he had gravely erred,
others had erred even more gravely but failed to repent as
he had done. A violent enemy of Rousseau and the Revolution, Joseph de Maistre, who was no mean psychologist,
once put that feeling, harbored in many hearts, thus: "When
I consider myself, I scorn myself. When I compare myself
to others, I esteem myself."

But, because his writings were traced with his own blood,
and marked with the burning search for sincerity of which
he boasted, they would, Rousseau imagined, be suitable,
not to serene egotists and sophists, but to those who had
suffered and were oppressed with a sense of the infinitude
of everything and of the futility of philosophical consolations. "I stifle in the universe" in his third letter to M. de
Malesherbes is one of Rousseau's famous and pathetic cries.
To those, and they were legion, who, in the second half of
the eighteenth century, were discontented by the prevailing intellectualist philosophy and filled to overflowing with
the moods which were later to be called romantic, Rousseau
answered that they could find comfort in that very feeling
of discontent, nourish themselves with the inner riches
which they could not impart to an understanding society.
"That internal void of which you complain is only experienced by the hearts made to be filled; narrow hearts never
feel the void, because they are always full with nothing"
(to Madame de Berthier). There is peril in such cultivation
of one's anguish, and dilettantism in toying with faith and
substitutes of faith. Rousseau did not encourage it, as
Chateaubriand and others were to do. Dissatisfaction to
him was a sign of election such as Pascal would have rejoiced in; it started a person on the road to seeking. But
in seeking, no arguments adverse to the reasons of the heart
had to be forcibly silenced. Good faith to oneself was the
golden rule. To Moultou who, from Montpellier, consulted

him on his own beliefs, Rousseau stated his own position in a letter (No. 3795) of November 14, 1769, and added the warning: "Take care, I beseech you, to be of good faith with yourself, for not to have believed and not to have wanted to believe are very different things. . . . I repeat, what I ask from you is not faith so much as good faith."

We believe that Rousseau reached a degree of good faith to himself unequaled in his time and not often if ever equaled by the romantics who were his progeny, in France, in Germany, in England, or by the great Russian, Tolstoi, who worshipped him, literally, as his saint. A Danish philosopher, Harald Höffding, who wrote one of the best studies of Rousseau's thought and was also an expert in psychology, declared: "If Rousseau had not given us his *Confessions* we should lack one of the most important contributions to the knowledge of human nature." Complacent he was at times, but far less than many a naïve admirer of his own greatness or of his petty idiosyncrasies, from Chateaubriand to Gide. Rousseau's moral theory, according to which "virtue only belongs to the strong" *(Second Dialogue)* and necessitates a struggle, shut him out from those whom he would acclaim as virtuous; his political doctrine stressed the devotion of that hard-won virtue to the general will and made it a prerogative of the citizen helping and loving, if possible, those who surround him. Jean-Jacques owned that he was not fit to fight. "Virtue supposes a struggle with our own self and the difficulty in triumphing makes its merit" (letter to M. L'A– de . . . , April 4, 1764).

But he experienced another state in which man may be, if not virtuous and even if not good to others, at least in harmony with himself and with nature. Rousseau, as a seeker after total sincerity, had proved most original in *Emile,* in the *Dialogues* which he pathetically and in vain attempted to lay on the altar of the Notre Dame cathedral, and in the *Confessions.* There he had known man, and himself,

through and through—"intus et in cute," as his second
favorite formula put it. He had come across the phrase, proverbial in Latin, in the third satire of Persius, in which a
teacher, upbraiding his lazy pupil who resembles Nero, then
being taught by Seneca, tries to bring him away from mundane evils to stoic virtue. But, as Rousseau grew weary with
the world and with thinking, he composed those ten *Rêveries d'un promeneur solitaire* (the tenth was interrupted by
death) which are a masterpiece of poetical prose and a mile-
stone in the history of introspective psychology.

Rousseau had always contended that there are in man
two categories of feelings: the relative ones, which spring
from comparison with others, and are therefore relative to
them and conditioned by society; and the absolute ones,
the natural ones: the absolute self depends in no way upon
life with others; it is the natural self to which we seldom
can or should surrender in active life. Only in the second
group of feelings is man sincere, for while other men seem
to urge us to become what we are not, natural feelings allow
us to remain what we are. The ideal society is that in which
man will recover as much of his absolute or natural self as
can be compatible with living in a collectivity; instead of a
fawning servility and a desire to please others and put on
a mask, man will assume his duties as a citizen and not abdicate his sincerity. As he drew near death, Rousseau refused to live for others or to be concerned with society; he
withdrew into himself and lived passively. The third *Promenade* ranks among the most precise and balanced analyses
of old age ever attempted: they are few in literature. The
fourth is a coherent and penetrating definition of lying and
of the degrees of sincerity which are compatible with life
with others. Rousseau admits that he lacked the moral
strength to follow his motto: to devote life to Truth, but
he does not swerve from the principle of good faith to oneself first. "If we must be just to others, we must be true to

ourselves." The fifth *Rêverie* contains the description of the most celebrated pantheistic ecstasy in literature. Wordsworth in *Tintern Abbey,* Shelley in *Mont Blanc,* the French romantics and those arch-romantics who followed them, like Rimbaud, owed much to those pages that describe how, on his tiny island, rowing on the lake or lying on the banks, Rousseau became divested of his own body and, his heart at last at peace, knew a "divine" state of self-sufficiency.

Wholly sincere man? No, Rousseau never was one, and he would not have aroused such passionate adoration if he had ever become that monster. But he went deeper and farther into understanding the value of sincerity, both to others and to himself, than anyone had done before. Thereby he justified his claim, in his early draft for a Preface to the *Confessions* and in Book X of that work, to have achieved what Montaigne had failed to do. With Rousseau, philosophy is not a way of showing off to others or of combining a comprehensive set of answers to the enigmas of life; it is lived. A new era is thus ushered in by him in the history of thought. He occupies a place, in our opinion, second to none among French philosophers, embracing more of the social problems than Descartes had done, opening roads for anthropology and for psychology which the seventeenth-century pioneer could not suspect, merging the man and the thinker into one even better than the author of the *Discours de la méthode,* who merely sketched the biography of a pure spirit. With reason could Kant, so unlike Rousseau in many respects, place him side by side with Newton. Kant, comparing him to Newton, wrote in his *Fragments,* "Rousseau was the first to discover, beneath the varying forms human nature assumes, the deeply concealed essence of man and the hidden laws in accordance with which Providence is justified by his observations. . . . After Newton and Rousseau, the ways of God are justified." Elsewhere Kant hailed Rousseau's ethical doctrine as "a great discovery of our age" and praised him for having, better than anyone else, lifted the mask off the face of man.[4]

4. Out of the mass of writings on Rousseau, we shall mention the few which afford help for an examination of Rousseau's sincerity and of his "Existential" position of philosophical problems: Pierre Burgelin, *La Philosophie de l'existence de J. J. Rousseau* (Presses Universitaires de France, 1952); Bernard Groethuysen, *J. J. Rousseau* (Gallimard, 1949); Jean Guéhenno, *J. J. Rousseau* (3 vols. Grasset, 1948); Georges Gusdorf, *Mémoire et personne* (2 vols. Presses Universitaires de France, 1951); André Monglond, *Vies préromantiques* (Belles-Lettres, 1925); Marcel Raymond, "Deux Aspects de la vie intérieure de Rousseau," in *Annales de la Société Jean-Jacques Rousseau*, *29* (1941–42), 1–57; Pierre Trahard, *Les Maîtres de la sensibilité française au XVIIIᵉ siècle, 3* (Boivin, 1932). The quotations from Kant's *Fragments* (*8, 6*30) and *Werke* (*2, 3*26) are borrowed from the little book by Ernst Cassirer, *Rousseau, Kant, Goethe. Two Essays* (Princeton University Press, 1945). The same Ernst Cassirer offers an excellent interpretation of Rousseau's thought (chiefly in its political and social aspects) in what is probably the most profound reinterpretation of eighteenth-century thought: *The Philosophy of the Enlightenment* (Princeton University Press, 1951; German edition, 1931). Another philosopher also favorable to Rousseau, Georges Beaulavon, wrote a clear and pregnant account of Rousseau's differences from and affinities with Descartes in "La Philosophie de Rousseau et l'esprit cartésien," *Revue de Métaphysique et de Morale, 44* (1937), 325–52.

CHAPTER 4

Romanticism and Sincerity

IF THE VITALITY of an artist or of a movement can be gauged by the number of foes it arouses, of all the European romanticisms, the French, which came last, may well have left the most enduring effects. To a far greater extent than in England, or even than in Germany, romanticism in France appeared to break with the national tradition and to be permeated by a revolutionary spirit which frightened those who had survived the Terror, the emigration, and the Napoleonic wars. Far more so than in England —where Wordsworth's and Coleridge's youthful illusion of living in "very heaven," when France shook off her chains, proved short-lived, and where Shelley's vituperations were promptly chastised—French romanticism, whatever creed was actually professed by Lamartine and Hugo in their early poems and by Balzac throughout his life, was in its essence revolutionary: it questioned the established order in religion, philosophy, politics and, most perilously of all in a country where literature embraces those three realms of discord, in literature. Marx did not err when he hailed as a revolutionary the monarchist and would-be Catholic author of the *Comédie humaine*. Stendhal is, to this day, a favorite with Communist intellectuals in France, such as Roger Vailland, Claude Roy, even Aragon. Victor Hugo is celebrated sonorously by the liberals of the Spanish-American continent, by those of the Middle East, and by Soviet officialdom. Michelet, that arch-romantic among the French, has nourished the democratic sentimentality and the faith in the common suffering man of many a modern socialist. The whole nineteenth century, with Rimbaud and Zola and Gauguin in the midst of the very bourgeois Third Republic, rang with those calls to arms or with those mournful complaints of defeated artists escaping to other lands, which had first been heard in the romantic era of the early years of the century.

In contrast, if English romantic poetry, from Blake to Keats, was deeper and purer than that of France, the novel (even with Walter Scott, who rendered only the more exterior aspects of romantic sensibility), history, criticism, the drama, and philosophy in Great Britain had not been powerfully affected by romanticism. The German romantics of 1800–20, unequaled anywhere for originality, for dissatisfaction with the finite bounds of life, and for vagueness and even occasional mawkishness, had remained isolated from the practical and political conditions in their country, and were soon to be disowned by the Hegelians and by the Young Germany group. In Russia, where romantic temperaments such as Lermontov and Gogol flourished, there cannot be said to have existed *a* romanticism in the singular; nor was there a widespread romantic movement in the country of Manzoni, Foscolo, Leopardi or in the Spain of which Mérimée and Hugo and Gautier then dreamt exotically. Judged by its poets alone, French romanticism between 1820 and 1850 certainly looms in retrospect unequal to Wordsworth and Keats, to Goethe and Hoelderlin; its speculations on poetry are shallow when compared with those of Schelling, of Novalis, and of Coleridge. But if romanticism was an upheaval of the whole of a people's sensibility as manifested in all literary or pictorial expressions, it may well be that—much to the grief of many a French critic who has, romantically, denounced romanticism as a foreign poison temporarily instilled into French veins—French romanticism effected the most profound change in the mood and in the outlook of a people. It came late, as the French Renaissance had done compared to the Italian; it triumphed, as so often individuals, peoples, and ideas triumph, with Laertes' weapons, exchanging swords with its adversary or absorbing much of what was still alive in classicism. Unceasingly indeed, and unlike what had happened in England or in Germany, and of course in Russia, it remained mindful of the French classical models it had to challenge in order to establish itself in a country where continuity is made up of the dialectical play of conflicting vicissitudes. But the French national temper was forever transformed by the successive romantic waves which, having advanced with Rousseau and Diderot as early as 1760–70, were to assail it again with Claudel and Saint John Perse, with the Surrealists, then with the Existentialist champions of subjectivity.

Such a comprehensive and chaotic movement cannot be encompassed within any definition that singles out one feature of the landscape and magnifies it into immobility. The impossibility of defining romanticism had already entertained Heine and Alfred de Musset, one hundred and twenty-five years ago. More wisely, Kierkegaard, as early as 1836, noted in his *Journals:* "I must first protest against the notion that romanticism can be enclosed within a concept; for romantic precisely means that it oversteps all bounds." Reducing multiplicity to unity, profusion to monotony, elusive qualities to a common denominator may be the irresistible need of some philosophical minds, but it is the falsest way of murdering the past in order to delude oneself into accepting a mutilated and betrayed view of it. Adding up eclectically all the definitions of romanticism proposed, from the return to nature or the revival of the Middle Ages to the spirit of revolt or that of prophecy, from the cult of imagination to that of symbol, may be permitted in a textbook; but no enumeration will ever account for the diversity of temperaments that are called romantic. Relating the historical sequence of cénacles, groups meeting in one salon or another, circles and schools gathered around Fichte or the Schlegels or classifying poets into generations that elected to reside in the Lake Country or happened to wander during the last years of their lives in Italy is not a useless task; but it has been accomplished too many times, as has the favorite pastime of French literary historians: the study of manifestoes, prefaces, doctrines justifying the works or hiding the timidity of the achievement behind the sharp assertiveness of the theoretical ideas. Musset's provincial dullards, Dupuis and Cotonet, were baffled by the contradictory definitions of romanticism offered five or six years after *Hernani*. Several forests have since grown their leaves, their bark, and their moss of critical exegesis over romanticism. More than once, the reader, or the perpetrator, of modern criticism is visited by gloomy thoughts such as Gibbon expressed when he surveyed the decadence of antiquity: "A cloud of critics, of compilers, of commentators darkened the face of learning and the decline of genius was soon followed by the corruption of taste."

We do not claim here to cut through the tangle of much accumulated growth in order to proffer, on the silver tray of sincerity, a new key unlocking the enigmas of romanticism. More modestly, we would first propose a few principles of negative prudence: romanticism must not be viewed by us today as it imagined itself to be: a clean break with the past, noisily justified, in France at least, in prefaces, declarations of principles, and doctrinal declamations by which young iconoclasts were trying to reassure themselves. Theories count ultimately for very little in art and literature, except for those of a few historians of ideas on art and literature. Romanticism was at first, with the *Sturm und Drang*, with the *Lyrical Ballads*, with the *Préface de Cromwell*, a confused but determined fight against the sclerosis of devitalized traditions. It had to resort to a panoply of weapons in a manner which was then fair play. The fortresses of literature once occupied by the neoclassicists in France (the Théâtre Français, the Academy, the monthly reviews) have long ago been taken by storm. We do not have today to see the romantics as they wished to be seen: resorting to Shakespeare or Schiller as shields, dignifying themselves with noble if illegitimate ancestors such as Ossian or Chatterton, seizing André Chénier, Klopstock, even Calderon and Dante as their allies.

Romantic polemicists were not necessarily hypocrites. Like all writers and not a few other men ("sic nos non vobis"), they did not guess where their revolt would ultimately lead them and what, in their achievement, would endure. They dared not always avow to themselves their pantheism, or their fascination with infernal powers, or the attraction that evil or sorrow held for them. They dared not, in their twenties or thirties (Lamartine, Hugo, Musset), break away from a sentimental piety or shallow religiosity inherited from their background and education. After all, the excesses of the Parisian mobs and the trenchant eloquence of the guillotine were not yet forgotten in their family's memories. Moreover, expanded as the language of literary discussion became in Europe, with the nineteenth century, it still had to grope for words that were not clearly defined (such as imagination, irony, organicity) and it did not use others (sincerity, symbol, myth) as liberally, or as loosely, as we do today. Critics of a later age may thus detect among romantic writers the germs of notions for which words did not then readily exist. They may also—provided they do not disregard the historical truth, inadequate as it is, too petulantly—interpret romanticism in the light of its splendid aftermath and include fecundity among the elements of significance or greatness of a writer or an age. We certainly would not hold today our view of classicism had it not been for the romantic movement and the romantic debate, which radically altered what had preceded it. Epigoni of romanticism such as Flaubert and Baudelaire, the Symbolists, Yeats and Rilke and Rubén Darío and Eugene O'Neill and the Fauvist painters, and many a current man of letters concerned with the authenticity of his unconscious or with the sincerity of his divided personality have afforded us a perspective on the romantic movement of the first half of the last century which it would be idle to renounce.

With the exception of Rousseau—who, though he used the word only once, was more truly a romantic than anyone in the early nineteenth century in France except Berlioz and Michelet—the moralists who had aspired after sincerity had searched for it in a cool and dispassionate observation of human nature. In contrast, most of the romantics were men in revolt. They fretted against literary rules, dramatic conventions, diction, and versification to which their predecessors had bowed. They rebelled against the constraints imposed upon individuals by society, by urban or civilized life, by the state, the family, or a religion that had turned into an institution. Their revolt, in more than one case, proved ephemeral: Wordsworth, Southey, Scott, Goethe, Hugo, Pushkin were temperamentally anything but *révoltés,* as became clear once they disengaged their true selves from the contagious exaltation of their youth. But in revolt first did the romantics, all over Europe, assert themselves. They were thereby driven to express what was most singular in them, and not what they shared with their group or with their predecessors.

Those rebels were also discontented men. Their discontent was at times nothing but the impatience of youth eager to dislodge, from positions of influence, too stubbornly established elders. Those romantics who were unfortunate enough to outlive the age at which romance fades (let it be forty, beyond which limit Dostoevsky asserted no great man should survive), like Wordsworth and Goethe, became placid conservatives. Lamartine, Hugo, Stendhal, George Sand withstood better the usual bowing of the heart to the head. But in a deeper sense that discontent which is disquietude, dissatisfaction with oneself primarily and with the order of things, nostalgia for a rose-colored past or for a glowing future, and angry refusal of the present, can coexist with conservative political views and with an outwardly bourgeois existence. *Sehnsucht* was a mood common to Novalis and Lenau, to Lamartine and Nerval, to Shelley and Keats. In it, those poets attempted to discover the most elusive, most personal quality of their psychological makeup and to express it with what countless critics have called the accent of sincerity.

That anguished self-centeredness radically separated the romantics from those writers of earlier eras in whom modern critics, reluctant to accept novelty in ideas or in feelings, have discovered pronouncements or complaints outwardly similar to those of the romantics: Shakespeare, Pascal, Calderon. Most nineteenth-century romantics dreamt Adam's plight anew: they wished to recapture innocence, to appear in a tired society ("Je suis venu trop tard dans un monde trop vieux," as Musset expressed it) as unsoiled, virginal men. Through kinship with nature, through travels among primitives or among those primitives they imagined the Greeks or the Syrians to have been, through love ("Et ton amour m'a fait une virginité," as Hugo's redeemed courtesan, Marion Delorme, will humorlessly put it), they hoped to frame for themselves a new soul. They withdrew from

the actual world in order to listen to their inner promptings. Their pathetic fallacy has been derided by aesthe-
ticians who were hardly more objective than they. Their
adoration of women was often love of love itself, or love of
their own selves. They were aware of it, for there almost always lurked a lucid observer of his own exalted flights inside every romantic poet. Byron, Shelley, Musset, Heine
were all split personalities who sat in judgment upon their
romantic half. The self was the ultimate reality for all the
romantics, from which all else radiated.

They did not however imagine that they could truthfully
render that tormented and imperialistic self through recording the minute factual events of their lives. They were
far remote from Pepys and from Boswell, even from La
Rochefoucauld and Marivaux. To them, man was a creature of passion; he could best be known by being lovingly
followed in his exploration of his limits. To the romantics
we owe the delving into the unconscious and the rendering
in literature, in painting, in music of what in man is semi-
animal or monstrous. Not only grotesque figures inspired
by Gothic gargoyles, dwarves, and demons, but centaurs and
minotaurs people their imagination. One of them, the painter Géricault, observed aghast: "I begin to paint a man; he
ends up a lion." There is more than a little eroticism, and
occasionally sadism, in what we conventionally or contemptuously term romantic love. But, if they descended lower
into abysses, the romantics also soared higher. There are
more angels than demoniac creatures in their universe.
They idealized woman at least as much as they reviled her.
Long before Rimbaud, they hoped to reinvent love. They
knocked at the bars of their mortal prisons, seeking the absolute, or the philosopher's stone, or the Devil's elixir, deny-
ing the narrow bounds assigned to man. Prometheus, Eu-
phorion, Icarus haunted their imagination. They were not
so much irrationalists, as their French critics later insisted,

as superrationalists or suprarationalists. Even when they resorted to inflated language or to exclamatory rhetoric to convey an experience they deemed unique, they were trying to render passionately and exaltedly what they had experienced ardently. Even more than with any of their predecessors, fidelity to their impossible aspirations and sincerity to their expanded selves were of greater import than truth, or were *their* truth. The mind, and particularly the mind in turmoil, heated by violent emotions, created for them its own world or transfigured a cold, enigmatic, repellent world through the power of imagination.

The romantic writers found themselves in an enormously expanded world, even more so than the men of the Renaissance, at the dawn of a scientific age, had been. Physics, chemistry, geology—soon paleontology and biology, anthropology, a broadening of their literary geography beyond the precincts of the Mediterranean basin and of Europe, the revelation of whole eras of history which had lain unexplored during the self-sufficient classical and Augustan ages —opened up new vistas around them. Novelists, historians, poets did not remain unaware of that expanded universe. Their imagination was on a par with that of the scientists, and they were no longer content with attempting descriptive sketches or painstaking catalogues, in periphrastic language, of nature. Goethe and Balzac more than once emulated men of science, and Shelley has been hailed as "a Newton among poets."

But that affinity with scientific imagination and that bold invasion of realms hitherto uncharted (the medieval cathedral, the mythological and the mythopoeic creativeness of youthful races, the poetry of the Old Testament and of Dante) originated in the projection of the romantic ego over the physical world and over a past into which, like the Homeric visitors to the world of shadows, they instilled a little of their own blood to conjure up its dormant life. The glowing ardor of the romantic ego endowed it with an insight into the secrets of other men and of the natural world which more objective observers had placidly left unheeded. Starting with the romantics, man set himself up, in literature, as the measure of all things. The reactions attempted by realism, the efforts of the Parnassian poets, the advocates of a "neue Sachlichkeit," and the painters of reality proved short-lived. Personality was the new universal cult. Four relatively new genres were cultivated assiduously during the century and a half that followed the French Revolution: lyricism (often taken to be synonymous with personal poetry), the personal novel (much less conspicuous in England, however, than on the continent), the autobiography, and the intimate diary. A fifth might be added: criticism, which, with a number of its practitioners, often consisted in relating the adventures of their souls, not among masterpieces, but apropos of them.

It is impossible and inadvisable to imprison the multifarious features of the romantics of several countries within the walls of a foursquare structure. Athirst for infiniteness, or for unbridled freedom, romantic temperaments unfurled wings to break away from their cells. The vagueness which they were intent on preserving in their passion, in their aspirations, in their sorrows, in the solace sought in religion, nature, and love, precludes our finding most of the essential romantic traits in neatly representative texts susceptible of an equally neat text analysis. But the factors that prepared an invasion of several branches of literature by romantic egos claiming a new and more sincere expression of themselves are easily recognizable.

The man and the author, as Rousseau had taught, were to be merged into one. An author ceased to be, or to wish to appear, as a fastidious craftsman, contriving his books, as La Bruyère had asked him to do, like a clockmaker. He lived, first, as intensely as he could, and enriched his writings by the experience thus gained. He traveled, to flee from himself, to stock his visual memory with new images, but also to search for adventures which he could then relate. He cherished the dream of heroic action; Chateaubriand, Byron, Lamartine haunt the imagination of Barrès, D'Annunzio, Lawrence of Arabia, Malraux, and other adventurers of our own hyper-romantic century. Long before the doctrine of commitment flourished, those romantics had aspired after political or military glory, so as to be loved all the more by the women of their day and by those yet unborn. Readers of earlier eras had cared little whether Leonardo, Ronsard, Racine, Donne, Bach had experienced the moods they rendered in their art. Not so after the romantic upheaval. Biography assumed a mythical value.

Humility had not necessarily been bestowed on ancient men of letters like Cicero, Horace, Juvenal, still less on post-Christian ones like Cellini or Aretino. But examples of that "endless" virtue, as T. S. Eliot calls it, were very scarce after Rousseau's advent. With romanticism, the French, the German, to a lesser extent perhaps the British, creator joined the Italian artist in arrogating for himself all rights. Not only did he bestow immortality on his sovereign, on his pensioner, or on his none too coy mistress; he felt more keenly than others and needed to look freely for creatures who would provide the new Don Juan, the new Faust with a temporary response to his overflowing feeling. Passion gave him special rights, and so did genius. He blatantly exposed the women who were honored by his love, for, like Zeus visiting Danae, his touch transmuted clay or flesh into gold, or into the more brittle metal of poetry. He implored nature to beat in sympathy with his own heart, to retain the memory of his ecstasies. He bid time stand still in impassioned appeals. If a dear friend had been ravished away from him, he wished, with Browning—

> There had died along with you
> Three parts of Spring's delightful things.
> Ay, and for me, the fourth part too.

Like Yeats calling for his beloved to join him in "the ragged wood," he offered to drive all other lovers away and he proclaimed: "No one has ever loved but you and I."

In order to adhere more closely to his lived experience, his much cherished *Erlebnis,* the romantic creator wrote rapidly. Stendhal, Balzac, Lamartine advocated speed in jotting down the promptings of their heart or in transcribing the flashes of inspiration, as the one secret for preserving naturalness and sincerity. Many of them attempted long poems, for their inspiration was unquenchable and "facility, that grace of genius" as one of them called it, had been granted them. But weariness soon afflicted those unquiet and highstrung creators. In their inmost selves, they knew that they were at their best in shorter lyrics or, indeed, in fragments. Painters multiplied sketches and often reserved the most precious side of their genius for those unfinished fragments, fearing nothing so much as the genteel, over-polished canvases of more pompous predecessors. Poets realized that they grasped the elusiveness and the intensity of their sensations most firmly in brief, unconnected snatches unspoilt by too much "oiling"; they even rejoiced in contradictions that mirrored their torn souls but also their broad spirits encompassing all the diverse facets of life. Novalis, in one of his *Fragments* (Heilborn edition, No. 578), asserted that "to destroy the principle of contradiction is perhaps the highest task of the very highest logic." Rimbaud, the Surrealists, and Gide had precursors in their plea for a liberation from the shackles of consistency and logic.

Few of the French and the English, and not very many more of the German romantics had read Schopenhauer. But they professed, without having to delve into the arcana of philosophy, that the world was their representation. The women they celebrated or cursed had to conform to their inner image of the woman who was a fit companion for them or a fit subject for their song. They all loved a muse far more than individual women, as a learned historian of medieval philosophy, Etienne Gilson, has contended in one of his lighter volumes, *L'Ecole des muses* (1951). Indeed, like Shelley when he confessed his disappointment with Emilia Viviani, whom he had just celebrated as "Spouse, Sister, Angel" in *Epipsychidion,* most of them were aware of the passing character of their affections; they sensed that sincerity does not necessarily entail stability or fidelity. In nature, likewise, they received but what they gave. Coleridge, and even Wordsworth, knew it and said as much. Shelley communed with nature more rapturously. His wandering poet, in *Alastor,* dies as the moon over the mountain mixes with darkness,

> his poet's blood,
> That ever beat in mystic sympathy,
> With nature's ebb and flow

at that very moment growing feebler. In one of his more profound poems, "Mont Blanc," he had described with remarkable psychological accuracy the mutual flow of the mind into the universe and of the universe into the mind.

> My own, my human mind, which passively
> Now renders and receives fast influencings
> Holding an unremitting interchange
> With the clear universe of things around.

Rationalists have scoffed at what they fancied to be the fallacy of passionate sensibilities and a distortion of inanimate nature, neither maternal nor loving. But the poets who recorded such a pantheistic ecstasy, Wordsworth at the

end of "Tintern Abbey," Byron in *Childe Harold,* Shelley,
Goethe, Lenau, Lamartine occasionally, had not failed to
observe nature with awakened senses. Their insight "into
the life of things" penetrated far deeper than the cold, prosaic contemplation of the Augustan and neoclassical poets.
Because they were tensely, vibratingly attentive to the exterior world into which they wanted to merge their own
selves, they aroused in it a life unperceived before them.
There is a truth of imagination, recreating the objects that
it suffuses with its own glow, and a truth of an exalted sensibility which are no less valid than the truth of rationality.
Such was the romantic creed.

Of one sin the romantics were guilty—a sin against sincerity and against art. What they felt intensely had, they
thought, to be expressed powerfully; and power, for them,
often lay in exclamations, interrogations, cataracts of images, litanies of invocations, debauchery of sonorousness.
The French, whose romantic movement had suffered most
from such an inflation of language and whose diction was
slowest in purifying itself of the remnants of neoclassical
style, were, between 1900 and 1930, the most relentless in
damning the excesses of the romantics. Their anti-romantic
crusade has now run its course, and Balzac, Michelet, Hugo
stand unscathed in their glory. Delacroix and Berlioz have
been restored to a very high estate, and Musset himself may
soon be due for a revival. There is excess indeed, and dross,
and an occasional insincerity of language in the romantics.
They played their part of bold adventurers who annexed
new provinces to literature, accumulating conquests which
a later age, more adept at sifting, organizing, purifying, was
then to assimilate. Such voracious explorers, who seek their
own selves in the whole universe, may be guilty of haste,
of turgidness, of confusion between authentic voices and
mere echoes of their own sonorous calls. Such was the price
to pay for the revolution they effected. In countries more

faithful to the legacy of antiquity, such as Italy, in remoter lands where literature was traditionally the elaborate and detached function of mandarins or of a polished, aristocratic, or sacerdotal class, a formal and almost hieratic beauty may be preferred. Mallarmé, Saint John Perse, and other moderns have dreamed again of such a "trobar cluj." Art is the supreme creation, enthroned above and apart from life, sufficient unto itself like a closed and unapproachable structure. Eastern and even Italian and French literatures may, however, have lost heavily when they cultivated such formal beauty at the expense of life with its disorder, its irrelevances, its abrupt invasion of personalities clamoring for a hearing. Unruly and impure as romanticism was in its search for the self permeating all else, it stood closer to the turbulence of life and it answered the call of an enlarged public insisting upon seeing itself portrayed in the literature of its times.

The preceding remarks, intended to set the stage for the invasion of literature by the self claiming greater sincerity than had found its way into the art of writing heretofore, probably read like so much criticism which cannot foretell or even recognize new works of eminence but which, once they have appeared and become accepted, discovers a number of cogent reasons why those works should have been as they were. Our purpose was to show that, during and after romanticism, a growing number of literary artists aimed at being truthful, or sincere if not truthful; they professed such an aim, and our judgment among other criteria (for sincerity alone grants no talent and no virtue in art), must be based on it. The word sincere has become so commonly accepted that very few indeed are the critics of the last hundred years who have not used it to "explain" the forcefulness or the impact of a work. Inversely, insincere is the most damning of all words of obloquy. If several writers have been called comedians without losing caste in our hierarchies, it is because the epithet tragic has usually been affixed to the word. Many have alluded to the masks that they assumed; but the masks implied a sense of modesty or of irony which intensified their sincerity through preserving it from profanation. We shall in the following pages, without any attempt at exhaustiveness (almost all of literature would have to be surveyed), mark the main milestones of that claim to sincerity in the country where the claim has been put forward most loudly: in France.

If we consider the works themselves, and more especially the poems composed by the romantics and by others since, we are faced with the unavoidable arbitrariness of subjectivity. First, a poem (or any work) is never beautiful or pre-eminent for one reason alone, but for a multiplicity of features which often elude analysis. Each of them proposes its own criterion, or imposes it, and has accordingly to be weighed. No great work—not even tragedy, the favorite toy of modern critics obsessed by Aristotle and Sophocles as not even the Renaissance humanists were—ever submitted to conditions laid down in advance. A critic cannot become a lawgiver decreeing what an ode or an elegy or a sonnet should be, except in its metric form. But the critic, however emotional he may be, can deny that a poem, or a picture or a sonata, must primarily be a work of art. No amount of personality could ever replace the talent or the work that strikes the reader as sincere, that is to say, as conveying adequately the experience, the feeling, the vision of the creator. Lastly, the prejudice should be eliminated which naïvely equates sincerity in a writer with his truthfulness or his veracity in recording what happened to him, what he felt, when and where. Not even in a diary is such accuracy to be found or to be wished, certainly not in an autobiography, in which the fragmentary meaninglessness of an experience formerly undergone becomes, in retrospect, part of a broader design and receives its significance from what followed. A lyrical poet or a novelist writing in the first person in no way has to cling to the myopic accuracy of the historian.

Let the reader collect his own anthology of a score of the most familiar romantic poems: one or two passages from Wordsworth's *Prelude;* Coleridge's "Dejection" or "Nightingale"; Shelley's "West Wind" ode or the rarer and more moving poems of his last two years, "A Lament" (O world! O life! O time!), "To Edward Williams," "The Zucca"; Keats' sonnet "Bright Star!" or one of his great odes; Lamartine's "Lac"; Musset's "Nuit de Mai"; Nerval's "Desdichado"; one of Goethe's briefer lyrics, "Nachtgedanken" (to Frau von Stein) or of Heine's sorrowful songs; Lenau's "Der schwarze See" or "Herbstlied"; Hoelderlin's "Abschied" ("Trennen wollten wir uns?"), etc. In all of them, differ as they do in other respects, we are struck immediately and directly by a tone that was not audible in the poets of the preceding centuries. The poet may be sentimental, or eloquent, or lack wit or the ability to smile at himself. He may verge on the ludicrous (Musset in the pelican parable), condescend to pathos or to obscurity (the second stanza of the "Ode to the West Wind"), yield to facility (Lamartine or Heine), truncate his autobiography (Wordsworth omitting from Book IX of *The Prelude* Annette Vallon and Caroline, the French daughter he had by her). But his own emotion grips us. We know at once that he is not playing a game and taking literature as a means of entertaining others or himself. He has lived his emotions and his thoughts intensely and rendered them in such a way that the intensity is disengaged from small incidents, raised on a general plane even when the first person is retained, multiplied by the language and the music of the poem. Indeed, not a little of the distrust evinced by British and even more by American critics of the last forty years toward such lyrical poems is to be set down to their gentlemen's training which dreads and hence scorns the manifestation of emotion. Instead of the security encountered in the poets of the seventeenth and eighteenth centuries, and even in those of the Renaissance, who bow to the rules of an agreeable game and seem to abide by the conventions of their age, the romantic individualists stand ready to startle the reader at every turn with an emotional inconsistency or the laying bare of some intimate recess of their hearts.

Biographers have ransacked the records of Lamartine's private life. They have published the letters in which Graziella—the Neapolitan fisherman's daughter who, in the novel that bears her name, died for love of the French poet —was called "a little girl as pretty as an angel and as stupid as a goose," and with whom he confessed being encumbered. They have revealed how the inconsolable poet, after Elvire's death and while he was composing the stanzas of "Le Lac," consoled himself with many a chance acquaintance among peasant girls. Frailty's name is not woman's alone. The conduct of a man easily carried away by desire or his banter in youthful letters to a friend often expresses a more shallow side of his nature than the poems in which he fuses the man that he was and the one, no less authentic, that he was trying to be. The prejudice of many a "debunking" biographer, prone to displaying a sense of superiority to the author whose secrets he has pierced, leads him to set greater store by what the author has confessed that is "human," base, deceitful than by his moments of idealism or of self-forgetfulness. The young man of twenty-seven who received from the dying married woman whom he called Elvire the burning love letters subsequently published by René Doumic, had reciprocated her passion. He rendered her feelings in "Le Lac"; and in the typical manner of French romantic poets—less purely concerned with their own selves than the German or the English, probably better able to balance the excesses of sentiment with the judgment of reason—Lamartine raised the lovers in a frail skiff, imploring nature and time to share their threatened ecstasies, to the symbolic and general plane of a man and a woman revolting against death. The impeccable, "classical" order of the development, even the vagueness of the adjectives and the indistinctness of the images, helped in obliterating the local setting and in enhancing the appeal of the first French poem of the last century in which the readers heard an authentic voice speaking to every one of them.

The same theme was treated by several other romantics, obsessed as they were by the momentous and mournful concern of all moderns, the passing of time and the engulfing voraciousness of death—even Virgil, Ronsard, Shakespeare, Rembrandt, Marvell had not experienced that fear with the anguish that gripped the romantic age and later Tolstoi and Proust. Once again, the discrepancy between factual accuracy and a broader faithfulness to what the poet knew himself capable of feeling need not awe us into expelling the word sincerity altogether from our critical vocabulary. Wary as we may be of words laden with imprecise connotations, we must admit that critical vocabulary in any language is not susceptible of much precision, because the notions it has to convey are themselves loose and apt to vary with each individual. The third stanza of the "Ode on a Grecian Urn," conjuring up the torments and joys of love; the third stanza of the "Ode to a Nightingale," which condenses a world of despair into one line ("The weariness, the fever, and the fret"); Keats' so-called last sonnet which, according to some researchers, may have been written before the poet fell in love with Fanny Brawne—these poems do not, of course, tell the minute, unessential story of a love affair. Nor does "La Belle Dame sans Merci," for we have known, since Fanny's own letters were at last published in 1937 by Frederick Edgcumbe, that Keats' passion was understood and returned, if not in its full morbid frenzy, at least with sympathy and feeling. But behind the art displayed in poems that come as close to perfection as anything in English lyricism, there is the restrained but explosive force of an uncommonly sensitive man pouring the whole of himself into his verse. He was more completely himself when his ardent imagination envied the steadfastness of a bright star hung aloft the night and the soothing rest upon a loving bosom, than when he actually hung on Fanny Brawne the too sumptuous cloak of his self-tormenting need for love in order to avert the death he felt approaching.

Sincerity in an artist would be a dubious merit if it were not accompanied by an exceptionally ardent personality, overflowing with the urge to enshrine into words an experience deemed unique but which, once expressed, may reveal to others that it is not alien to them. With most romantic poets, that interest in their own ego led them to discover microcosmic correspondence with the outer world. In fact they, and not their classical predecessors, proved to be the new Titans scaling peaks, flying with the clouds and the wind, embracing trees and the waves of the ocean, ravishing from the gods the secrets of nature. The same poets who descended deeper into their own souls than their predecessors also ventured outside their own monads and portrayed other individuals similar to themselves or ascended those summits on which serenity, "Ruhe," was supposed to dwell: Goethe, Novalis, Hoelderlin, Hugo, Vigny (in "Eloa"), Lamartine (in "La Chute d'un Ange"), Keats (*Hyperion*), Shelley (fourth act of *Prometheus Unbound*). All of those and others less gifted created a new cosmic poetry in which the universe, instinct with a surge of creative life, responded to their passionate search for new gods. "Any descent into oneself," noted Novalis in one of his best known Fragments, "any inward glance is at the same time an ascent."[1]

1. Elsewhere in the same volume of Fragments the poet whose pronouncements anticipated the French symbolists, wrote: "No one knows him-

The new sincerity of the romantic poets indeed had to be nurtured by a faith: a faith that, even when they lamented their solitude ("L'Isolement," "Moïse," "Childe Harold," "Stanzas in Dejection near Naples," Lenau's two sonnets entitled "Einsamkeit"), they would not remain without communion with others whom their complaints would encourage to feel like them and with them. A creator can hardly be drowned in a pond of despair, for he trusts that unknown friends, now or later, will understand him. Because the romantic creator respected the acuity and the originality of his own sensations and was almost overpowered by them (Shelley's repetition of the verbs "to swoon," "to fail"; Keats' profusions of gustatory and olfactory sensations; Tennyson's marked sensuousness in his early poems), he had to be endowed with an abnormal impressionability. Much has been made, and yet not enough perhaps, of Keats' profound concept of "negative capability" and of his more whimsical comparison of the poet to a chameleon. His readiness to impersonate another character, on which all their friends have commented with surprise, implied an uncommon ability to live a vicarious or imaginative experience, a power of loving, and thus of sharing, which broadened their egotism into universal charity.

> By love, for here
> Do we begin and end, all grandeur comes,
> All truth and beauty, from pervading love;
> That gone, we are as dust.

The lines first appeared in Wordsworth's *Prelude* (xiv, 168–71) and later were altered. There is hardly a romantic

---

self as long as he is only himself, and not at the same time he and another." And again: "How could a man understand a thing unless he has its germ in himself? What I want to understand must blossom forth in me according to organic laws."

poet who has not written a hymn to love, seldom celebrating pleasure—unlike the Elizabethans or some of the Metaphysicals—but seeking in love a fuller self-revelation and the pretext for a confession which, shared by the partner to whom it was addressed, and by the public which became the poet's confidant and accomplice, received its own absolution.

Two consequences will derive from the displacement of the center of literature to the self. The claim is put forward by several romantics that their greater sincerity endows them with a peculiar merit and makes them more vulnerable to the scoffings and the scorn of the world. Sincerity also becomes a critical criterion, and in it lies the higher value of some works. One does not easily picture artists of earlier eras asserting that their work was destined to survive because in it they had mirrored their souls or poured their hearts unreservedly. Such a view would have been incomprehensible to Raphael, Titian, or Velásquez. El Greco—in whom, early in the twentieth century, many admirers thought they had discovered a genius closest to their anguished selves—after he settled in Toledo (we fondly imagine that it was because that city of ascetic monks was a fitting decor for his own torments), behaved exactly like any commercial artist, painted just the saints and martyrs he was asked to portray, followed to the letter the prosaic instructions of the patrons who ordered the "Burial of the Count of Orgaz," and grew rich thereby. Mozart composed precisely the religious music requested from him, utilizing lighter and purely pagan passages from his other works in a Mass or a Kyrie. In one of his letters he bluntly confided: "Make as much money as possible; next to good health, that is the best thing." He would not have posed for a disheveled, haggard artist waiting for inspiration to strike his forehead. Like most musicians of his day, and others since, he filled orders. Emperor Joseph II commissioned "Cosi Fan Tutte" and Mozart delivered it.

There have been artists since romanticism who liked to have it believed that they carried within their heads unlimited potentialities which a chance circumstance (the occasion which prompted all great works, Goethe asserted), an order from a publisher, or entreaties from a friend (as in the case of Paul Valéry) transformed into an actual work. Such a detached, or impersonal, attitude was naturally accepted by all in a century when the artist had not yet deified himself; it has become with us a coquettish contempt for too pompous a worship of art. The majority of creators have, for one hundred and fifty years, preferred to proclaim, or to hint, that they have poured the truest of themselves in their works and that, naturally, the public has failed to recognize it. Baudelaire made such a declaration, in angry and outraged tones, in his famous letter to Ancelle of February 18, 1866. Thackeray defended his novel *Pendennis* in a preface which stated that the reader's questions should be: "Is the author honest? Does he tell the truth in the main? . . . Is he a quack, who shams sentiment, or mouths for effect?" His book might be criticized as lacking in art or in interest, he added, but it told the truth and met the one requirement that passed before all others: "In his constant communication with the reader, the writer is forced . . . to speak out his own mind and feelings as they urge him."[2]

Pendennis was completed in 1848–49, and a number of the *Fleurs du mal* were probably composed by then. That same year (1848) there had died in Paris the acknowledged

2. Thackeray also upbraided Byron severely, because he had sung oriental beauties in preference to those of England. "That man never wrote from his heart," he declared in his *Notes of a Journey from Cornhill to Grand Cairo* (1845). See S. C. Chew, *Byron in England* (London, Murray, 1924), p. 256.

father of French romanticism, Chateaubriand. He was leaving behind him the most important work of confessions since Rousseau's, the *Mémoires d'outre-tombe*. In the Testament which served as a preface to the long relation of his life and loves, he declared boldly: "Of the French authors of my age, I am almost the only one whose life resembles his works." In the eleventh book of those memoirs into which, for the first time in literature, he boasted, all his life was allowed to be reflected, he sketched the "Defects of his character," excusing them as fast as he discovered them. They were redeemed by the two adjectives he applied to himself: "sincere and truthful." Indeed, in spite of the eternal posturing the melancholy Breton affected, and which was part and parcel of his "sincere" nature (sincerity is not necessarily simplicity, still less is it modesty), Chateaubriand offered a strangely truthful portrait of himself in his memoirs. All is vanity, he said, but indefatigably pursuing honors and women, an assertion based on his having established his fame as an apologist of Christianity and subsequently having become an ambassador to the Holy See, at the same time parading a mistress in Rome and punctuating the narrative of his life with that of the adulterous affairs of his heart.

Of the French romantic poets, Alfred de Musset is the one who most consistently claimed that sincerity was his originality and the source of his woe. After displaying, in his very early poems, the keenest irony of all his contemporaries and mocking romantic sentimentality with gusto, in 1830, with "Les Vœux stériles," he began to describe the poet's soul as reduced to the level of a prostitute and to complain dramatically that he who yearned for success with an indifferent public had better "boldly expel all sincerity, and not allow drops of blood to fall from his heart." An author prematurely broken by grief and prone to complaining could only reap scorn. In 1833, in the second canto of a light oriental tale, *Namouna*, he harped playfully on his favorite theme:

> Sachez-le,—c'est le cœur qui parle et qui soupire
> Lorsque la main écrit,—c'est le cœur qui se fond.

His romantic hero, Frank, in *La Coupe et les lèvres*, uttered a line which the poet's biographers were often to use as their epigraph: "L'histoire de ma vie est celle de mon cœur." And he laid, as the primary condition imposed upon a poet, the necessity of knowing one's limits and of keeping within them. The first of the great poems to follow upon the Venetian adventure with George Sand, *La Nuit de Mai*, contains the oft-quoted declamation on the pelican which, having found no food for his little ones, offers to their hunger his heart and his entrails and hastens his death by a last moan, a farewell that shakes the firmament. The poets, likewise, immolate their hearts to a listless, all-devouring crowd. From then on, Musset did not waver from the creed that suffering alone makes a man, and an artist, and that all the rest is sophistry. In the famous stanzas to the singer La Malibran, in light but revealing tales such as *Emmeline* (1837) and *Les Deux Maîtresses* of the same year, Musset returned to the question of sincerity. He laid bare much of what, in his life, made him a *poète maudit* and a self-tormented wretch in his underrated *Confession d'un enfant du siècle*, which ranks among the most acute romantic analyses of the quality of a man with two souls in his Faustian breast. All his life he was faithful to the advice he had given in 1832 to his friend Edouard Bocher: "Ah! Frappe-toi le cœur, c'est là qu'est le génie!" From Taine—who preferred Musset to all the French romantics (and also, in a famous parallel in his *English Literature*, to Tennyson) because "he was more than a poet, he was a man"—to the most solid works of critical erudition on Musset such as Pierre Gastinel's, his commentators echo the same formula of praise: his sincerity was total and redeems whatever weakness afflicted his character and his art.

The notion that sincerity is the hallmark of quality in art and that it is easily perceptible to any reader who has a heart as well as a mind became so pervading and so insidious with the romantics that a collection of the pronouncements by distinguished critics in which sincerity is resorted to after other criteria have failed would be tedious. No less calm and judicious a critic than Wordsworth in his fortieth year, in the second of his essays "Upon Epitaphs" (1810), after explaining that epitaphs must above all be simple and sincere, submits:

> These suggestions may be further useful to establish a criterion of sincerity, by which a writer may be judged; and this is of high import. For, when a man is treating an interesting subject, and one which he ought not to treat at all unless he be interested, no faults have such a killing power as those which prove that he is not in earnest. . . . Indeed, when the internal evidence proves that the writer was moved, in other words where this charm of sincerity lurks in the language of a tombstone and secretly pervades it, there are no errors in style or manner for which it will not be, in some degree, a recompense.[3]

3. Ironically enough, the volume of *Wordsworth's Literary Criticism* in which this essay is reprinted (London, Froude, 1905) is preceded by an introduction in which Nowell C. Smith solemnly declares: "No better instance than Wordsworth's prose could be found of sincerity in writing . . . Wordsworth's writing was, like his character, absolutely sincere."

A few decades later, in his chapter on "The Study of Poetry" included in the *Essays in Criticism,* Second Series, Matthew Arnold, ever striving for laws or objective and immutable criteria that would reassure his taste (next to Sainte-Beuve, he probably is the one critic who erred most signally in rating the authors of his time, from Burns to his own generation) laid down the requisites for "supreme poetical success." The powerful application of ideas to life cannot suffice, unless it is made "under the conditions fixed by the laws of poetic truth and poetic beauty." Those laws in their turn impose "high seriousness, the high seriousness which comes from absolute sincerity. The accent of high seriousness, born of absolute sincerity, is what gives to such verse as 'In la sua volontade è nostra pace . . .' its power."

Of such "sincerity," Arnold decrees, Burns, like Chaucer, came woefully short; both failed to reach "high seriousness." In the same volume, in the essay on Byron, Arnold approvingly quotes Swinburne, and joins him in applauding in Byron (of all poets!) "the splendid and imperishable excellence which covers all his offences and outweighs all his defects: the excellence of sincerity and strength." All his life the son of the Rugby school principal attempted to set up standards for greatness in poetry: a great theme was essential in his eyes, and a robe of outward charm should cover "thought and austerity within" (sonnet on "The Austerity of Poetry"); greatest of all is the moral virtue which makes the artist equal to the thoughtful man inside him. He took Keats and most romantics to task for being wrongly fascinated by the Elizabethan tradition and preferred to seek for models in Goethe and among the moralists of France such as Joubert. Pleasure he banished, or he accepted it only if purified and spiritualized. The reader, alas! avenged himself: *Empedocles* left him cool. In a disillusioned quatrain, "A Caution to Poets," first sent to

Clough in December 1852, the poet, turning to criticism
and to cultural predication, prosaically admitted that

> What poets feel not, when they make,
> A pleasure in creating,
> The world, in its turn, will not take
> Pleasure in contemplating.

The ablest critics of the last century, even those who endeavored most determinedly to deprive literary judgment
of its changeable subjectivity, like Taine, preserved romanticism in their hearts and ultimately resorted to sincerity
as the hallmark of greatness. Taine's tastes, it has not been
sufficiently noticed, more than once wrestled with the rigid
doctrines in which he valued art as the expression of a society and saw in it the convergence of race, environment,
and "moment." He could not contain his tears when he read
Lamartine's prose novel, *Raphael,* and he wound up the
fifth volume of his *English Literature* with a brilliant and
altogether unconvincing contrast between the British nation—prim, neat, orderly, sanely balanced, moderate, faithfully mirrored in its favorite poet, Tennyson—and the
French public—disorderly, quick, unstable, witty, skeptical,
passionate, whose beloved poet (so Taine asserted, although
both *Les Contemplations* and *Les Fleurs du mal* had appeared) was Alfred de Musset. "Was there ever a more vibrant, a truer strain? . . . He experienced the inner tempest
of profound sensations, gigantic dreams and intense joys.
. . . He suffered but he invented; he sinned, but he produced."

Long after Matthew Arnold and Taine, journalists and
scholarly commentators of literature will daily hit, or fall
back, upon the criterion of sincerity when they "explain"
the reason of a work's impact. Such sincerity they will de-

clare to be "unmistakable." Woe to dull-souled creatures
who look elsewhere for the secret of literary art.[4]

4. A most learned philologist and critic, James Darmesteter, writing in
1896 on George Eliot (*Nouvelles Etudes Anglaises,* Calmann Lévy, pp.
111–63), whom the French then tended to prefer to all their own novelists,
quoted from a sentence in Eliot's letter of March 1, 1860, in which she confessed to having wept torrents of tears on human suffering, and commented:
"There lies the secret of her power: her work lives because she put her
heart's blood into it." The *Times Literary Supplement* of February 18, 1955,
declared of T. E. Lawrence's *The Mint:* "Its sincerity and honesty are unmistakable." We have seen the term used as a criterion of value as often as
four times in a single issue of a respected Paris daily. Among the British
poets, Robert Burns asserted as firmly as Musset was later to do in France
that no author has the right to sing love who has not first felt it. "Misery
is like love; to speak its language truly, the author must have felt it," he
wrote in one of his letters. In his *Commonplace Books,* he jotted down:
"Shenstone observes finely that love-verses writ without any real passion
are the most nauseous of all conceits; and I have often thought that no
man can be a proper critic of love composition, except he himself, in one
or more instances, have been a warm votary of this passion." I am indebted
to my colleague F. W. Hilles for bringing those two passages to my attention.

CHAPTER 5

The Poetry of Introspection

SHRUGGING ONE'S SHOULDERS at the flood of sincerity from which the romantics hoped to draw new inspiration, dismissing as loosely uncritical the use made of that ambiguous word by romantic and unromantic criticism alike, would be all too simple. The truth is that, in spite of half a dozen moves of revolt against the romantics staged since 1830, most lyrical poetry still is judged relatively to the romantic, and that the concept of sincerity is for us inseparable from literature. Catullus appeals to the moderns more readily than Horace, Donne more than Cowley and even than Pope, Hoelderlin more than Schiller, in no mean measure on account of the romantic intensity we seem to descry in them. We have lately acclaimed the baroque poets and artists of several lands, without always admitting that we cherished in them several of the features of the romantics under a mask which struck us as new. Claudel, Machado, Dylan Thomas are all alike imbued with the best, occasionally even with the most spurious, elements of romanticism. We find it in Rilke in his oracular definition of the beautiful "als des Schrecklichen Anfang," the almost intolerable beginning of the terrible in his first *Duinese Elegie* and, in the last of his sonnets to Orpheus, in his calls to the magical force at the crossroads of all the senses. Nor is it lacking in T. S. Eliot himself, that archromantic in disguise. We call them modern because a shiver emanates from their verse and their personality shakes ours. Their ego intrudes into our own lives; they force us to share in their passions and, momentarily, to suspend our sense of restraint, if not of disbelief.

But, for all their rhetorical devices and the frequent impurity of their glittering ore, the romantics were far from lacking insight into human nature, read in the mirror of their own. They fought against one set of conventions and one form of insincerity, and did not fail to question their own claims to a fuller or bolder truth. At no time since St. Paul have there been more human beings rent asunder by an anguishing schizophrenia. The very poets who yearned to be metamorphosed into disembodied angels, to merge their corporeal frames with the wave or the wind, to ascend into the skies with an ethereal minstrel, or to borrow the language of the visionary cuckoo, proved to be the most acute analysts of their aspirations. They lucidly dissected their sorrows and perceived the inevitable lag between their idealism and the conditions laid upon their finiteness. Romantic irony has been studied chiefly by the Germans and hence with some excessive gravity. Like much of the theoretical baggage of German romanticism, it derived from Fichte's *Doctrine of Science;* the Schlegels, Tieck, Novalis, Jean Paul pondered over it. Through that irony, the creator stressed his independence of his own creation precisely as he was accomplishing it. He was aware of the lag between his limited and static mind and the loftiness and freedom of the ideal model which his art could only clumsily approximate. Irony was not the monopoly of German romantics, even if theorists of other nations failed to speculate over it. In a less philosophical manner, perhaps with a deeper gloom at falling short of their goal, Shelley, Vigny, Baudelaire experienced it, as did Heine, Musset, and Pushkin with more playfulness. For all of them, irony served as an antidote to their temptation of parading their sincerity. The question that was to obsess Gide, Julien Green, Pirandello and other later introspectives, "Can one know and tell the full truth about oneself?" had already tormented the more inquiring minds among the romantics.

Heinrich Heine was one of them; sentimentality and irony were bedfellows with him. He lamented unrequited love, woman's perfidy, but the complaints of his swollen heart were silenced by the realization of man's privilege, which is, unlike that of the sun and the moon forever pursuing their divorced courses, to submit to death.

> Ich aber der Mensch
> Der Niedriggeplanzte, der Todbeglückte,
> Ich klage nicht länger.
> (*The North Sea*, "Sunset")

He was aware of the obstacles that stand on the path of our knowing, and telling, the truth about ourselves. "When a man wants to blow his brains out, he always has excellent motives. But does he know those motives?" Heine asked in his *Reisebilder*.

Goethe had, early in his career (in a letter in French to his sister, in 1767), youthfully asserted that a poet need not feel the love that he describes. Later, however, he outgrew that Anacreontic view of poetry as a light-hearted game. He confided to Eckermann thus: "What I had not lived, what had not burned the tips of my fingers and had not made me think, I never dreamt of turning into poetry." Such an experience need not be actual, but imaginative, and literary inspiration may foster it. More courageous than many romantics, Goethe ventured to express pleasure as well as the nobler emotions of sorrow; he included sensations, even

erotic ones, as well as feelings. In the most brutally frank
of his works, the *Roman Elegies,* he appeared to challenge
the notion of many timid critics for whom allusions to
books or to works of art are less sincere than the stark record
of lived experience. His sensuous enjoyment of the docile
woman of scant culture whom he was later to make his wife
had brought to him a keener delight in Ovid, Propertius,
and ancient art. He never feared submitting to influences;
he did not seek to preserve the soul of his originality through
ignoring others or fighting his own plasticity. His personality was powerful enough to be merged into his work and
grow enriched thereby. The artist whom he depicts in
Kuenstlers Erdewallen gleefully identified himself with the
Venus Urania whom he had endowed with artistic life.

> Wo mein Pinsel dich berührt, bist du mein;
> Du bist ich, bist mehr als ich, ich bin Dein.

It was Goethe's fate to outlive many of the German romantics who had vainly appealed to the "Stürmer" in him,
the author of *Werther* and *Goetz,* against his older and
serener self. Heine's long struggle with physical torment
ended in 1856; Nerval had hanged himself in Paris one
year before, and the other French poet who is often compared to Heine, Musset, died in 1857. By the middle fifties,
in Western Europe, a sharp reaction had set in against the
exhibitionism into which the romantic cult of the self at
its most sincere had degenerated. A weary doubt lurked in
the minds of many: did not a poet incur dull monotony by
singing his emotions? Could the self, expressed in the first
person singular, for long appear able to renew itself? Would
readers meekly agree to recognize themselves in that exceptional creature, the poet, while on every side melodrama,
journalism, fiction were courting the readers of a mass age?
Several of the romantics of Germany and France, and less

successfully, on the stage, those of Britain, endeavored to win the dramatic audiences. In their poetry they eschewed the dreariness of the omnipresent "I" through impersonating their dreams in heroes thrown into ambitious spiritual adventures. In France, which had long smarted under the indictment of being unfit for the epic muse, epic poems, not very readable today, flourished on Prometheus, Ahasuerus, Psyche, Empedocles, Centaurs and Bacchae, fallen angels and Satan.

Tennyson dramatized his youthful despair in poems in which the form of direct confession was avoided: "Supposed Confessions of a Second-rate Sensitive Mind" and "The Two Voices." When the death of a dear friend, Arthur Hallam, in 1833, forced him to reconsider his view of life, he assumed a solemn tone, strove for generality, and multiplied symbolic allusions so as to avoid too direct an expression of his feelings. The question obsessed him whether he was justified in chiseling images and contriving rhythms to convey, through words which inevitably betray, a grief that was strictly his.

> I sometimes hold it half a sin
> To put in words the grief I feel,
> For words, like Nature, half reveal
> And half conceal the Soul within.[1]

Words act like a dull narcotic, numbing pain, but also turning a sincere sorrow into a meretricious game. Other sections of Tennyson's long elegy (XXI, XLVIII) reveal him as dreading the insinuation of readers that he was parading his sorrow as a convenient theme for a poet. He disclaims any calculation for facile affect.

> I do but sing because I must,
> And pipe but as the linnet sings.

---

1. Tennyson, *In Memoriam,* V.

If artifice must enter into art and fancy lend its hues to feeling, writing *In Memoriam,* he contends, has deepened his suffering.

In Memoriam, significantly enough, marked the exact middle of the century, as did the passing of the oldest survivor of the great English romantics, Wordsworth. Five years later, Browning's lyrical masterpiece, *Men and Women,* displayed brilliantly the new genre of the dramatic lyric, which broke away from the narrowness of subjective poetry. Few volumes in the whole range of nineteenth-century lyricism display such insight into the subtleties of love in all its shades but the most violent, the most sensuous, and the most jealous ones. "Love among the Ruins," "By the Fireside," "In a Year," "One Word More," and even less directly autobiographical poems such as "The Statue and the Bust" are the outcome of a profound experience, deepened, sublimated, and broadened (hence more likely to arouse echoes in the reader) through Browning's intellectual transfiguration of his emotions.

The origins of the interior monologue, which enjoyed a sudden vogue between 1920 and 1940, soon to be turned into a threadbare, laboriously contrived device, are to be found in several of the meditations lent by Browning to Italian painters, Greek skeptical observers of early Christianity, British Catholic bishops, medieval rabbis. Striking as those monologues are, and none probably comes closer to perfection of form than "A Grammarian's Funeral," it is our belief that Browning's ultimate survival as a great poet will be due to the more "sincere" poems in which he voiced his complex feelings directly, without attempting to preach a Victorian message of hope. In the love poems of *Men and Women,* Browning sedulously avoided flying into an empyrean of impassioned rhetoric while he ventured into the most perilous of all the territories of love poetry: married love. Sincerity in love, in poetry and, generally speaking, in life, cannot be measured out, as Mr. Prufrock would say, in coffee spoons. It is not reached by a bare recording of facts or even of impressions, or by a symbolic rendering of such impressions. A certain dose of artistic or pathetic fallacy may enter into the synthetic compound dubbed by critics and readers "a sincere work." Lie, "le mensonge de l'art," may in art grow into a higher truth, as ugliness may turn into a strange beauty. We shall debate the question later in this book. We may however provisionally submit that, among the English poems published between 1830 and 1880, the finest are precisely those that convey a personal experience, intensely felt, searchingly analyzed, and expressed with restraint: those of Browning primarily; the elegies of Matthew Arnold, far more secure in the memory of posterity than his frigid narrative, dramatic, or philosophical attempts like *Merope* or *Empedocles;* two or three lyrical passages from *Maud;* a dozen stanzas from Swinburne's regrettably long "Triumph of Time" and about as many from his "Garden of Proserpine," his "Forsaken Garden," "Ave atque Vale," and the close of *Tristram of Lyonesse.*

Parallels between writers of different countries are as tempting as they are misleading. The French and the English poets of the middle years of the nineteenth century may however be considered together from the angle: how sincere can or must poetry be? how much direct expression of the self can it bear? Leconte de Lisle undertook to burn what most of the romantics had professed to worship with more trenchant haughtiness than any of the champions of classicism in England or Germany. His dogmatic preface to the *Poèmes antiques* in 1852 demanded impersonality, scientific objectivity, the wiping out of all the literary decadence which had followed the golden age of Greece. Several of the romantics were branded as boisterous histrions, ad-

dicted to sham self-idolatry. Elsewhere, in a vitriolic sonnet, "Les Montreurs," they were likened to beasts on a
leash dragged around a circus, or to charlatans and prostitutes selling their "sincerity" to the populace for venal
applause.

Rimbaud very probably remembered the preface by the
leader of the Parnassians when he echoed the same horror
for Alfred de Musset, the same yearning to return to the
pristine freshness of Greece and blasted all subjective poetry, in his famous seer's letters of 1871. Flaubert's correspondence untiringly proclaims a similar creed: impersonality is the hallmark of the very great artists; the creator must
be like God in nature, nowhere visible but everywhere
latently present. He is not entitled to have any personal
feelings, to be of one country or of one faith. "The less he
feels a thing, the better equipped he is to express it as it is;
but he must possess the ability to make himself feel it."
Like science, literature must strive for impersonality and
reach generality. Emotion never proved anything anyway.
"I wept at melodramas not worth a sou and Goethe never
wetted my eye with a single tear, unless it was a tear of
admiration."

Flaubert's fiction is nevertheless filled to the brim with
its creator. Flaubert *is* Emma Bovary, and Salammbô, and
Frédéric Moreau, and even Saint Anthony. He was well
aware of his own insidious affinity with those two ludicrous,
caricaturally Faustian heroes, Bouvard and Pécuchet, ponderously acquiring knowledge and buying experience, only
to sink in the end in the Preacher's mournful admission
of universal vanity. Flaubert, too, had heaped up information, ransacked archeological libraries, pored over theolog-
ical folios, before composing his Carthaginian epic and his
Tentation. As had Leconte de Lisle, he had proceeded on
the assumption that beauty lay in remoteness and that aesthetic distance should prevent too hasty an identification

of the reader with his characters. He had distilled a rare elixir out of the trivialities of modern life. In the end, however, he found that the most alive of life had eluded him. It had only served as a pretext for the laborious erection of a palace of art. Flaubert's letter of sympathy to a fellow novelist, Feydeau, who had just lost his young wife, is touching in its naïve callousness:

> Poor little woman! It's ghastly! You have and will have good scenes, however, and you'll be able to make some fine studies. It's a dear price to pay for it. The bourgeois fail to realize that we serve them the dish of our hearts. The race of gladiators is not dead, every artist is one of it. He entertains the public with his death-agonies.

Literary fate has its ironies. The few poems by which Leconte de Lisle is likely to survive are his rare personal ones, those which seem to talk "sincerely" to us, without the screen of Vedic, Hellenic, or barbaric mouthpieces: "Dies Irae," "Ultra Coelos," "Le Manchy," "Epiphanie." Flaubert wins us most engagingly when, as in *L'Education sentimentale,* he forgot about knowing and allowed himself to feel.

The contemporaries of Baudelaire who, almost to a man, failed to appreciate the poet's originality—Sainte-Beuve, Mérimée, Taine were among them—branded him as an insincere comedian. Since 1917 when the poet's work, having completed a prolonged stay in purgatory, emerged out of copyright and of relative disgrace, a multitude of men and women have hailed Baudelaire as the poet who best anticipated and voiced their moods. The new generation of commentators, with Gide and Thibaudet at their head, chided their dull-witted predecessors such as Faguet and Brunetière who had failed to see through the mask put on by the poet and to discover his total sincerity. One of the precursors of the Baudelaire cult, an uncommonly perceptive one, Jules Laforgue, had already discerned the secret of an appeal to the rebels of the Symbolist generation which no other poet equaled. Without any trace of grandiloquence, Laforgue remarked, without any flights of lyricism, Baudelaire seemed to whisper into the ears of each of them as in a confessional. Paul Claudel, approved by Jacques Rivière, an arch-priest of sincerity, lauded Baudelaire for having expressed the only passion which the nineteenth century could experience with sincerity: remorse. Is Baudelaire's privileged position among French poets due in some measure to his higher sincerity?

No unambiguous answer is likely to be offered as long as the word sincerity itself remains such an ambiguous one. We happen to have, in Baudelaire's letters to his mother, the fullest and most agonized confession of a poet's abjection in modern letters. Those letters express the truth of the moment at which they were written, as the poet, weak-willed, torn between self-pity and remorse, attempted to move his mother to forgiveness and to coax her into paying his debts. Like most letters, they are attuned to the personality of the recipient. They leave out what might have angered Baudelaire's mother or not been understood by her. The picture they present of Baudelaire's mental misery is a painfully true one. And yet it is partially true, for other facets of Baudelaire's character do not appear. One sees nothing of the lover, the cynic, the art enthusiast, the patient chemist refining his evocative witchcraft, the critic of other writers' work, the bon vivant that he probably was even in the depths of his agonies. That self-portrait is touched up, so as to mirror the personage that Baudelaire thought he was at that moment, or that he wanted to be.

A truer, because deeper, picture of Baudelaire's feelings and aspirations is offered in *Les Fleurs du mal,* over which the poet labored instead of rapidly and movingly laying his heart bare as one does in a letter. Even in letters less intimate than those addressed to his mother, those in which the poet vowed to mend his ways, to imitate those who, like Sainte-Beuve, Mérimée, Victor Hugo, had won worldly success and honors but who looked down upon Baudelaire's nonconformity, he must have realized that he was trying to lie to himself. He never really hoped, or perhaps wanted, to reform. Even in the poems of idealizing worship addressed to Madame Sabatier the reader descries an undertone of self-deception of which all lovers, and most idealists, have probably been guilty. Surely he knew that her confiding to him her sorrow under a Parisian moonlight ("Confession") was the pose of a professional beauty capriciously attracted by a grave poet, and that he was lending her more than her superficial mind deserved when ("Semper Eadem") he was magnifying her banal weariness into ". . . cette tristesse étrange / Montant comme la mer sur le roc noir et nu." Baudelaire may not have been the most virile of lovers, as has often been hinted; still he had seen enough of life and of women of all milieux to realize that he was going a little far when he breathed the fragrance of the angels in the "spiritual flesh" of Madame Sabatier, an opulent and buxom Baccha. But he needed a woman to serve as a pretext for his momentary idolatry of some Madonna; she happened to be at hand and he seized upon her. The reader avid for sincerity is embarrassed by what might be termed by a moralist a slight duplicity. But soon he is carried away by the imagery and the harmony of those flowers purified of all evil, by a beauty which becomes truth. Artistic sincerity, that is to say, the felicitous expression given to a mood the poet wanted to experience and which indeed he did experience in a state of voluntary and imaginative exaltation, is there; it makes up for the slight self-deceit that underlies it.

The poems dedicated to Satan and singing in black strains the delight of perdition, the entrancing horror of destruction, the torment of the self-chastising sufferer and the refinements of erotic cruelty, may well strike readers as more directly sincere; for Baudelaire conveyed in them a rarer experience. He himself laid stress upon uniqueness as the ultimate proof of originality. In his fine essay on Richard Wagner, he advised the critic to pay less attention to the systematic aspects of the works of a deliberate artist than to the impalpable element *sui generis* through which he is himself and not another.

In the same masterpiece of musical criticism by a poet who had scant musical training but who analyzed his own pleasure searchingly, Baudelaire claimed the right to use the first person singular unashamedly, so as "to enclose himself within the strictest limits of sincerity." Once more, however, the notion of sincerity is laden with complex and contradictory meanings. With an insolence akin to that of Byron or of Poe eager to assail the "cant" of the society which had ostracized them, Baudelaire proudly exaggerated the devil's sway over him and the lures of sin. No doubt he was in part acting like the scientist who magnifies what he wishes to observe and dissect; but he was also aware of the fact that sincerity lies in an artist's ability to produce an impression of truth.

Paul Valéry will later drive that statement to the paradox that the poet has no need whatever to experience the poetic state, provided he can create it in other men. More reasonably, Baudelaire admitted that emotion is not produced in a reader without a good deal of effort, of combination, almost of artistic and higher trickery. In the second draft of a tentative preface to his volume of verse, he alluded to the futility of revealing to the reader "what dosage of instinct and sincerity blended with rubrics and charlatanry is indispensable to the amalgam which a work is." Two years after the publication of *Les Fleurs du mal,* commenting on the low quality and the decreasing number of religious paintings in the fifth chapter of his 1859 *Salon,* he observed that such decadence is not necessarily linked with any decline of faith. Flaubert likewise remarked that drinking songs are not necessarily written by drunkards or by drinkers, or Sunday school stories by pious vestrymen. The one requirement, Baudelaire decreed, is "that the poet, the actor and the artist, at the moment when they are accomplishing the work which they have undertaken, believe in the reality of what they are portraying. . . . Art is the one spiritual domain in which man may say: 'I shall believe if I want to, and if I do not want to, I shall not believe'."

The most splendid of *Les Fleurs du mal* are not necessarily the most personal. Art does not allow of such facile inferences. Baudelaire's sincerity is not necessarily greater than Lamartine's or Musset's, or even than that of Hugo in his poems on his daughter's death or on the mysteries of the ocean, of evil, or of God. But Baudelaire added restraint and density, an explosive force, a wealth of rare imagery to the poetry of his romantic predecessors. While they had been inclined to pose as better men than they were and to appeal to the public's sympathy through the consecration of a sorrow that singled them out of the common herd, Baudelaire affected to be worse than the average man; he forced his reader, "Hypocrite lecteur, mon semblable, mon frère," to admit that he, too, was prey to evil. At the same time, he realized that, since it would have been vain to try to equal the lyrical flights of the romantics in a more prosaic age, the new function of the poet at mid-century was to probe more pitilessly into himself and to exasperate feeling through analyzing it cerebrally. That new type of sincerity, springing from an attempt to remove the mask of self-deception often assumed by desire, characterized much of the love poetry written after Browning and Baudelaire.

Early in his career, in 1847, in a curious short story entitled *La Fanfarlo,* Baudelaire had pictured a character very much like himself, Samuel Kramer, whose plasticity was such that he could imitate others, borrow passages from their writings and honestly believe they were his, yet "in spite of that comedian's ability, be deeply original." Sensations and emotions grew doubly acute when memory worked its transfiguration over them and when the intellect had refined upon them. "Affections in me spring mostly from the mind," Baudelaire was to confess to Jules Troubat the year before his death. Herein lies the superiority of Baudelaire's love poems over any others in the French language. Lamartine's Elvire, Hugo's Juliette, Vigny's Eva and even his Dalila, vituperated against by the wrath of the new Samson, real as they were in life, remained vague as portrayals of women.

But Baudelaire's contemporaries had read Stendhal and Balzac. They insisted upon finding in poetry women who could rival those complex characters, infernal as well as angelic, whom the novelists had been representing. They balked at the facile idealization which spares the poet the difficulty of analyzing the person he claims to love and which, all too promptly, pictures desire as adoration of spiritual goodness.

Baudelaire's pitiless rending of the veils of self-deception led him to uncover the mutual misunderstanding on which idealized desire often rests. He anticipated modern psychoanalysts by portraying with the same courage the aggressiveness of the lover bent upon inflicting pain in order to subdue his partner, and the childish weakness that throws him into the arms of a mistress in whom he wants to find also motherly protection or sisterly tenderness. "Soyez mère" is his imploration to the loved woman in "Chant d'automne," and he addresses her as "amante ou sœur." In the most frighteningly lucid of all his poems, "L'Irrémédiable," he plumbs the depths of that gulf to which the determination to see himself unflinchingly has led him:

> Tête-à-tête sombre et limpide
> Qu'un cœur devenu son miroir . . .

One beacon alone will flash gleams of light into those dark abysses, and it is "La conscience dans le Mal."[2]

It would be tedious to review a long series of French or English poets of the latter half of the nineteenth century and naïvely mete out praise or blame to them according to the degree of their sincerity. Let us rather stress the few points we have tried to elucidate.

From the romantic age onwards, lyrical poetry is set apart from fiction and drama as well as from the pictorial and plastic arts. From poets, because they often resort to the first person singular, the public has been inclined to demand that they express their emotions and feelings as they have experienced them. Personality was considered as the better half of genius. The spontaneity and the intensity of the inspiration are valued above all else. The poet ceased to try to conform to a preconceived model set up in front of him or to abide by rules of poetic diction. He yielded to the capricious contradictoriness of his most fleeting impressions. A revolution was thus effected in our ideas on literature. James Thomson, Gray, Akenside, Voltaire the poet, Parny, Delille, once exalted on a pinnacle, are now rel-

2. Five years after *Les Fleurs du mal,* George Meredith published his sequence of fifty poems, *Modern Love,* which, alone perhaps in English literature, matches Baudelaire's clearsightedness in analyzing love's illusions and tragic misunderstandings. Sometimes, as in the concluding poems, there are distinct Baudelairian undertones:

> Lovers beneath the singing sky of May
> They wandered once; clear as the dew on flowers . . .
> Then each applied to each that fatal knife,
> Deep questioning, which probes to endless dole.

egated to a less glorious rank from which they are not likely
to emerge.

Antiromantic reactions have come and gone. They have
denounced the declamatory expression occasionally given
to that aesthetics of the heart, the excessive reliance upon
their own powers and the scorn for poetic tradition which
led several romantics to fall abruptly from their soaring
flights and to leave too many fragments behind them. Failures indeed abound among them. Still the great romantics
were far more assiduous workmen than we often believe.
They knew that the rendering of an intense emotion requires the virtues of order, of submission to a pattern, of
rhythms and melodies orchestrated, of obstinate polishing
such as Horace and Boileau had advocated. Such a "simple"
and apparently ejaculatory short lyric as Shelley's "Lament"
"O world! O life! O time!" was persistently reworked by the
poet.[3] True sincerity requires the relentless pursuit of the
best, or the only, form (musical, plastic, metaphorical) that
can convey the full emotion experienced by the poet, without banalizing or weakening it. The "Ode to the West
Wind," with its combination of terza rima followed, at the
end of each fourteen-line stanza, by two closing lines reminiscent of a sonnet, its treatment of the effects of the wind
on earth, in the sky, on the ocean, all taken up again in the
fourth stanza and ending in the fifth with the identification
between the wind and the prophetic poet, may well be the
most majestically ordered poem in English. "La Belle Dame
sans Merci" is no less faultless, as suggestive to the imagination as it is satisfying for the analytical intellect.

In France likewise no seventeenth-century classicist ever
composed as impeccably as did Lamartine, Hugo, even
Musset. Through their art, very remote from improvisation,
those poets, and Brentano and Eichendorff in Germany,

3. Bennet Weaver, "Shelley Works Out the Rhythm of 'A Lament',"
PMLA, 47, (1932), 570–77.

Hoelderlin in his ambitious *Hymns,* invested their burning emotions with a generalized appeal. Their self aroused brotherly echoes in many a reader. Victor Hugo, moved in *Les Contemplations* by personal experience of joy and sorrow, universalized his emotions and could proudly upbraid his reader, if he objected to a personal inspiration, with the famous cry: "O insensé qui crois que je ne suis pas toi!"

Since the most genial of the romantic poets became, around 1850–60, imitated by less talented epigoni who merely exaggerated their defects, the more perceptive authors of the age distrusted the pitfalls into which the aesthetics of sincerity could project them. They aimed at objectivity. They stressed the powers of analysis, even of dissection. They prolonged the romantic discovery of the subconscious by delving even deeper into evil, eroticism, and the dark layers in ourselves in which moral censorship is silenced.

The French Parnassians clamored for scientific objectivity and proclaimed art for art's sake; the English poets of the middle Victorian era listened with even more gravity to the Goethean lesson of serious resignation. Matthew Arnold and his friend Arthur Hugh Clough, in didactic tones which often played havoc with their well-meaning talent, admonished their countrymen to cling to knowledge. "Let us seek knowledge. / Knowledge is hard to seek and harder yet to adhere to," advised the sincere Clough. Even more sincere, as well as more imaginative, was Matthew Arnold in "Dover Beach," "Resignation," "Obermann." Few writers since Saint Augustine have felt so hopelessly anguished by their inner cleavage "between two worlds." Orthodox or liberalized Christianity was a temptation, but doubt was not to be eradicated from their minds. Their duty seemed to be to preach to Englishmen the Goethean ideal of intellectualizing themselves; but the refuge of isolation and silent thought was an equally strong temptation. Of two desires, remarked Arnold, "One drives him to the world without, / And one to solitude." But it would have taken more than sincerity and pangs of conscience to turn the poetry of Clough, of Sully Prudhomme, of Arnold himself into pure gold. Sinners like Verlaine, adolescents unfit as yet for abstract thinking like Rimbaud, passionate believers like G. M. Hopkins were to shake poetry with far more vigor. What was sincerely thought was not intensely expressed.

The aesthetics of sincerity was to count for much less in the poetry of the last decades of the nineteenth century and in the twentieth. Poetry, in France especially, then became a highly conscious art, soaring away from human emotions and from communication. The most paradoxical of those doctrinaires of inhuman poetry, Paul Valéry, discarded sincerity as a meaningless concept for an artist. The emotions of a poet in presence of nature were, around 1910–30, practically excluded from his verse. Mallarmé, Valéry, and their followers railed cruelly at the feelings of a man in love as poetical ingredients henceforth to be dispensed with. All the easy means of arousing emotions were scorned by artists in love with difficulty. Nature and love thus banished, death alone, of the three main traditional themes of romantic lyricism, was deemed worthy of the challenges thrown by the thinking spirits who composed "Toast funèbre" and "Le Cimetière marin." Countless private diaries, formless autobiographical novels became the refuge for indulgence to sincerity. Poetry could not thus be soiled.

Critics of poetry themselves are wary of bringing into play the notion of sincerity to account for the power of Claudel or of Saint John Perse, of Rilke or of Eliot. They are mindful of the rashness of their predecessors who lavished praise on poets who had more sincerity than genius, more sentiment than talent: Ernest Dowson, Oscar Wilde, Rupert Brooke, Edna St. Vincent Millay or, in France, Albert Samain, Anne de Noailles, Louis Aragon. Moreover,

ransacking the biographies of the poets who had appeared
as most spontaneous, scholars had discovered that many,
among the most "sincere" of inspired bards, had labored
very hard in order to attain naïveté.

Verlaine is a case in point. He was for many years, along
with another "sincere" rascal, François Villon, the favorite
French poet with the English, the one whom *jeunes filles*
of several countries recited most rapturously or sang at their
piano. Religious anthologies gave him the lion's share as
the main Catholic poet of France. Many of us, to be sure,
continue to admire him today, although not for his simplest
and most magical "romances," which have worn thin. After
an eclipse caused by his insufficient obscurity and by his
cavalier disregard of symbols, he is again enthroned among
the true, if not among the supreme, singers of France. Who
knows if he may not outlive Claudel, and Valéry himself?
The word most often used to praise him was sincerity.

Yet, "if ever a writer was *not* sincere, Verlaine was that
writer,"asserted one of the authorities on the poet, André
Fontaine, who undertook to prove it in a little book, *Verlaine, homme de lettres,* in 1937. Verlaine, indeed, was primarily a man of letters. In incessant penury, unable to ply
a trade or unwilling to practice one, poor Lélian, as he
called himself, wrote cynically for money. He aimed at
pleasing the scant public that bought volumes or pamphlets
of verse; in 1875, for no other reason, he projected a book
of patriotic poetry, which then sold well. One of his letters
(*Correspondance, 3,* 104–05) is disarmingly candid on his
intentions: "It will be very brief and simple, . . . very sweet
and very touching, . . . very naïve of course, and I shall do
my utmost to be absurdly sincere." In his autobiographical
notice, he brazenly explained that, after 1880, "my work
was cut into two very clearly distinct portions . . . volumes
in which Catholicism displays its logic and its illecebrancies,
its blandishments and its terrors, and others of a purely

worldly and sensual character. I believe and I am a good Christian one moment; the next minute I believe and I am a bad Christian."[4] One of his best known volumes bore the title *Parallèlement*. He thus made no secret of the contrast between the flesh and the spirit wrestling in the book as in his soul; he combined the religious and the most brutal pagan strains, nostalgic regret for the young bride whom he had in fact martyrized and his obsessive passion for Rimbaud.

Verlaine disregarded factual truth, forsook impartiality in the pretty poems with English titles, "Birds in the Night," "Child Wife" in which he perfidiously ascribed to his wife all the wrongs in their estrangement: "Vous n'avez rien compris à ma simplicité, / Rien, ô ma pauvre enfant." Nevertheless those poems and others in *Romances sans paroles* rank among the finest—may we say the truest—that Verlaine composed. He momentarily saw himself as he portrayed himself, and he probably came to regard as the only true one the image he had given in verse of his behavior. Like many poets, Verlaine was endowed with the privileges of the chameleon. His acute senses perceived outward impressions so strongly that he yielded to them. He took in the most tenuous nuances of light; he lost himself in the dizzying whirl of a merry-go-round ("Bruxelles: Chevaux de bois") or of a folk-dance ("Streets"); he emptied his being of all will to withstand outside impulses. He knew that therein lay his originality and he nurtured it sedulously. His power of expression and of music was such that he could produce an impression of utter sincerity on his reader.

4. Elsewhere again, in *La Revue d'aujourd'hui*, March 15, 1890, and in a letter to Félicien Rops of February 11, 1888, Verlaine shamelessly declared that "Sincerity was now [his] rule" and that he settled "all squarely and candidly in [his] vice, so sincere it was, so free from sadism." The word "illecebrancies" was coined by Verlaine, no mean Latinist, from the Latin *illecebra*, seductive charm.

His naïveté was deliberate. His sincerity was to portray him-self as he thought he was, substituting in the process an authentic literary personality for the vacillating, childish, and—childlike in this too—calculating and mendacious personality that he was.

In becoming impersonal and dehumanized in its pursuit of metaphysical and cosmic truths, modern lyricism gained in dignity; but it also lost in breadth of appeal to that por-tion of the public that responds best to a personal note in poetry. Other literary genres meanwhile were being prac-tised by egocentric authors, passionately eager to be pitied, envied, admired, loved: the personal novel, the autobiog-raphy, and the private diary.

CHAPTER 6

The Personal Novel

THE NOVEL is doubtless, next to the drama, the literary genre to which the notion of sincerity might appear to be most alien. No adequate definition of the novel, embracing all that a novel may be and applying to the novel exclusively, has ever been proposed. But the legislators of literature have usually concurred on the two features deemed essential to the craft of fiction: a narrative of events likely to bring forth the growth and decay of characters and their reactions to the vicissitudes of life, and the creation of beings independent from the author or given free rein by him after his imagination had launched them on their adventurous careers. The novel in several of the literatures of Europe (or the romance) has been considered as the ignoble but natural heir to the most objective and highly generalized literary genre of ancient literatures: the epic. In others, like the French, after a long and fruitless series of epic attempts at a meandering fiction, peopled with all too idealized heroes, the modern novel appeared to have discovered its true vocation when it established itself as the successor to Corneille's and Racine's tragedies. *La Princesse de Clèves, Manon Lescaut, Les Liaisons dan-*

gereuses, Balzac's and Flaubert's masterpieces have traditionally been glorified by French critics as the rightful successors to classical tragedy: psychologically searching, objectively presenting crises of passion and conflicts between
sensuous unreason and the admonitions of the will or of a
torn conscience, artistically condensed. As the novel developed into a more sophisticated genre and heeded the
strictures of critics and their endeavors to codify, hence to
ennoble, a parasitic late comer of letters, its plot became
more detached from the events which its author might actually have witnessed or lived; the setting acquired more
realistic vividness, with DeFoe, Lesage, Fielding; the characters affronted each other in dialogue, and the novelist's
ambition was to probe into their hearts and to analyze their
thrills or their agonies, but also to watch them from outside,
fondly at times, at times detachedly, occasionally in a gently
ironical or in a bitterly satirical mood.

However, the great age of fiction that dawned with Jane
Austen, Stendhal, and Gogol was to belie all efforts at curb-
ing and at classifying an unruly form of literature. As books,
and works of fiction in particular, conquered the vast new
reading public created by the spread of literacy and by the
advent of serials in magazines and daily papers, their authors stressed the strangeness of adventures and the credibil-
ity of the apparently incredible, which a public that had
known the Terror, the Napoleonic Wars, and the ascent of
the "rabble" to financial, social, and political power wished
to find in fiction. At the same time, they realized that they
had to provide common readers—who no longer belonged
to an idle and privileged class but who earned their daily
living in offices and factories—with a convincing picture of
the cities, of the countryside, of the environment with which
they were familiar. Realism, of very diverse sorts, is found
in Victor Hugo's romances as in Balzac, in Flaubert, Tolstoi, and Thackeray.

Our own age has derided the shortcomings of realism. It has clamored for a novel *démeublé,* unencumbered by elaborate descriptions of homes, streets, and scenery. It has, most patronizingly, smiled at the naïveté of novelists who took the comings and goings and petty doings of their characters with ponderous seriousness. Foes of the traditional novel, ironical like Virginia Woolf, scathingly scornful like Paul Valéry, earnestly eager to transcend realism like Marcel Proust, have been numerous and influential. Still, periodically, an offensive return is staged by the "pure novel" in the country where the onslaught against it has been the most vehement: France. In the 1940s, when there raged a wave of admiration for the American novel for its worship of facts and of violence impassively recorded, then in the middle '50s when Georges Simenon, Jean Hougron, Alain Robbe-Grillet, Nathalie Sarraute advocated the strangulation of psychology in the art of fiction and steeped fiction again in visual details minutely described and hauntingly magnified, objectivity became the hue and cry of the adversaries of psychology in fiction. The ego and its inward gaze were hunted out. The novel rivaled the paintings of the Cubists and of the Abstractionists, the poetry of Francis Ponge, electing, like them, "le parti pris des choses," siding with objects against the descent into the inner man.

These advocates of a new objectivity, as were the Realists and the Naturalists before them, were irked by the exuberant growth of a new type of fiction, the personal novel, which, since the romantic movement, has been challenging the epic or dramatic narrative. That type of novel, in which the first person singular was usually substituted for the third, in which the tone was one of intimate confidence, asserted itself as readers expected more sincerity from those literary works which had once been dismissed as mere innocuous entertainment. Here, too, Rousseau's example fascinated his successors; Stendhal, George Sand, Balzac, as

well as Goethe in *Werther* and Hazlitt in his *Liber Amoris,*
admired *La Nouvelle Héloïse* this side of idolatry and
hoped, in another literary form, to rival the pathos and the
introspective depth of the *Confessions.* Memoirs, autobiographies, fragments of private diaries, lyrical raptures,
dreams of rebellion against an understanding society which
appeared to crush the individual were all merged into the
new personal novel of the romantic age.

To be sure, many a work of fiction before *René* (1804),
Obermann (1804), *Adolphe* (1816), *Louis Lambert* (1832),
Lélia (1833), *Volupté* (1834), Stendhal's *Henri Brulard* (begun in 1835) had already been written in the first person
singular, in France and elsewhere. Moll Flanders and the
Vicar of Wakefield, along with many a Spanish or French
picaresque hero, had said "I" not "he." The device is a convenient one to prop up deficient imaginative power in the
novelist. With the over-inventive story tellers, who wish
to astonish their readers with the narrative of hardly credible adventures, like those of Gordon Pym, or to win cred-
ibility for fantastic episodes, the resort to "Ich" instead of
"Er," as the Germans say, is equally effective. Eighteenth-
century novelists, whom we like to picture as innocent of
all the wiles and the torments through which modern fiction writers attempt to endow their labored products with
structure and a point of view, had of course realized that a
narrative told in the first person provided them with a
natural order (that in which events succeeded each other in
life), with unity through the variety of episodes and the
picaresque avatars of their heroes, and with the organizing
point of view of an author who knew whither his characters
were heading and what reassuring or woeful fate was to be
meted out to them in the end.

Different is the spirit behind the many personal novels of
the century of hypertrophied egos: the nineteenth. Their
authors then aimed not at truth (as Marivaux and Laclos

had done), not at the exact and searching exploration of motives unknown to the heroes themselves, not at the creation of a rounded and vivid character such as Marivaux's Marianne had been,[1] but at sincerity. Gone is the boyish relish in colorful and bewildering exploits and in the impetuous ravishing of not unwilling ladies with which one of the most curious predecessors of Casanova and Alexandre Dumas, Courtilz de Sandras (1647–1712), had romanced D'Artagnan's memoirs. Gone is the sentimental and insipidly moral series of tales about women seduced by French grandsons of Richardson's prolific Lovelace, such as Madame Riccoboni and other Anglophile eighteenth-century ladies poured out in the midst of their own stormy careers; even their autobiographical novels remained unctuously didactic and remote from the sensuous and emotional pangs their creators must have endured. These novelists, not excluding the whimsical author of *Tristram Shandy* himself, seem to be fearful of delving into their own selves, or too diffident of the immodesty that outright self-revelation entails to portray themselves without some ironical or aesthetic distance. The English Puritans, the Catholic confessors and moralists in France, and the Swiss and German Protestants had all warned against the sin of pride which was the pitfall of contemplating one's ego too leniently. Novelists and even writers of memoirs still considered that they owed it to their public to improve it or to entertain it, in any case to remain mindful of its existence and of the conventions to which it still subscribed. Only with the romantic revolution did the writer revolt against his audience and society in general, proclaim the higher rights of the individual, and color outward nature, religious aspirations, history, psychology, with the blinding light of his own burning ego.

1. Saintsbury calls Marivaux's heroine "the first nearly complete character of the kind that had been presented in a novel at her date," in his *History of the French Novel* (London, Macmillan), *1* (1917), 349.

The "douceur de vivre," insofar as it designated the re-
morseless enjoyment of one's pleasures, the compensation
for the loss of innocence with the shedding of one's prejudices, as Diderot put it, even the resignation to some pain
if the sufferer's intellectual awareness was heightened thereby ("the knowledge of one more truth amply repays for the
loss of a pleasure," wrote Laclos) vanished for many a decade from life, or at least from literature. The marvelous
lucid prose of the eighteenth century, which seemed to race
along nimbly and to reduce all enigmas to easy terms, was
immolated to more turgidly declamatory tastes. Enjoyment
of life was hardly ever again simple. Philosophy as well as
ethics, pride in anguish, and brooding on remorse raised
modern fiction to the heights of metaphysics. Madame de
Choiseul's warning to her age, which was about to crash
headlong against the scaffolds of the Terror, soon ceased to
be heeded. "Let us beware of metaphysics applied to simple
things," she had pronounced.

France did not enjoy the monopoly of the personal novel
in the romantic age. Foscolo wrote the hyper-romantic
Letters of Jacopo Ortis; Fr. Schlegel, Novalis, Hoelderlin,
Goethe, later Gottfried Keller and Stifter composed novels
on adolescents whom life and their loves (and not a little
aspiration after unattainable Diotimas or unpluckable blue
flowers) were supposed to educate. English fiction proved
more wary of such sentimental declamations and clung
harder either to a precise historical setting (Walter Scott,
but also Thackeray's tender *Henry Esmond*) or to the depiction of Dickensian reality. Not only overstatement but
also lyrical prose such as Rilke and Gide later practised on
the continent, even when wielded faultlessly by DeQuincey
and Pater, appear to be less benignly tolerated by British
taste. Our remarks here will be limited to a few of the
French personal novels in which claims to more ardent
sincerity were put forward.

Posterity is inclined to smile at the personal novels of Chateaubriand, as Stendhal (who had far more in common with him than he would acknowledge) did unweariedly in his diary and notes. The setting and the invention of details in the narrative betray indeed much stilted awkwardness in the novelist, in *René* or *Les Aventures du dernier Abencérage*. The tone is too consistently lyrical, the invocations to nature and solitude bombastic; the sorrows of René baffled by his sister's mysterious attachment to him, and the tenderly chivalrous melancholy of the Moor in love with a Christian virgin in the *Dernier Abencérage* bear the imprint of the *style Empire* a little too markedly. The avowed intention to serve, however strangely, the return to Christian faith, in novels short of breath and diffusely built, toned down the initial boldness of the theme. Literature had to wait several more decades before portraying abnormally warm affection between brother and sister with the tragic naturalness of Somerset Maugham in the story entitled "The Book Bag." Both René and Aben-Hamet belonged to a curious class of fictional characters, akin to those in Stendhal, that martyr of shyness; like his, they are tender, passive, prone to idealizing women as elusive Sylphids, yet fully conscious that their will to love is stronger, and more deceptive, than any love actually felt by them. But their creator failed to delve deep into the inconsistencies or the pre-Proustian intermittences of his heroes' hearts. He preferred to pour out his gloomy jeremiads, to indulge invocations to the primeval American forests, to laud overcivilized "savages" or conventional hermits offering the consolations of faith. Only in his *Mémoires d'outre-tombe,* and then only at occasional moments, did Chateaubriand dimly realize that his talent lay in his ability to recapture lost or faint memories and to be entranced by them, or in his attempt to elucidate his own complexity to himself through writing:

The better part of genius is composed of that sort of memories. The most beautiful things which an author may put into a book are the feelings which come to him, through reminiscence, from the early days of his youth. (*Génie du Christianisme, 3,* Book IV, Ch. v.)

In a sketch for a preface to his then as yet unwritten *Mémoires,* drawn up in 1809, he wrote words which again have a Stendhalian ring: "I write chiefly in order to account for myself. . . . I want, before I die, . . . to explain my unexplainable heart." But he had fallen into the habit of posing, and he seldom dared face himself in the nude with austere sincerity.

Sénancour owes his dim halo of fame among English-speaking readers to Matthew Arnold's two poems on him. Van Wyck Brooks printed, in 1947, a brief and fervent essay of his youth on Obermann, as one of three French victims of the "malady of the ideal." In a preface to that volume, Robert E. Spiller defined Obermann's predicament in terms very similar to those used nowadays by Camus' host of biographers and commentators: "What choice has an idealist in a world that has lost faith in absolutes?" Sénancour lived the *mal du siècle* perhaps more desperately than any other French romantic. He was born in 1770, the same year as Wordsworth, Hegel, Hoelderlin, and Beethoven, two years after the Breton enchanter. His generation, nurtured on Rousseau's *Rêveries,* experienced the sorrows of modern man more intensely than the impetuous children of the new century, Hugo, Berlioz, Michelet, Balzac, who consoled themselves in action as well as in their greater fecundity as writers. The latter, the romantics of France, moaned over their aloneness, but, in fact, encountered an audience attuned to their complaints and finding in political and business activity a diversion to an ennui in which much impatience entered.

The true victims of romanticism, and the genuinely sincere ones, were those whom we dub today the French preromantics. There is much less about their writings that is meretricious or sparkling tinsel; their solitude "among men, but not of them" hurt them the more burningly, as they lived in a social age and attempted to uproot the social man in themselves. Their failure was one of language. They lacked the vocabulary, the caressing style, the intoxicating cadences which alone could have rung true to their readers. They stood up in revolt against the rationalism of their century but could not, unlike Chateaubriand and Lamartine, make themselves believe that they had found religious faith. Their wish to believe was not matched by the disregard of what impeded their intellectual ascent to faith. Their wish and their will to love were corroded by their secret awareness that love demands much self-delusion and more outgoing spontaneity than they were capable of recapturing. Madame de Staël and Maine de Biran, Benjamin Constant and Sénancour, and a host of more obscure talents born like them between 1765 and 1770 yearned for sincerity in literature as much as any French writers did between Rousseau and Gide. The word recurs in Matthew Arnold's notes on his French predecessors ("Of all writers, he is . . . the least attitudinizing" he jotted down in annotating his own poems on Sénancour). As late as November 12, 1867, Arnold recalled, in a letter to Mr. Dunn, what an extraordinary impression he had received from Sénancour's "gravity, sincerity and feeling for nature" when he was twenty-five. From him indeed he had first realized how torn he would remain all his life: between Homer and the Judaeo-Christian tradition, between culture and the anarchy of the heart's promptings, between increase of knowledge and increase of sorrowful doubt, between the others with whom and for whom a writer turned reformer must live and the purity of his own ego.

> Ah! two desires toss about
> The poet's feverish blood;
> One drives him to the world without,
> And one to solitude.

Obermann is never likely to be more than one of those "books of the second shelf" which amateurs of psychological documents and students of romantic moods unwrapped in literary adornments jealously cherish. It is not an autobiography, and the author himself protested against Sainte-Beuve's hint that it could be; it is an autobiographical novel, with no plot, in the form of letters and an attempt by the author to watch his ego grow in depth and radiate on outward but never allow itself to be inflated so as to absorb the outside world and to refract it. Sénancour's fear was that which haunted Baudelaire: the fear of one's ego being "vaporized" instead of its being concentrated. But Senancour possessed neither the will power required to prevent his yielding to the vertigo of pantheistic merging into nature nor the verbal gift that could have found an imaginative and sensuous expression of what he felt with acuity. He upbraided his successors, the romantics, for lacking sincerity; he drove sincerity to himself as far as any man was to do in the nineteenth century. Such an attempt devoured his power of imaginative creation. Artistic sincerity differs from psychological truth to one's inner life. In an obscure early novel of his, *Aldomen,* Sénancour had already anticipated that the intention to see oneself nudely and unflinchingly destroys spontaneity itself, hence impairs sincerity.

There are several women among the authors of "personal novels" in the early nineteenth century in France, and there are even more today when French women have taken it to their hearts to outdo all males in boldness and brutal self-revelation. Mme. de Staël confessed herself in *Delphine*

(1802) and in *Corinne* (1807); but her heroine remains throughout a lifeless one. The didactic purpose intrudes incessantly and the characterization is pale. The style is slipshod and colorless. Necker's daughter was the mistress of her age as a literary and political thinker (the most eminent in French until Mme. de Beauvoir) but hardly as a novelist who, as the French like to put it, would have extended or deepened our knowledge of the human heart. Like most women, she lived novels better than she wrote them.

The same year as *René* (first an episode in *Le Génie du Christianisme* of 1802) and *Obermann* appeared, in 1804, a strange Russian-born lady who was later to exercise a strong mystical influence on the Czar, Mme. de Krüdener, published a melancholy epistolary novel, *Valérie*. A young woman of that name, married to an elderly gentleman, involuntarily lights a romantic passion in a chaste and shy young man, the son of one of her husband's best friends. That French Werther, prosaically called Gustave, will only reveal his love to a friend with whom he corresponds; with Valérie, he can but weep, grow pale and wan, and finally die, without Valérie's having guessed his not-too-well-hidden secret. The novel clearly belongs to the lachrymose genre which was beginning to seduce the very same French who were hardily fighting in Napoleon's armies over ten European capitals. The Emperor himself had shed buckets of tears over *Werther*, had worshiped Rousseau and, like Chateaubriand's *René*, had recited *Ossian* to the moon and the stars.

Edouard (1825) by another great lady, Mme. de Duras, is less insipid, and the author would deserve the attention of a monograph by a young scholar. On a ship bound (like the one which took Chateaubriand to America) for Baltimore, two young gentlemen meet. One of them, Edouard, who will be killed in the American War of Independence, entrusts his newly made friend with a manuscript. His con-

versation, which recurred on topics such as death, the infinite, solitude, revealed that a secret lay buried in his
bosom. He had fallen in love with the Duchess of Nevers,
whose father he served as secretary. But her station was so
far above his and his own respect for her was so much
stronger than his male conquering instinct that he moaned
over the differences of class and left for the army. When
the lady begged him to return and marry her, slander accused him of having actually enjoyed her favors; her father
was incensed. Edouard leaves to fight for the freedom of
the Americans and she, at twenty-one, conveniently perishes
from a "maladie de langueur." Mme. de Duras' novel
opened no new chambers in the palace of sincerity, but it
stands out as a not altogether unworthy predecessor to
Fromentin's *Dominique* and Gide's *Porte étroite* among a
surprisingly large number of French novels whose theme
is the fear of love and the refusal of consummating it—
usually on the part of men.

In the eyes of its rapturous admirers, such as Marcel Ar-
land today, the late Charles du Bos, and John Middleton
Murry,[2] the masterpiece of French fiction at all times is
Adolphe. Its author is one of the most enigmatic in the
whole range of French literature. His *Journal* reveals him
as one of the most self-centered of men, cruel to the women
whom he had ceased loving or desiring, a lucid practitioner
and analyst of the strategy of *le désamour* or the art of extri-
cating oneself from an affair that palled on him, in order
to enmesh himself in a worse one and enjoy more suffering.

2. In his volume *The Conquest of Death* (London, Peter Neville, 1951)
John Middleton Murry hails *Adolphe* as "a meditation on problems of love
and death and an assertation of the reality of 'revelation'." The English
critic, Katherine Mansfield's husband, who, like the author of *Adolphe,* was
constant only in the vacillating inconstancy of his opinions, proclaims in
his tenth chapter: "I find in *Adolphe* a new revelation of the eternal truth
of Christianity." Frenchmen are occasionally embarrassed by Britons whose
francophilia tramples upon their proverbial phlegm!

It may even be, as one of his few posthumous adversaries, Henri Guillemin, contended in *Benjamin Constant muscadin,* a volume published in 1959, that he added greed to his other faults and was out for Mme. de Staël's fortune. Yet his complexity will always fascinate his readers and endear him to them; many recognize themselves in his contradictions, in the aridity of his heart coupled with a vivid sentimental imagination, in his mixture of pride in his superior intellect and self-hatred. The remark made by Mme. de Beaumont, as early as October 1, 1797, in a letter to Joubert, was pathetically true: "He cannot even succeed in loving himself." He disarms our severity through his own lack of charity to himself, and without his relentless pursuit of sincerity to himself, which drove him to record every one of his weaknesses, we should not be in possession of the evidence with which to indict him.

The word sincerity is central in any discussion of that supremely intelligent personal novel, *Adolphe.* The author uses it a few times, and he was not addicted to grandiloquence or to verbal looseness. In Chapter IV, he notes that, while vacillating between restlessness at being chained by Ellénore's love and the desire not to hurt her, while he reassured her and blandly promised what he could not hold, "he was sincere" while he made those promises. In the very next chapter, he coolly admits being impelled by no more springing from his heart and takes pity upon his own plight. "It is a dreadful misfortune not to be loved when one loves; but it is a much greater one to be loved passionately when one has ceased loving." Twice in that Chapter V, he owns having been weak, kind to the woman whose love imprisoned him but thereby "insincere." Paul Bourget, who in his youth revered the novel as he revered Stendhal and who, like Constant, was to turn into an apologist for religion while powerless to believe, gave him this eloquent testimony in 1889: "Benjamin Constant gave unto the last the example of a virtue so rare that it takes the place of many others, for it supposes a nobleness of soul which has persisted, untouched, among the worst aberrations. He was *sincere;* he had that higher sincerity which must be called the great one, toward others and also toward himself." Forty years later, in an address given at the Entretiens de Pontigny on "Autobiography and the Novel," expanded in 1946 into a book, *Grandeur et misère de Benjamin Constant,* Charles du Bos, "anima naturaliter christiana" and an indefatigable keeper of a private diary himself, contrasted the false sincerity of many moderns (which serves as a cloak for yielding to one's weaknesses and sliding down one's slope) with the true one of Constant, which includes moral strength and courage; it is a virtue against one's self. It goes hand in hand with nobleness of soul.

The opinion is typical of many others, pronounced by some of the most exacting, morally speaking, of French critics and often by the most deeply religious ones. In such a laying bare of one's foibles and of one's contradictions, the French—in whom some insidious Jansenism so often pierces through orthodox Catholic faith or through stubborn unbelief—discern a courageous cleavage, to which a fuller Christian revelation might perhaps put an end. The kind of confessional literature that Constant practised is, to them, an ascesis, *une ascèse.* The Protestant novelist Jean Schlumberger, not usually a boastful man himself, took pride, in an article written in 1937 (included in *Jalons*), in the literary education dispensed to French youth, nurtured on Flaubert, Baudelaire, or Constant. "Just as Sparta inflicted upon its young men, through a whipping in front of the altar of Diana, an ordeal of endurance, we submit ours to such reading," he said; art and literature, in his view, filled the astringent role once assigned to moral or religious disciplines: not just to provide delight, but to chastise. If some day a philosophical history of the Protestant spirit in French

literature is written, many common features should be de-
scried among those Protestants: Rousseau, Mme. de Staël,
Constant (all Swiss, but the latter of French origin), Loti,
Gide. All were unstable, vacillating from one pole to another of their being, tormented by the demon of analysis
and by fitful objurgations of their conscience, eager to depict their faults sincerely and thus to win absolution for
them.

The sincerity of Constant in *Adolphe* is manifold. First,
but there is scant originality in that, he had lived his novel
and the story was "bone of his bone and flesh of his flesh."
Scholars have engaged in heated controversies to maintain
that Ellénore was either Mme. de Staël or Mrs. Lindsay.
She was both, and also Constant's second wife, and even
Mme. de Charrière, Geoffrey Scott's "Zélide" who, as Belle
de Zuylen, had once been courted by Boswell. She was forty-
seven when Constant, at twenty, knew her, was fascinated
by her mind, and probably, as Sainte-Beuve hints, owed her
a rite of initiation such as young Balzac, later, obtained
from Mme. de Berny who was more than twice his age.
Scholars' most passionate quarrels on the loves of writers
long since dead seldom eschew childishness. A novelist cannot disassociate one mistress from another when creating
a heroine who embodies them all; all his women were made
to love as Constant, through his pleadings, his threats of
suicide, then his weariness and boredom, forced them to
love him. "Zélide," at any rate, had the good sense to help
him mold his style while he was young, and to orient his
experiences and his sorrows toward a literary utilization of
them.

Constant's sentimental education, which was a stormy
one, and his precocious growth in spite of the most irregular intellectual education, soon taught him that most men
wear masks and, even when alone, are insincere, "factitious." They do not literally pretend; they are not capable

of showing themselves to themselves as they are. Notations
to that effect recur in his *Journal,* for instance on December
1, 1804. On June 12 of the same year, he had asserted the
most radical solipsism. "We are only known to ourselves,
we can only be judged by ourselves: there stands an invin-
cible barrier between others and ourselves." Hence, unlike
Sénancour and most of his predecessors who hoped to discover in their own selves what Montaigne was the first to
call "the human condition" in all its generality, Constant
is content to find himself fascinating and to accept his illogic, his duality, or "his successive or simultaneous sincerities" in the plural, as Gustave Rudler expresses it. There
is duplicity there, no doubt; but Constant was a "homo du-
plex" if ever there was one. Thus, in his diary of February
12, 1804, at the very moment when he saw Goethe almost
daily at Weimar and was charmed by him, Constant, the
only really informed German scholar among the French-
speaking writers of his age, confided his tepid admiration
for Goethe's frigid *Iphigeneia* and his aversion for *Faust.*
"I find that it is less good than *Candide* and that, while it is
as immoral, as arid, as desiccating, it has less lightness of
touch, fewer ingenious jests and much more mad taste." He
certainly was not afraid to think against the grain.

His independence from all current vogues shows equally
clearly in his style: the most perspicuously precise, the most
deliberately monotonous, yet vibrating with restrained
emotion and heightening the emotions it appears to stifle
through cerebral analysis. Mme. de La Fayette appears
courtly, too nobly controlled, much too sedate, loose in her
choice of words and fearful of the abysses which too relentless an analysis would open up, when compared to Constant.
Camus' phrase, "a passionate geometry," fittingly describes
such a novel. Descriptions are few and far between, but—
as in the wintry walk with Ellénore, laden with ominous
silence, concisely related in Chapter x—unforgettable. No

episodes, no secondary characters distract the narrator from his cruel mission. All preaching is banished, although the author's attitude is remote from cynicism and his awareness of moral values that he is unable to live up to adds a dimension to the story and fills the reader with a sense of its import which twentieth-century fiction, except in Proust and Mauriac, has regrettably lost. The answer from the imaginary publisher to whom *Adolphe,* supposedly found in an abandoned casket in a Calabrian inn by a traveler (the only conventional feature of the novel) had been offered, printed at the end of the book, castigates the very faults of which the author knew he should be accused: the conceit of him who hopes to attract pity through describing himself without any veils and who secretly hopes that what he explains with utmost sincerity will thereby be excused. "The great question in life is the pain which a man inflicts, and the most ingenious of metaphysics does not justify the man who has torn the heart which loved him."

By laying himself bare to the reader, in his diary and even more in *Adolphe,* Constant went deeper than anyone since Racine, certainly much deeper than Stendhal in his overrated and naïve treatise on love, in removing the masks which usually disguise the complexity of relations between man and woman. All that pertains to the senses, it is true, is omitted. It is clear that Constant was an inflammable creature and that Platonic loves were hardly for him (he had to live through only one, in his late and almost abject passion for the arch-coquette, Mme. Récamier, whose wiles he should have known better how to elude). But he implicitly admitted that love of the senses fails to matter if imagination, fomenting desire and transfiguring the woman, and then cerebral analysis providing complexity and self-torture, are absent. He bowed to his fate, aware that his sorrow was thus increased; and his fate was to need women. "The main cause for the agitation in my life," he noted on June 19,

1806, "is my need of women. That need must be satisfied at all costs."

Constant's analysis of the intricate nuances of love remains the most acute before Proustian fiction, because all the causes that had impeded full sincerity in such a revelation were coolly removed by his searching dissection. First, with a candor few men have dared display, he showed himself as he was when his imagination had been fired by a certain lady and his amour-propre stung to the quick by her resistance: he cried, implored, threatened suicide.[3] (He had attempted it in his youth and seems to have earnestly considered it several times rather than not be fully accepted by the person by whom he knew he would be bored the next month.) He appealed to feminine pity to rescue him. "I see every day my reason and my talents perish. The misfortune not to have been loved by you is fatal. . . . What is life worth when one can no longer be loved?" Such runs one of his many shameless protests to Juliette Récamier, when he was close to fifty and she close to forty, and after

3. Suicide was for several decades the favorite hunting ground of sociologists; but literary suicide, while not reducible to statistical methods of inquiry, would be a curious subject for study. A few preromantic or romantic French writers attempted it, from Chamfort to Baudelaire (perhaps), and to Charles Barbara and to Nerval, who carried out the attempt. A few logical fanatics of passion fulfilled in death alone, such as Heinrich von Kleist and his beloved in Germany, Claire Desmare and her lover in France in 1832, actually preferred taking their lives to witnessing the probable degradation of their loves through disillusionment and the wear and tear of time. But fictional suicide has a rich history: Stendhal's *Armance*, Vigny's *Chatterton* and *Stello*, Petrus Borel's *Champavert*, Lassailly's *Les Roueries de Trialph*, Maxime du Camp's *Mémoires d'un suicidé*. Flaubert, Louis Bouilhet, Alfred Le Poittevin, and many young and exasperated romantics, around 1845–55, pondered over suicide. Our contemporary novelists have to resort to automobile accidents and to stoical and inordinate absorption of whisky to replace the former means of dismissal of fictional characters, which were suicide, consumption, and general paralysis exacting the wages of sin.

he had observed her for years in Switzerland without experiencing any warm feeling!

To show more convincingly the extent of the sacrifice of his honor, of his career, of his life if need be, to the person who is not yet moved by his protests, he proceeds, like other men but with fewer restraints, to declare to her how valuable, how essential to France and to the cause of freedom he is. The date is 1814. In January of that year, Constant had published an extraordinarily lucid and profound pamphlet, *De l'Esprit de conquête*. It is directed against the French Emperor but transcends immediacy and is probably second only to Tocqueville's writings among the French political writings of the last century which survive. Constant is at that very moment jeopardizing his chances, even his life, by attacking the returning Emperor, fast advancing toward Paris after his landing from Elba. He begs Juliette to realize the peril that he is running, and his own worth. "I challenge Buonaparte. I remain here to prove at least to you that there is something in me which is courageous and good. . . . You do not know what I am worth." In short, he reveals to what extent he is a spoiled child who must have what he wants or threatens a scene, perhaps puts on an act of self-slaughter.

Yet he never for a moment dreams of finding idyllic peace in mutual love, quietude for his work, release from the nightmare of his masochistic tortures. Love, in his eyes, is a war. Laclos had showed how much strategy enters into it and that woman's two favorite passions are "the glory of defence and the pleasure of defeat." Constant's vocabulary is that of the battlefield: encirclement, siege, scheming, storming the fortress, then, in anticipation of satiety, withdrawal. "She was no longer a goal; she had become a bond," Adolphe writes of Ellénore. And, the more signs the lover gives of wishing to untie those burdensome bonds, the more stubbornly does the feminine partner fight to chain him more securely. All men have perceived their capacity for such oscillations, yearned for or feared the depression of their spirits which may follow the physical relaxation of desire, and either hated the woman after having prized her too highly or turned to God for a love less demanding, or less readily answered, than that of woman. Some have advocated deferring fulfillment and prolonging the sweet pain of desire, like young Gide. Young Goethe, more pagan or more robust, content to let his Faust wrestle with the two souls in his breast, dreamed of staggering back and forth, rapturously, from desire to enjoyment and in the midst of enjoyment to pine for new desire.

> So tauml' ich von Begierde zu Genuss,
> und im Genuss verschmacht' ich nach Begierde.

Constant was less easily duped by his own desires. His truth was alternation; his axis was the least rigid of all, mobility itself. He drove sincerity toward himself to the admission that he could not long prize a good of which he was certain, and that to possess means also to be possessed. He suffered in thought the sufferings that he inflicted upon others far worse than his own. And, better than his two rivals in the analysis of love among the French romantics, he was clearsighted enough to apply sincerity as a scalpel to disassociate the very different elements men and women cover by the same word, love. The two sexes understand almost opposite feelings by that fallacious word and, as they reach middle age, they diverge even farther. In a moving while beautifully restrained and grave letter written in 1805 or 1806, on Julie [Talma], the actor's wife (long separated from him) who had died at forty-nine, Constant wrote:

Almost all women talk well on love: it is the chief affair of their lives. . . . But as they are very directly interested, they cannot be impartial. The greater the purity of their souls, the more inclined they are to grant an exaggerated importance . . . to such relationships. . . . Julie knew that that imperious inclination, the natural state of one of the sexes, is but a fever for the other one; she understood and owned that women who have given themselves and men who have won are in a precisely opposite position. It is only when women have, as the phrase goes, consented to their defeat that they begin to have a precise goal: to retain the lover for whose sake they have made what must seem to them a great sacrifice. Men, on the contrary, at that same time, cease having a goal: what used to constitute one of them has turned into a bond. It is hardly surprising that two persons placed in such unequal positions promptly cease to understand each other; that is why marriage is an admirable thing, because, for a goal which no longer exists, it substitutes common interests which always persist.

The last sentence is not ironical, although Constant, when he wrote it, had divorced his first German wife ten years earlier, was anxious to attempt an amazing marriage with stormy Madame de Staël, and was to marry secretly another German wife, Charlotte von Hardenberg (portrayed as *Cécile* in a novel thus entitled, published only in 1951) in 1808!

Other French personal novels pale beside *Adolphe,* if viewed from the same angle of the novelist's utter wrecking of all the illusions and self-delusions which might keep him from seeing himself as he is. *Emile* is the least known of those that deserve a niche among the many sentimental grandsons of Rousseau.[4] It was written by Emile de Girardin, the illegitimate son of a count and general of Napoleon who suffered from his irregular birth and from the hostility of his stepmother. The author, born in 1806, was twenty when the novel was published; while immature and too Byronic as well as Rousseauistic in tone, it bears reading even today. Emile de Girardin claimed to be fully true to the description of his inner turmoil and of his moods (of a pitiable character pursued by fate), because he refused to impose order and consistency upon them. Ten years after the youthful *Emile,* and after a memorable duel in which he killed another journalist, Armand Carrel, the author embarked upon the biggest undertaking of modern journalism in France: he created the inexpensive press and the serial novel. Many men of action have likewise begun by laying bare their languid boredom and their yearning for understanding and love, then rushed to dominate forcibly those same men and women who had failed to respond to the calls of their sobbing hearts.

Another one of those sturdy workers who, after exhaling his melancholy under the thinly veiled disguise of Joseph Delorme, conveniently packed off his double to an untimely end through consumption and then labored relentlessly to leave some forty or fifty volumes to posterity, is Sainte-Beuve. In 1830, while spending some time with his friend Ulric Guttinguer in Normandy and collaborating with him on a personal novel, *Arthur,* Sainte-Beuve was led to under-

---

4. Rousseau's fascination for the English, the Germans, for Tolstoi and the Russians has been fully analyzed, as well as his impact upon the literatures of those peoples. But Rousseau's influence on French romantic poets, on novelists, on writers of memoirs and confessions, even on political thinkers has daunted scholars. Four books, at least, would be needed to cover such a wide field, and they could contribute much to a spiritual and sentimental history of the last century.

take his own psychological analysis and to put an end to his own poisonous conflicts through the catharsis of a personal novel. He preferred the phrase "intimate novel," of which he claimed to be the creator; in fact, he had admired *Obermann* and hoped, as his mouthpiece Amaury confesses it, to emulate René, in whom he recognized himself. Guttinguer was a débauché to whom women flocked (while Sainte-Beuve brooded over his lack of physical charm and his inability to conquer without stooping low); but he also had strange mystical velleities, and, like his hero Arthur, he ended by entering the priesthood. Sainte-Beuve had, at that time, declared his passion for his best friend's wife, Mme. Victor Hugo, both to her and to the poet. The poet had shown a magnanimity which probably humiliated Sainte-Beuve. A would-be lover who undertakes such a "sincere" *démarche* with the beloved's husband is likely to be vexed if no jealousy is evinced by the threatened husband. These biographical elements, and many others, enter into the novel *Volupté* (1833). They are not felicitously fused together and it took little time for the hypercritical author to discover that his novel was "scarcely a novel." It moves at a funeral pace; it is replete with indigestible stories of political conspiracy; it ends awkwardly with the hero's taking the Holy Orders for which he is hardly fit. The style itself is overlabored, devious and twisted, and if "sincere" its sincerity lies only in its faithful rendering of a calculating and affected personality, not devoid of cowardice and more than once guilty of double dealing. Still, Sainte-Beuve had the five letters of the English word "truth" engraved on his seal!

The irreparable weakness of *Volupté* is that it fails to retain our interest. Yet there is much psychological acuity in the explanations and digressions on the conflict that Sainte-Beuve was living through and which a more creative talent might have dramatized into an exciting work of fiction. A young man has, early in life, discovered that his sensuality is irrepressible; carnal pleasures sway him; he enjoys them with a fullness enhanced by his taste for reverie and for idealizing the women who might be his partners of good will, and by his refined and cerebral analysis of his enjoyment. But he lacks all physical charm; he is perhaps afflicted with some anomaly that may impede full sexual union; he cannot be a straight, healthy Don Juan. He skirts along oblique paths, listens to women's confessions of their passions for other men (as Sainte-Beuve did to George Sand's and others'), insists upon idealizing women and lending to them more intricate and perhaps more mystical motives than are really in them.

The hero of *Volupté*, Amaury, worships a lady whose generous but irascible and queer husband continues to trust his wife's suitor. He deludes himself into believing that she might provide him the impossible combination of a great soul and a responsive sensuality. Thus could his own inner cleavage between respect and *volupté*, spiritual adoration of the woman and carnal love be reconciled into some unity. "To love, to be loved, to join pleasure with love, to feel free while remaining faithful, to retain my secret chain even through passing infidelities; to polish my mind, adorn it with knowledge and grace only to make myself a dearer lover, to give more to the woman possessed and to explain the world to her: such was the scheme of a soft life which I envisaged as the ultimate happiness" (p. 157). Greater sincerity might have pointed out to the hero the inanity of his dreams. Sainte-Beuve—born after his father's death, brought up by two women, tender, plaintive, successively seduced by many literary, religious, and philosophical doctrines which he should have known he would desert soon after espousing them—was indeed torn between pleasure and respect, carnal lust and mystical or fraternal respect for woman. Gide will later live such a conflict but make better literature out of it. After two or three experiences in which Sainte-Beuve hardly shone as a man of honor (with Mme. Hugo, later with Mme. Hortense Allart), the critic understood his bachelor's incurable selfishness lucidly. He dealt only with such "venal nymphs" as were ready to meet him two-thirds of the way, and reserved his intellectual admiration for the women of the past who deserved one of his *Lundis*. *Volupté,* curious as a psychological document, lacked the imaginative force and the vividness of style without which autobiographical sincerity fails to become convincing literary sincerity. But the subject ranks among the most tantalizing ones for a writer of fiction. When Balzac, angered by an unjust critique Sainte-Beuve wrote on his *Recherche de l'absolu,* exclaimed: "I shall take my vengeance; I shall do *Volupté* over again," he was paying tribute to the wide possibilities offered by the theme, but which were left unexploited by the critic who had not yet resigned himself to being, like Iago, "nothing if not critical."

There are too many other elements that account for Balzac's towering greatness over other French novelists for us to dwell on the three personal novels he wrote, each a masterpiece in its way: *La Peau de chagrin* (1831), *Louis Lambert* (1833), *Le Lys dans la vallée* (1835). In the latter, he undertook to redo *Volupté,* with ten times more vividness. Many other Balzacian novels, *Gambara,* and the splendid *Illusions perdues,* rest on a personal basis; but what novels do not? *Le Lys dans la vallée* has had its detractors, usually among the more fastidious academic critics. Most readers, at a time when, having been nurtured on Dostoevsky, we are less concerned about excessive feelings, inconsistencies and ambivalences of the heart, hasty but effective style in novels, would today agree with the philosopher Alain who hailed the novel with raptures as "perhaps the most beautiful novel that exists" in his *En lisant Balzac*

(1935). Mme. de Mortsauf, the chaste, mystically pure married lady whom the college boy once impetuously kissed on her shoulder at a ball, thus incurring her wrath, inspires the boy with a spiritual but all-consuming passion. Like the hero of *Volupté*, he is linked in political plots with her husband's affairs, introduced into their home. Like him, but with fewer incursions into bad taste than in Sainte-Beuve, his senses, exacerbated by his chaste spiritual adoration, offer him as a prey to a fierce carnal Englishwoman, Lady Dudley. But the unfulfilled love is the stronger of the two. "The flesh lusteth against the Spirit, and the Spirit against the flesh; and these are contrary the one to the other," St. Paul had written to the Galatians (5:17). The lust of the Spirit is the only total one. The closing scenes, with Mme. de Mortsauf dying from her struggle against temptation, unable ever to forget the brutal and clumsy lips once applied by the adolescent on her back, rank among the most genuinely moving in Balzac, who did not always succeed equally well in making his angelic women credible and true. But the sincerity of the novel is of the indirect kind: it illustrates the superiority of fiction, reaching a more intense truth, over autobiographical fiction, which clings to subjective sincerity.

Subjective sincerity may be said to have been Stendhal's goal. For many years, he kept his diary, jotting down a few revealing remarks amid a sea of inconsequential details, storing up material and training his style for his critical and fictional works. When in 1814 he began publishing, he neglected that *Journal,* to which Beylian fanatics have ascribed exaggerated importance. His aim was to view himself without any illusions, to record his immediate and spontaneous reactions to people and books, and probably to utilize those notes some day in order to compose an autobiography in which fleeting impressions would receive their significance from the perspective of memory organizing them and weighing them. His perennial concern was to follow the ancient advice: *Nosce te ipsum.*

It was not easy to be oneself in an age when individuals had not yet fully earned their right to rebel against society, aesthetic rules, or psychological categories inherited from the century of Condillac. Stendhal unweariedly encouraged himself in the pursuit of his truest self. "To be great in any genre whatever, one must be oneself" (*Pensées,* March 1818); "All that is worth while in this world is 'soi' " (*Souvenirs d'égotisme*). First, and he took some time before realizing it, style must be alert, swift, eschew the polish of many a practitioner of the *style Empire* or *style troubadour,* which young Henri Beyle scorned. One of Stendhal's several natures was to dream, to draw deep sighs from his heart so as to move (so he thought) women who proved singularly unresponsive to that romantic worshiper of love writing like a clinical analyst of it. But he avoided expressing that facet of his character directly. "I am always fearful lest I may have only written a sigh when I believe I have noted a truth," he remarks in a four-line chapter, in the first part of his book on *Love.* His heart, which yearned to talk, had to be silenced. The sincerity of his style consisted in excising, in toning down, in sobriety, and also in avoiding too carefully concerted a structure, too stately an order. In an 1830 article on "Walter Scott and *La Princesse de Clèves,*" published in *Mélanges de Littérature,* Stendhal burst out impatiently against all clichés: "Any work of art is a beautiful lie." For its naturalness is addressed to a reader, who has to be pleased.

The winning quality that has endeared Stendhal as an egotist to so many men of our age is that desultoriness, sedulously cultivated, he had admired in Sterne. In *Henri Brulard,* written at a time when he had recently gone through that momentous crisis which grips those who have just lived half a century, he related his life with utmost disorder and nonchalance; the accuracy of the facts did not concern him, only the truth of what he had felt, and, as he warned in the very first chapter, "how many precautions must one take in order not to lie!" In that book, he attempted to remember the moods of his childhood up to the age of fifteen. The *Souvenirs d'égotisme,* supposed to cover the years 1821–30, were begun at the age of forty-nine. The striking title may have come from Lady Morgan. Stendhal was proud of it, and of the literary genre which the word connoted, the only one perhaps in which the moderns could boast of any progress. "Egotism, but sincere [egotism], is that manner of depicting the human heart, in the knowledge of which we have effected gigantic strides since 1721, the year of the *Lettres Persanes.*"

In *Henri Brulard* and the *Souvenirs,* both destined only for the posterity from which he hoped so much, Stendhal attempted to keep clear of selfishness and of egocentricity. He had two pet hatreds: hypocrisy and vagueness. And he thought he could shun those vices if he knew himself thoroughly and wrote in the first person singular. But he apologized to his reader. For was he so certain of knowing himself? The thought that he did not "desolated" him at night, he confesses. And the only antidote to the recurring "I" of his *Souvenirs d'égotisme,* he stated in his preface, "is a perfect sincerity."

Had Stendhal attained it? In his autobiographical writings and in his journals, clearly not. Too much is left out of what mattered most in his life: his failures in love (and not just the fiascos of an imaginative cerebral), the insight he must have had into the scant value of many women he had pursued, the failures of his career, the fallacy of his Italian vision (for did he ever really enjoy Italy, even the famous days of 1800 in Milan, with Angela, on which *Henri Brulard* closes, since he lacked the words to convey his rapturous bliss?), some twinges of uneasy conscience about his outrageous stealing of ideas and of whole passages from previous writers. "Marriage has many pains, but celibacy has no joys," Dr. Johnson once said. Stendhal's anguish at his loneliness, the sense of his failure in literature (his first great novel did not come out until he was forty-seven) while the young romantics who were born when he was twenty were dazzling Paris, the woeful inadequacy of his attempt to write the life of the man whom he deified most, Napoleon, the formlessness and apparent insignificance of his diaries and other minor writings—all these must have plunged him more than once into fits of doubts about himself and about the vanity of his daily "hunt for happiness," doubts which find little or no expression in his intimate papers.

Paul Valéry, prefacing *Lucien Leuwen* at an age when he had ceased being an enthusiastic, or even a benevolent, reader of novels, expressed himself tartly on Stendhal's claims to sincerity. Stendhal's lifelong concern was to reach greater sincerity through greater spontaneity and, by refusing to organize his confessions, by sudden reversals which he normally expected, to be more natural than the more elaborate and more regular authors. The assumption, which later pursuers of sincerity will challenge, was that there is a criterion to determine what is natural: presumably, the promptings of the senses or of feelings being more "natural" than those of our intellect. It is certainly a challengeable assumption. The emotions and the gestures of love have often been learned through imitation, if not through books, and may serve as a mask for underlying aridity of heart.

Can the man be sincere who is determined and attempting to be so? Stendhal's tone is unique and ravishes Beylistes as much as Cimarosa's music enchanted "Arrigo Beyle, Milanese." But there was affectation in that tone, retorts Valéry coolly, which is "three or four times too sincere; I perceive in it the project to be oneself, to be true to the

point of falseness." And the arch-skeptic in matters of inspiration and of naturalness in art continues: "In literature,
truth [le vrai] is inconceivable. . . . Whoever confesses himself lies." The claim to being sincere flatters the one who
puts it forward, for it implies that others are not.

Stendhal, the most intelligent of creators next to Goethe,
did not fail to become aware of the inadequacies of that
kind of sincerity. After filling volume upon volume of
notebooks, memoirs, anecdotic biographies of artists, he
realized that only in fiction could he reach truth and launch
into the world living persons who would be endowed with
unity, mystery, and that fullness which the pathetic six
characters in Pirandello's play envy in the creations of imagination. His three great novels are not truly personal
novels. But his three central heroes are projections of the
author which compensate him generously for what he had
not been in real life: ardently loved by aristocratic ladies,
handsome, rich (Lucien Leuwen), brilliantly successful,
they act and live their sorrows or their joys instead of analyzing them. In a fragment entitled "Comedy is Impossible," written in Rome on May 24, 1854, and printed in
Mélanges de Littérature, Stendhal at fifty-one confided:
"Truth on the greatest as well as on the smallest things
seems to me almost impossible to reach, at least a *somewhat
detailed* truth. M. de Tracy used to tell me: truth can no
longer be attained except in the novel."[5]

5. An exhaustive treatment, leaving literally nothing to be added and
perhaps disproportionate to Stendhal's importance as a psychologist, is
found in Georges Blin's *Stendhal et les problèmes de la personnalité* (1958),
an immensely learned volume, listed in the Bibliography. The most penetrating single essay on Stendhal is Jean Starobinski's "Stendhal pseudonyme"
(1951), collected in *L'Oeil vivant* (Gallimard, 1961), in which the Swiss
critic comments upon the varied masks under which Stendhal hid himself
and nurtured his singularity: he resorted to more than one hundred
pseudonyms! Starobinski shows how Stendhal fulfilled the famous Paradox
on the Comedian of Diderot, experiencing a feeling all the more fully for
acting it. "It is impossible to act passion better [than I did that day], since

Romanticism did not vanish from French fiction after the deaths of Stendhal (1842) and Balzac (1850). It has often been contended that the generation born around 1820, that of Baudelaire, Leconte de Lisle, Flaubert, lived its romantic dreams with more wholehearted determination not to compromise with an ugly reality; it was exacerbated by the lack of sympathy it encountered in a utilitarian public. Practitioners of the personal novel are to be found among the writers of the Second Empire, and they had successors among the novelists of the late nineteenth century. But their originality paled; the spark of novelty was extinct; the personal novels of Anatole France, Paul Bourget, Maurice Barrès are the least distinguished part of their achievement. The mysterious trend that seems to sway the most creative talents of an age along a certain path carried them, after 1850, toward a new objectivity and the emulation of science (usually at its least scientific). After 1880, poetry again attracted those who wanted to analyze their emotions with self-pity or with irony. The novels, if they deserve that name, of Mallarmé (*Igitur*), of Villiers de l'Isle-Adam (*Axel*), of Laforgue (*Hamlet*) are more preoccupied with symbols than with an exact and relentless delving into the secret of their authors' souls. Minor novelists of the Symbolist era are among the most disappointing of any period of modern French literature. Teodor de Wyzewa (in *Valbert ou les récits d'un jeune homme*, 1893, *Le Cahier rouge*, 1917), Remy de Gourmont in his many cerebral attempts succeeded chiefly in showing how men of superior critical intelligence can be mistaken about their talent. The private diary had already sapped the art of fiction.

I actually felt it," Stendhal curiously remarks in his *Journal*. Elsewhere, he remarks that the hardest thing is to depict from memory what in us was natural. "We succeed better with what was factitious and 'acted,' because the effort which was required to 'act' engraved it in the memory." (Quoted in Starobinski's volume, pp. 224 and 229.)

During the Second Empire, the public for fiction had
been considerably enlarged to include many more women
and *jeunes filles,* and the bourgeoisie was demanding, and
securing, the kind of sentimental, placid, reassuring novel
that it wanted to read. Never has French literature been
closer to the Victorian temper than with French-Swiss writers like Édouard Rod and Victor Cherbuliez, French ones
like Feuillet, Ohnet, even Georges Feydeau—although his
portrayal of a lover's infuriated jealousy of his mistress'
husband, *Fanny* (1858), and his longer story, *Daniel* (1859),
revolted the public but pleased Sainte-Beuve. Lamartine,
with his *Raphaël, pages de la vingtième année* (1849) constructed little more than a potboiler in that lyrical and
hollow retelling of his love for Elvire. "It was like a second
virginity of my soul which I acquired in the rays of the
eternal virginity of her love." Such trash could not suit the
more exacting readers of Constant and Stendhal. Flaubert's
Mémoires d'un fou are little more than juvenile moanings
of a weary young man who declares life vain and pursues
the phantom that, after many an attempt, he was to endow
with life; she became Mme. Arnoux in *L'Education sentimentale.* Maxime du Camp, his friend, intoxicated himself
with his own dreams in *Mémoires d'un suicidé* (1855),
though his gift for self-analysis is not slight in that book.
He spoiled a later personal novel of failure, *Les Forces perdues* (1867), through too commonplace a love plot and too
platitudinous maxims and reflections which slowed the narrative to a snail's pace. Ages that display the most feverish
activity in opening up new sources of wealth, expanding
economically beyond their frontiers, building up for the
future with energy are also those (the Second Empire in
France, America between the two World Wars) whose literature is most thickly peopled with *ratés,* vacillating will-less
characters, dangling men bewildered by life and ending as
failures, even in their loves.

A personal novel must have some features of a novel while using the first person lavishly and reaching for a sincere transcription of the moods of the self; and many of those who attempted writing such a novel after Balzac's *Louis Lambert* (in which Flaubert thought he recognized with dismay his friend Le Poittevin, dead at thirty-two in 1848) were too often devoid of the minimum of vulgarity, or of grasp of the exteriors of existence, which a novelist must possess. Nerval's *Aurelia* (1855) is a symbolic tale of rare beauty, but sincerity is hardly the word to apply to its mythical transfiguration of moods and events into a dream world. The book has truth, provided it be interpreted, and that truth often is found more abundantly in a mythical than in a confidential work, as Giraudoux noted, following one of Nerval's biographers, in *Littérature*. The same Giraudoux, among the most discreet and *pudiques* of twentieth-century authors, added that the French are seldom intimate enough with themselves to produce intimate writings and that they fear boredom with their own selves to an extent that Protestants never reach. If that were ever true, they have outgrown that fear in the present age.

Among the epigoni of the romantics who molded the intellectual clay of their generation and subsequent ones, Renan and Taine, two notable thinkers, attempted fiction briefly, and unsuccessfully. Their aim was a valid one, one for which more imaginative thinkers may some day try with better luck: to compose a personal novel in which the pathetic struggles of the intellect and moral conflicts would hold the center of interest. For literature, dwelling complacently on a very limited number of themes and situations, fails to reflect the main concerns of the age it purports to portray: religious, metaphysical, political, moral issues. Existentialists have come nearest to succeeding, but they had predecessors: William Hale White, the author of two of the most impassioned volumes of transposed auto-

biography in English letters; Mrs. Humphrey Ward in
Robert Elsmere (all novels written in the eighteen eighties,
after the crisis caused by higher criticism of the Scriptures
and the shattering of traditional faith); and, in the early
twentieth century, Edmund Gosse's admirable *Father and
Son*.

Renan, four years after his abandonment of his project
to take Holy Orders, having gone through an extraordinary
fervid period of intellectual contention and written his
Future of Science, was sent on a mission to Italy. His travels
in that country, in search of manuscripts and documents,
mollified his enthusiasm for sincere and pure scholarship.
He feared the drying up in himself of spontaneity, humility, tenderness; he toyed with the desire to retain the best
of Catholicism, its poetry and its sentiment, while unable
to believe in it as truth. He was vaguely drawn to chaste,
sentimental love for woman as an antidote to the perils of
desiccating criticism. "The misfortune of my life was," he
wrote at twenty-six, "to be critical to a fault. . . . I have
killed youth and naïveté in me; I cannot escape from myself. But naïveté makes for the energy of human nature."
Such regrets however were vain, and probably not altogether sincere, in the sense that they voiced only a superficial and passing mood in Renan. The attempt to write a
personal novel on his dilemma soon proved abortive. He
expressed his self, thereafter, through history, moral speculation, or conscientious philosophical examinations.[6]

Taine, a much more complex personality than he is often
taken to have been and a more tormented one, apt to think
with his heart as much as with his head, was probably more
richly gifted for creative literature. His *Voyage aux Pyré-
nées,* his passionate evocations of the Ardennes forests, his

6. Renan's fragments of an attempted autobiographical novel, "Patrice"
and "Ernest and Béatrix," did not appear until 1914, in the volume *Fragments intimes et romanesques* (Calmann Lévy).

sensitiveness (he wrote a series of sonnets on cats), his love for art show him to have been endowed with an artistic temperament fully as strong as his philosophical one. He undertook in his youth to write a thinly-veiled confession novel, *Etienne Mayran,* which Paul Bourget esteemed highly and of which an edition was once offered as fit reading for American college freshmen. It is the story of a boy who opens himself up to the life of thought, as do so many French teenagers sent to Paris to prepare themselves for the "Grandes Ecoles." An orphan, deprived of affection at home, poor and unglamorous, he asserts his intellectual superiority as a compensation; he cultivates stoical invulnerability to spare his tender sensitiveness some hurts; conscious of his own worth, he stands up as an intellectual rebel against a superficial society, like Julien Sorel or the more destructive hero of Jules Vallès' trilogy, *Jacques Vingtras* (1879–86). But Taine lacked power to depict the concrete, or even emotions of bitterness, of hatred, of spiritual despair and religious longing; Jules Vallès, Jules Renard, Huysmans were to do that more convincingly. Taine's sincerity, confined to the drama of the intellect, could not by itself give life to a fictional attempt. An early enthusiast of Stendhal, he gave up an endeavor which would have been too permeated by Stendhal and never completed his novel. Soon after, he came to dread Stendhal's impact on French youth, and he omitted from his critical essays the ardent eulogy of the creator of Julien Sorel he had written earlier, fearing he might demoralize French youth, whom he then preferred to have read less disturbing works, such as George Eliot's, or Elizabeth Browning's verse novel, *Aurora Leigh*.[7]

---

7. The temptation to select intellectuals as heroes of their novels, as Renan, Taine, Vallès did, more obsessive with the French (and probably the Russian novelists and storytellers) than with the Anglo-Saxons, has been analyzed with rare talent by Victor Brombert in *The Intellectual Hero* (Philadelphia, Lippincott, 1961).

The last notable personal novel with which this chapter need be concerned, Eugène Fromentin's *Dominique,* counts many fervent admirers to this day. Its heroine, Madeleine, is mentioned in Proust's saga-novel. André Gide, in 1913, included it unhesitatingly among the ten French novels that he preferred to all others. "It is not a sublime book, but a friendly one. . . . Nothing in it is artificial; Fromentin appears as an artist in it, no doubt, but not particularly as a man of letters; all the qualities of his pen are precisely those of his intelligence and of his heart." In several respects, the *pudeur* and modesty cherished by Gide as the most precious classical virtues characterize this novel of renouncement, an ancestor of Gide's own *Porte étroite* and of Alain-Fournier's *Grand Meaulnes.* Some of its fragrance has evaporated for us. It is a polished period piece. Fromentin, who was a painter and art critic, published it in 1862, at the age of forty-two, when Flaubert, the Goncourt brothers, and Zola were offering stronger fare to the reading public. The sensitive evocation of landscapes near La Rochelle, done with expert discreetness rare in painters who wield a pen as well as a brush, and the restrained tone in which the author-hero relates the history of a romantic passion and of an unconsummated love are the most original features of the novel. The narrator looks back at his youth with no complacency but with a melancholy which he seeks to free from the declamation and the self-deceptiveness that accompanied romantic sorrow. He loved and idealized a young woman who married a gentleman richer, socially more prominent, and more self-assured than he. His respectful passion was shared. A single kiss is exchanged, and both partners, mindful of the perils of romantic love, aware that happiness could hardly be reached at another person's expense, too sensible to be carried away by melodrama or by heroism, choose forbearance and resignation.

The heroine is too idealized and too well-behaved to appeal to the fancy of modern readers, and too vaguely delineated by the novelist. But the narrator himself probes deeper into his own vacillations. He is one more of those numerous Hamlets who proliferated in France even more than in Britain at the end of the romantic era and again after World War I. He longs for action and for the audacious conquest of the palpable advantages of life which seduced Balzac's heroes and a character, Augustin, who, in *Dominique,* serves as a foil to the introspective narrator and is offered by him as a model of shrewd practical wisdom. He loses no opportunity to offer a moral lesson on the vanity of revolt and on the need for discipline; that bourgeois didacticism is in part what has aged the book and causes us to prefer Fromentin's travel sketches in North Africa or his appraisal of Flemish and Dutch painters. Yet the novel, if less acutely lucid than *Adolphe* and regrettably lacking in cruelty, is more courageously sincere—probably too much so, and its faults are those of the personal novel that refuses to lie in order to appear true.

Its supreme courage is in its acceptance of provincialism, unabashed and placid, in contrast with the attitude of young men like Julien Sorel and Rastignac who were drawn to Paris by the glittering splendor of the Second Empire and the newly opened possibilities for success in industrial and financial speculation. Few avowals are harder to make for a Frenchman than that of his inveterate provincialism. Equally few writers could be candid enough to reject all hypocrisy in love, all dramatization of their desires and of their feelings, every urge to pain or to vex or to dominate the young woman whom they know to be at their mercy. Neither religion nor ambition restrains the hero. But adultery would be, for that gentleman farmer, a violation of the laws of property, a reckless risk imposed upon the woman, since happiness could not lie in the acceptance of the natural and social order and in a clear conscience. The reader is irked by such sincerity which stifles passion, eschews struggle, chooses the way of prudence, and dares praise chastity. "Je suis un chaste en art," Fromentin wrote to a contemporary poet, Armand Silvestre, who had sent him amorous sonnets which stressed the carnal side of love.

Nothing is ever strained in *Dominique*. Even the novelist's bag of tricks, which Fromentin could easily have borrowed from his predecessors, remains unopened. Technical weaknesses are obvious, and accepted by the author. He describes himself with no pose whatsoever, no attempt to please or to transfigure. But a sincerity which thus fails to dramatize itself into anguish or to assume the extreme frankness of cynicism lacks the intensity that moderns appear to need in art. A lover who consents to abdicate is soon suspected of not loving ardently enough. "Lying," says Proust in the part of his novel in which he has pondered most eagerly on the topic, *The Fugitive* (once translated as *The Sweet Cheat Gone*), "is essential to mankind. It plays a part at least as large as the quest for pleasure; it is conditioned by that very quest. . . . We lie all our life long, even chiefly, perhaps solely, to those who love us."

The personal novel did not bring forth the greatest masterpieces of nineteenth-century fiction; but it constituted the most original addition to the novel as that century inherited it, and nowhere, not even in Germany, was it treated with such earnestness, such talent, and such insight into inner life as it was in France. It bears rereading to this day far better than the historical novel, which stimulated Balzac and Hugo, emboldened historians to resurrect the past, rivaling Walter Scott and Chateaubriand themselves, and which periodically finds, as it should, determined champions. It had the audacity to break away from most of the conventional requirements of the novel as understood by earlier ages: a plot, a series of fights with exterior obstacles, picaresque and often incredible but boisterous adventures through varied milieux, descriptions of nature, cities, houses, clothes, faces. Practitioners of that novel, aiming at more searching sincerity toward themselves than previous ages had ever dreamt of, did away with the myth or the assumption of an omniscient observer who knows all about his creatures and explains them to the reader, while they foolishly rush about and indulge their passions. The pretense of objectivity, bequeathed by the epic and by tragedy to the art of fiction, was dropped. A graver loss, from which literature has not recovered, notwithstanding the efforts of devotees of the comic spirit such as Flaubert, Meredith, and Proust, was that of humor, and of the ability to see others, and oneself, relatively and mockingly. The narrator, who is the author's *Doppelgänger,* must begin by taking himself seriously and by eliminating most of the outside world and the network of social relations which would normally hem him in, in order to probe into his own self in aloneness. With that search for sincerity, that extraordinary interest in and cultivation of the self, the conviction grew in writers that, as Proust was one day to proclaim, each of us only knows himself alone and no two human beings ever communicate. The desolate consent to an inescapable aloneness as the anthem of novels is to be found not only in Proust and Thomas Mann and Julien Green or, earlier, in Chekhov and Turgenev, but in Hemingway and Dos Passos and Nathaniel West and Norman Mailer and almost every modern American novelist. Eras and cultures in which community living and communications and stereotyped cheerfulness are the words most frequently and glibly bandied about also appear to be the ones least capable of emerging from their well of loneliness.

The balance sheet of the personal novel is, however, a positive one. Like lyrical poetry, which dwells on sorrows more successfully than on joys, it took it for granted that a higher capacity for suffering is the hallmark of superior individuals and is rewarded by the intellectual pleasure of watching oneself suffer. Only the very small minority of individuals endowed with a refined gift for analysis are capable of unraveling their own intricacies and of reaching to their hidden authenticity. Being thus analyzers to a fault and pitiless dissectors of themselves and of others, they do not hesitate to inflict suffering upon others; they refuse to play the comedy of love, or of family affection, or of respect for their progenitors if they do not feel, or have ceased to feel, those conventional emotions. Their struggle is with those who impede the free expansion of their authenticity. Only Gide's *L'Immoraliste* will, at the dawn of the following century, equal the cruelty evinced by *Adolphe* early in the nineteenth.

Gide, like Constant, like Fromentin, and many another hunter for full sincerity, will naturally need to imagine characters with enough introspective acumen to serve also as the narrators of their fiction. Aldous Huxley remarked somewhere how much he envied France that privilege of her novelists, to be able to count on a high degree of analytical self-awareness in their reading public. Henry James before him had stressed his own need for "finely aware characters" and for excluding "headlong fools" from his novels with a sophisticated point of view. Only recently have the French become fascinated with the idiots of epic stature who people Dostoevsky's novels of tragic buffoonery or who soliloquize in William Faulkner's. And their counterparts to those characters (Camus' *La Chute* or Claude

Simon's Faulknerian novels) cannot be kept from waxing intelligent in their turn—and unconvincing. Indeed, the question which, especially since Freud, we are led to ask when rereading the personal novels of the nineteenth century is: is enough of an allowance made for the surges of the unconscious and its manifestations through dreams and involuntary lies or lapses of the tongue or symbolic betrayal of what the characters have attempted to censor? Do not those novels eschew irrationality and mystery too easily? They win the reader's credence with little trouble, through resorting to the first person singular and confiding to him in the engagingly insidious tone of a man confessing to a friend. They enjoy the benefit of smoothness and of effortless unity in the narrative, of espousing the flux of time and finding events, seen exclusively through the lenses of one person, very easily ordered. But do they not shirk the difficulty of seizing life also in its raw, disorderly irrationality? Will not a later reader feel a little duped, will the reader not refuse, in a later age, to lend credence to the view that life can be described and conceived as thus smoothly lucid and sheltered from coarse hazards?

A personal novel constitutes a confession under a thin disguise and therefore also a vindication of oneself and a subtle apology for the behavior of the weak-willed heroes of Constant, Sainte-Beuve, Fromentin, and of Flaubert's protagonist of *L'Education sentimentale*. It has given French literature several minor masterpieces, and it will inspire major ones in the twentieth century, but only when expanded and enriched as it will be by Proust, Mauriac, and a few others. It is difficult for the author of such a novel to attempt a second one without repeating himself. Or else, as Gide shrewdly perceived, he should sketch several successive, perhaps contradictory, delineations of himself, touch up his self-portrait over and over again, be alternately

Ménalque, Michel, Lafcadio, the Swiss pastor, Edouard, and Bernard.[8]

8. Our allusion is to a curious letter of Gide to François Paul Alibert, January 17, 1914, in the Bibliothèque Jacques Doucet, quoted in the *Revue des sciences humaines,* July-September 1952: "The use of the first person singular, which allowed that sort of apparent effusion in most of my writings is, as you know, deceptive; or rather, for it is nevertheless sincere, it is only partly revealing. My true portrait can only be reconstructed if all those successive avowals of my work are taken to be simultaneous. When I try to hunt myself out, to reduce myself, it is a yawn, never a confession which I obtain. Outside the faculty for sympathy (which is all my intelligence), it seems to me that I do not exist and that my moral personality is limited to diverse possibilities which, each in its turn, bear as a title: Ménalque, Alissa, Lafcadio." — On the personal novel (and similar kinds of fiction), the best critical works are: Joachim Merlant (a scholar whose death in World War I was a severe loss for French criticism), *Le Roman personnel de Rousseau à Fromentin* (Hachette, 1905), and, in a subsidiary way, *De Montaigne à Vauvenargues. Essais sur la vie intérieure et la culture du moi* (Société française d'Imprimerie et de Librairie, 1914); Jean Hytier, *Les Romans de l'individu* (Les Arts et le Livre, 1928); Pierre Moreau, *Autour du culte du moi* (Archives des Lettres modernes, no. 7, 1957); Leon Edel, *The Psychological Novel* (London, Hart Davis, 1955).

CHAPTER 7

Autobiographies and Private Diaries

MEMOIR WRITING has been a favorite occupation of warriors (ever since Caesar), of condottieri and adventurers like Benvenuto Cellini, of chroniclers like Froissart or like many a sturdy sixteenth-century French fighter such as De La Noue, Montluc, Brantôme and D'Aubigné. Every literature can boast hundreds of volumes in which disgruntled politicians, statesmen out of office, generals without an army, even humble captains and sergeants yield to the temptation to record for posterity the events, "quorum pars magna fui," as each of them might put it, to enumerate the mistakes which, if given the chance, they could have spared their country, to offer the counsel their experience entitles them to dispense to others. An American scholar, Anna Robeson Brown, listed over two hundred titles of such autobiographical writings for French literature alone in her 1909 volume, *The Autobiography;* and two world wars and their aftermath have easily doubled the figure. Another American compiler, Louis Kaplan, added up 6377 entries in his *Bibliography of American Autobiographies* (University of Wisconsin Press, 1961), disproving the myth that

Americans might have inherited from their British cousins the virtues of understatement and of modesty.

The originality of the French probably lies in the number of women, endowed with a gift of style, who, during the seventeenth and the eighteenth centuries, left fascinating memoirs: Madame de Motteville, Madame de la Fayette, that vivacious German Palatine princess who became the second wife of Louis XIV's brother, then Madame Roland). George Sand, with her long and revealing *Histoire de ma vie*, brought up the rear. Few women of our age would dare compare themselves to that galaxy of memorialists who had witnessed life at the court of glorious kings and lifted the veil to observe, with a keen feminine eye, the reverse of the glittering decor; Simone de Beauvoir, calmly audacious, will, in the nineteen sixties, be their imperturbable successor. Not many male memoir writers of the twentieth century equal the more robust and less inhibited talents of the Classical Age (Retz, La Rochefoucauld, Saint-Simon) or those who, born in England like Gibbon or in Italy like Goldoni and Casanova, chose to write the record of their adventures in French. Witnesses to the Revolution and to the Napoleonic wars had enjoyed rich opportunities for observing human passions, ranging all the way from ferocious cruelty and cold-blooded plotting to heroism. Our feel of those times, though perhaps not objective history, owes much to the memoirs of those highly placed personages, Talleyrand, Fouché, Ney, Bonaparte's brothers, the fallen eagle of St. Helena. Most of those recorders of events, intent upon their own glorification, cared little about total sincerity to themselves; their self-portrayal is all the more truculent as a result. It must be conceded that memoirs left by the defeated generals of a more recent war (Gamelin, Weygand) or even by the victorious ones (Eisenhower and several other American and British artisans of the 1945 victory, and of the bungled peace) pale beside the more talented military memorialists of the past. So do Poincaré, Paul Reynaud, Léon Blum, Mendès-France, to mention the French alone, beside less scrupulous but more fiery politicians of an equally garrulous bent in the past. Winston Churchill perhaps and, in the finest passages of his third volume in particular, De Gaulle, alone may long continue to be read with relish by the common reader, and eyed with a suspicion all the keener by puritanical historians wary of rhetoric.

There is scant question of total sincerity in memoirs. That literary genre is not usually indulged by artists, writers, intellectuals in general, and very few professors have been addicts to that mode of self-justification. Memoirs are by definition a retrospective genre: the author is a man of action who, retired from the struggles of life by age, by events, or by changes of political fortune, perhaps forced to the contemplation of his career through imprisonment or exile, undertakes to reinterpret his achievement in the light of the present. He has little difficulty in endowing his volume with consistency and with unity, since all is centered around his own ego. He records events (conspiracies, battles, negotiations, sieges laid to feminine fortresses which seldom refused to parley), but he seldom analyzes his own thoughts or his own sensations. His gift has to be that of a picaresque storyteller, touching up life so as to make its narrative exciting and his own ego more exalted, not that of an introspective. Since most memoirs are composed by aging persons casting a prolonged backward glance at their careers and often blending the imaginary and the real, the conquests that a libidinous old man like Casanova would have liked to make being undistinguishable from those he actually made, they are arranged by the author with an eye to his present situation. Even an amateur of genius like Saint-Simon, or temperate masters of the art of omission like Goethe and Renan, relate past events—in Saint-Simon's case, incidents of a court doomed to decadence because he was not asked to play a leading role in it—or their own sentimental or intellectual education, from the vantage point of the present. They do not allow the unknown or the contingent to erupt into their orderly story. Their temporary aberrations or their mistakes take on an air of rational necessity when envisaged from the serene heights of detachment they have reached. The chapters written in the past tense lead to the future which was to invest them with significance. The wisest and most urbane authors of memoirs are those who warn us at the outset that they are mixing "Dichtung und Wahrheit" and that, as Renan gently hinted in the preface to his own *Souvenirs,* "What one says of oneself is always poetry."

The age of emigration, which compelled many French aristocrats to break with their leisurely social life and to forsake their friends, their past, the setting of their youth, and the wars which followed each other until Waterloo, was in France the last golden age of memoir writing, now wistful and melancholy, now arrogant and self-vindicating. Autobiography, rather than memoirs, was to become, next to fiction, the privileged vessel for nineteenth-century outpourings. Some of those autobiographies will be in verse, either directly in the first person *(The Prelude)* or thinly hidden under a symbolic projection of the author *(Childe Harold, Alastor, Julian and Maddalo, Jocelyn).* Greater flexibility and variety are found in the many autobiographies in prose left by Englishmen as different as De Quincey, Haydon, Mill, Newman, Ruskin, Herbert Spencer, by Benjamin Franklin, Thoreau, or Mark Twain, by a dozen Frenchmen. The latter, however, will prefer the private diary to a genre in which sincerity was almost impossible of attainment.

Indeed, not a single one of the French autobiographies of the nineteenth century rivals the arduous attempt at telling the whole truth about one's inner self which Jean-Jacques had made. His *Confessions* long weighed upon all similar endeavors by his successors. Musset wrapped his own avowals in a half-fictional garb, thus transfiguring George Sand and his other mistresses to his heart's content, condoning his own weaknesses or vices more leniently than Rousseau had done his; even his exploration of the degeneracy of a man through sexual indulgence fails to bring forth the acute flashes of insight which illuminate Rousseau's mournful chapters. He was only half-satisfied with the book in which he had tried to universalize his disease and confided to Liszt, in a letter dated June 20, 1836, that "that sort of work, interesting or not, lies outside art; not true enough to be memoirs certainly, and not false enough to be a novel." Hazlitt, a fanatic of Rousseau as he was one of Napoleon, related his pitiful love affair with a lodging-house maid with far more intemperate exhibitionism than his Swiss predecessor, so discreet on his own relations with Thérèse, had done; but his *Liber Amoris,* curious as a document on the lack of restraint which the English can evince when they disregard their ideal of a gentleman, fails to become a deep, or a sincere and unadorned, record of his miserable passion. There is too much of *La Nouvelle Héloïse* in it. Benjamin Haydon, the painter, devoted three volumes to portraying himself according to "exact truth"; he took his own life, at a rather advanced age, pathetically quoting Lear in his diary, "Stretch me no longer on this rough world." But suicide as Goethe, and Gide long after him, argued when confronted by the suicides of sincerely desolate young men around them, can hardly bestow authenticity on a fake talent. With Rousseau, the quest for sincerity had not served as a paltry excuse for unreserved acceptation of all in oneself. In a letter to Sophie, Jean-Jacques aptly phrased his deeper concern, which was to use sincerity as a means of moral reform. "Whoever has the courage to appear as what he is will sooner or later become what he should be."[1] De Quincey's autobiographical sketches have a playful charm, but his more romanticized *Confessions of an Opium Eater* is the book through which he fascinated his age, and Musset and Baudelaire in another land. Ruskin's *Praeterita* show him at his seductive best, but afford no inkling of the somber sexual and mental derangement that preyed upon the Puritan aesthetician and finally engulfed him.

Most autobiographies are selective in more ways than one: the author underlines his singularity and leaves out those features in himself in which he resembles others. At all costs, he must be interesting: if he was sane, wise, sensibly successful, mildly passionate, he would not deserve a moment's attention from us. Then, the autobiographer naturally relies upon memory; he records the struggles of his youth against society, injustice, conventionality; often, too, he fondly varnishes his account with the magic of wistful regret and extenuates the sorrows and the frustrations of even the most privileged children (Sacheverell Sitwell's *All Summer in a Day,* Osbert Sitwell's bulky *Left Hand, Right Hand,* Cecil Day Lewis' *The Buried Day*). But very few are the authors who show themselves to disadvantage. Stephen Spender has been more candid than most in *World within a World,* but he soon turns into a moralist and a reflective critic of his age. Middleton Murry eliminated much from his private life in his personal records; so did the flamboyant South African Roy Campbell. Nowhere do autobiographers accuse themselves of coxcombry, of silliness, of cowardice; nowhere do they observe pitilessly and render the symptoms of their own decrepitude. Relating

1. The reference is to Rousseau's letter (No. 383) of July 13, 1757. Quoted in Jean Starobinski's remarkably penetrating book, *Jean-Jacques Rousseau: La Transparence et l'obstacle* (Plon, 1957).

one's own internal progress implies that one was no ordinary mortal, for evil or for good.

The fondness of our age for the autobiographical literature stems from its ease. The author finds a book almost ready made in the narrative of his youth. If he fears his powers of depiction of persons and places to be inadequate, his gift for vivid rendering of his passionate emotions to be uncertain, he can, as Stendhal's Henri Brulard notes when reminiscing over amorous desires in Milan, analyze what he cannot paint. He can remain unconcerned with other people, their sordidness, their clumsy sensibility, their pathos, and treat only his own more refined moods. What is more, in an autobiography, while giving an impression of faithful portrayal of himself, he links the shreds of his past, connects the disjointed pieces, analyzes, interprets what he must have been, stops up the gaps. The past, thus endowed with continuity and leading to the present, becomes rationally limpid. Everything is explained to the satisfaction of the inquiring reader.

But the loss is grievous. The common, presumably less sophisticated, reader will prefer a novel to the elaborated sincerity of an autobiography. For a fictional character is tense toward the future; he is carried away to his success or to his failure by an élan with which we want to commune. The goal, which is the vantage point of the aged writer recording his life (nowadays autobiographies are written and published by writers in their twenties, who probably consider themselves as more mature at that age), is not clearly envisaged all along. There are gaps, fluctuations of light and darkness, moments of mystery and of suspense through which the reader is enabled to believe that the author knows no more about his characters than he, the reader, does. Others exist around the protagonist, and he does not dispose of them so easily as the autobiographer does. Joyce's *Portrait of the Artist as a Young Man*, D. H.

Lawrence's *Sons and Lovers,* Stendhal's Julien Sorel, Flaubert's Frederic Moreau, even Zola's *Confession de Claude*
show us a richer, and also a truer as well as more mysterious,
character in his setting than any autobiography by these
authors might have done. Details are arranged; Lawrence's
Miriam was not exactly the girl who was then his companion, nor was his mother in the book exactly as in life.[2]
But the truest fidelity is not to take all life away from what
was intensely alive. No autobiographer, not even Cellini
nor Casanova, and no biographer, not even Boswell, ever
created a character such as Shakespeare, Balzac, Dickens,
Dostoevsky conjured up with their imaginative force.
Proust's narrator is real for us, while a mere autobiography
by Proust would probably be forgotten today. Albert Thibaudet, in Chapter IV of his *Gustave Flaubert,* uttered in-
controvertible truths on this subject when he wrote:

> Autobiography, which at first appears as the sincerest
> of all genres, is perhaps of all the most false. To nar-
> rate oneself is to cut oneself up, put into one's work
> the only part of oneself which one knows, that which
> reaches consciousness. . . . Autobiography is the art of
> those who are not artists, the novel of those who are
> not novelists. And to be an artist or a novelist consists
> in having the miner's lamplight which enables a man
> to go beyond his clear consciousness and to ransack the
> obscure treasures of his memory and of his possibilities.
> Writing an autobiography means limiting oneself to
> one's artificial unity; doing a work of art, creating the
> characters of a novel is feeling oneself in one's pro-
> found multiplicity.

The private diary, which tends to become the favorite
genre of the twentieth century, voraciously absorbing the

2. The point is made by Roy Pascal, in "The Autobiographical Novel
and the Autobiography," *Essays in Criticism* (Oxford), *9* (1959), 134–50.

philosophical treatise and the novel itself, was born of the rage for sincerity which causes many modern devotees of literature furiously to burn their very idol, literature. We cannot easily imagine Dante, Shakespeare, Racine, or Voltaire keeping a diary and jotting down their petty doings and readings, ideas for a play or a poem, reflections on love, ambition and death, sarcastic remarks on their literary enemies. Montesquieu's *Carnets* contain mostly aphorisms on general matters of history and politics, but represent no attempt to portray their author. Dangeau, the courtier whose insipid diary inspired Saint-Simon to write his more vitriolic memoirs, jotted down minute and often inconsequential details on the Sun King, whom he detested but who fascinated him. Sterne and other whimsical authors of humorous or sentimental travel diaries laid no claim to exposing their nude selves to readers; their reflections often concerned other people and exterior events.

With the advent of romanticism, however, a new urge impelled sensitive writers to confide their innermost thoughts to a diary and to retain those secret notebooks among the papers they bequeathed to their heirs, when they had withstood the temptation to publish them in their lifetime. Some such diaries are nothing less than a time bomb, carefully calculated to explode in the literary world after their deaths: the Goncourt brothers staked a great deal on the appearance of their *Journal* and its petty scandals twenty, and even sixty, years after their death. Their scheme proved a good one. Without their *Journal,* ever since grossly overrated and disappointing to the seeker of sincerity, and the annual prize bearing their name which seems to go to lamentably poor novels three years out of four, they would be well-nigh forgotten today. Delacroix, Vigny, Michelet owe many of their admirers to their *Journal,* although Michelet's loudly heralded intimate record again failed to come up to the expectations of the amateurs

of erotology. With Gide, Julien Green, and the unbearable
Léautaud—who never wrote a single book of any worth
but whose volumes of inconsequential notes on cats, wom-
en, and third-rate casual literature appear posthumously
at the rate of one annually—journal writing was turned
into an industry. Sincerity paid off. Outside France, Kierkegaard, Tolstoi, Kafka, Katherine Mansfield, and several
British valetudinarians like Denton Welch or brooding introspectives like Virginia Woolf have left diaries that rival,
or outdo, anything written in France. But only in France
thus far has there been established an annual prize for the
best intimate diary (how intimate it can remain after thus
competing for publicity is debatable), and imaginary private diaries, heirs to Landor's *Imaginary Conversations* and
old-fashioned *Dialogues of the Dead* or to imaginary or fab-
ricated memoirs, entertain the sophisticated reader. The
Journal intime d'Hercule (endowed with the robustness of
a docker or longshoreman, but also with brain and not un-
friendly to the Muses) was written by André Dubois la
Charte in 1957. We may count on reading someday the intimate diaries of the Creator of the world, while resting on
the Seventh Day, with those of Satan, of Aphrodite, and of
Cleopatra to follow in due course.

Prying into the secret motives of other people, discovering from her jottings whether George Sand actually indulged Lesbian loves or was afflicted with frigidity, whether
Kierkegaard was impotent, what Michelet or Julien Green
may have revealed about their sexual life, how much hatred
for his wife Tolstoi could harbor, why Kafka balked at
marrying Milena or how Katherine Mansfield, alone in the
South of France, was treated by Middleton Murry—such
a legitimate if slightly unhealthy curiosity lies at the source
of our avidity in devouring these diaries and others. But
undeniably many of us have gone to that kind of writing
for higher motives. We are irked by all that is artificial,

touched up in novels, in autobiographies, in much of poetry; we want the screen, which affords the author his aesthetic distance, to be eliminated, and to identify ourselves unreservedly not only with his imaginary characters but with himself. We fondly believe that, in the notations which Stendhal (greedy as he was for "the small authentic facts"), Hawthorne, Baudelaire, Amiel recorded for themselves alone, we are privileged to watch the raw materials of literature, what cannot possibly lie. "Facts speak for themselves" is one of the most fallacious assertions repeated by the wisdom of nations and the gullibility of many historians and scientists. They do not, in truth, speak for themselves, for they are to be interpreted, linked to their causes, envisaged in their consequences, weighed against just as many opposite facts. But modern readers are reassured by journalists usurping the role of novelists and by "factual" diaries expelling autobiographies. They cherish the illusion that, in a diary which the author presumably kept for himself, unbeknownst even to his wife, to his secretary, or to his confessor, they stand closer to the tormented writer whispering into their ears an ineffable or a monstrous revelation—"as if by one man for one man," as the claim of the anonymous team of journalists fabricating *Time* magazine used to put it.

In earlier ages, many of the remarks, often profound, which now stud the private journals of our writers, used to be phrased more epigrammatically and objectively and, severed in appearance from the author's self, they became maxims and thoughts aimed at universal validity. La Rochefoucauld, La Bruyère, even more Vauvenargues and Chamfort, could keep and perhaps publish their diary if they lived today, but we might well be the losers for it. The practice of confiding to a diary in the first person, instead of extracting the bitter lesson of one's experience in the form of maxims, came with the self-centeredness that won franchise among us with the romantics. The stylization of one's experience was resented as detracting from the immediate communication of an experience to a reader who no longer was a pupil to be instructed, a worldly courtier to be entertained, but a brother to console the egocentric author or an accomplice to be contaminated by the evil of self-examination and of self-pity. Other factors played a part in that change: the new taste for fragments and for the unfinished. A broken column moved the romantics more than a whole portico left untouched by years; prose poems, elegies, sonnets celebrated "colossal wrecks" in some Eastern desert and found bitter consolation in the passing of empires and the mystery of "two vast and trunkless legs of stone" half immersed by the desert sand. Sketches by artists and unfinished symphonies became invested with a glamor that failed to seduce equally in completed and harmoniously composed works. Brief snatches of verse, shorter and shorter pieces, a few sinuous lines traced in Vinci's *Notebooks* afforded ampler food for reverie than the long poems, branded as inevitable bankruptcies, or than finished works by Raphael or Poussin, from which the mystery of the artist crushed by the magnitude of his undertaking seemed to be absent. Pascal's fragmentary Thoughts, in which the torment of a "sincere" and tragically committed writer pierced through every line, became, with the advent of romanticism in France, the secret goal toward which Maine de Biran, Maurice de Guérin, Alfred de Vigny, Baudelaire, Nietzsche himself exerted themselves.

It is easy to be sarcastic at the expense of diarists: the great majority of them (Novalis, Hebbel, Platen in Germany, Amiel in Geneva, Maurice de Guérin threatened by premature death, Poe, Baudelaire, Marie Lenéru) were diseased persons who passionately needed that form of dialogue with themselves or of contemplation in an objectifying mirror in order to survive. Their journals read, under the appearance of self-indictment, as a desperate appeal to our pity. Some pose lingers in all of them, even in Stendhal, who reached elusive naturalness better than most, even in tortuous, laboriously naïve Amiel. But they are aware of it and their display of self-complacency itself is a form of sincerity; an affectation of unreserved humility would be more mendacious. None of these sedulous keepers of "journaux intimes," "private diaries," "Tageblätter," and "Tagebücher," not even the pessimist Leopardi, not even Kafka, had the heroism to destroy the record of his reflections or of his failures. Kafka must have dimly realized that, if he were determined to have his literary remains doomed to oblivion, he could have trusted himself and a chimney fire rather than Max Brod. We are told that Maurice de Guérin used to read excerpts from his diary to friends. Gide's *Journals* are his most insidiously calculated work. Julien Green fastidiously balances what he wants to omit from his *Journal* and what he agrees to reveal. Mauriac, who in his *Vie de Racine* had severely judged the intimate journal as necessarily a work of complacency and of falseness, in which the diarist dupes himself even if he does not expect to dupe posterity, subsequently published volume after volume of his *Journal* followed by volumes of his *Bloc-Notes*. But he had the honesty to warn the reader that he was, not unambiguously, using the word *Journal* in its French meaning of newspaper; his gifts are indeed those of a polemicist and of a chronicler commenting upon incidents and books, often with the acidity which a man of faith feels allowed by higher powers to manifest, not those of an introspective.

Most diarists are also narcissists, as is to be expected. They would compose dramas or novels if they could forget themselves and become engrossed in other people. They would be men of action if they preferred molding others and changing the world to observing every minutia of their mental or physical digestion, every complaint of their liver or of their heart. We may well expect to find few robust optimists among them, and may be grateful to optimists not to offer to us endless notations on how happy they feel in their work, how prosperous in their accounts, how easily they pour out book after book or how much pleasure they impart to those partners whom they fatuously honor with their love. All literature has always stressed sorrow rather than joy, melancholy brooding, remorse and anguish rather than serenity and confidence. Fiction itself, after all, is made up of the misfortunes of others, related with ebullient or mournful zest by Zola or Hardy. It may appear ludicrous to read, page after page, such jottings as "nothing happened to me today," "nothing salient this week," "saw no one of interest and had not one worthwhile thought," or, as in Léautaud's pages, "would have written a superb novel and won the Goncourt prize, if I had really cared" followed by a whole volume with inconsequential diary notes. But, as Leopardi puts it, the reader's reflection is: "Non so se il riso o la pietà prevale." He is pleased to feel superior to those pitiful diarists; he does not begrudge them his pity.

A French characterologist, Michèle Leleu, attempted, in 1952, a characterological study of the authors of private diaries. She reached no startling revelation in her book and no vertiginous profundity. Clearly, the literature of day-to-day self-revelation is a favorite one with sensitive and nervous natures, with those in whom the inevitable joltings of brutal life arouse prolonged reactions and cause inner wounds, with introverts who are reluctant to face, or to provoke, obstacles and prefer to cherish their own past and their sensitiveness as their own private world. These brooding individuals fear or ignore the future. "Whence," not "whither," is the question which concerns them apropos of themselves. Every detail of the past, or of the present as it is turning into the past, looms important to them. They spurn the mutilation of part of the self, the sacrifices, which the achievement of any work entails. They console themselves through writing, loquaciously, interminably, formlessly, as others do through garrulous talk or through their interior monologues. The inward descent into their own abysses points the way to their possible escape from their prison, as it did for Novalis, for the often suggestive journals of the Austrian dramatist Grillparzer (he commented upon the difficulty of seeing the past *purely,* without letting what happened since interfere, greater than the difficulty of looking into the future), for Hebbel, whose acute and concise aphorisms often anticipate Nietzsche. For many of those diarists, writing as they did, probing into their complexities, offered the only salvation possible for them. Without such an outlet, Delacroix perhaps would not have painted so much, Baudelaire would not have unburdened his poems of all that might in them have been superfluous, elegiac, sentimental, or bitterly satirical, Grillparzer and Hebbel would not have composed their dramas, Kafka his novels; Lyautey would not have cured himself of his obsessive boredom and of his shyness to turn into an empire builder.

No diary, of course, portrays the whole man as he appeared to his relatives and friends. Even when the diarist had a wife (bachelors are in the majority among introspectives), one mistress or several (Delacroix, Baudelaire, Montherlant, Léautaud), close friends (Kafka), he is tempted to stress his aloneness. He gapes at his own vacillations, marvels at his own mobility, scorns action as too plebeian, dwells on moments of melancholy but seldom on his ability to transcend such moments and to merge them into the dialectics of life. Kafka, we are told by Max Brod, was much less gloomy in his daily existence than in his journal; he could be playful and humorous, apparently, and, without sarcasm, he would laugh aloud when he read *The Trial* to his friends. Kierkegaard was endowed with rare comic tal-

ent. Charles du Bos and Julien Green must have yielded
to moments of cheerfulness. The sincerity of diarists does
not have to lend equal representation to all their moods,
particularly not to those of inebriation with life, with love,
or with beauty; but it penetrates deeper into their moments
of masochistic sorrow or of icy observation of their failures.
The uncontested advantage of the private diary over all
other literary genres lies in its total and perilous freedom.
It need follow no rule, no order, obey no consistency whatever, submit to no unity of style; the diarist can juggle time
to his heart's content, pass over whole months or years as
the mystic would over periods of dryness, magnify a wart
into a Himalaya and forget cataclysms raging in the outside
world as serenely as Goethe did when he chiseled his *Divan*
or Virginia Woolf when she kept her journal in bombed
London.

A few figures of the representative French *intimistes,*
striving for more sincerity in their approach to themselves,
should be reviewed here. Rather than Joubert, occasionally
acute in his literary and aesthetic remarks, often timid or
stiffly formal in manner and overdiscreet about himself,
Maine de Biran may be hailed as the first important such
writer in the last century. He is less well known abroad
than he deserves to be. Bergson, more recently Jean Wahl,
ranked him among the greatest thinkers of France; "one
of the summits of French philosophy," declares Wahl. His
stress on "an intimate sense" in man, a tension or "an effort" which transcends the organic and places us directly
in contact with our own existence, parallels Coleridge's
imagination and anticipates Bergsonian intuition. He was
born in 1766, just before Benjamin Constant, Bonaparte,
and Chateaubriand. An ailing temperament, abnormally
sensitive, this compatriot of Montaigne and of Fénelon
married his cousin, whose husband had emigrated during

the Revolution and was assumed to have died. He had three children by her. But in 1802 the first husband reappeared and the unhappy wife, afflicted with guilt, haunted by the thought of suicide, died soon after, having lost her reason. Obsessed with the urge to seize himself in his innermost secrets, relying less on analysis that dissects feelings than on the strange, ambivalent power of habit that sharpens our perception of what takes place inside us, Maine de Biran endeavored to unravel his true self from the appearances of it that struck others and which in turn became the mirror in which he saw himself. He kept his philosophical *Journal intime* from 1792 to 1817 and died in 1824. "No man," he noted, "has ever seen or watched himself pass as I have." Certainly no French romantic philosopher proved his equal.

George Sand's *Journal intime,* published after her death (in 1926) by Aurore Sand, is less analytical, less relentless in search for self-knowledge, than her long autobiography. It quotes curious advice dispensed to her by Delacroix, before whose easel she was posing for her famous portrait (in 1834), on how to cure oneself of heart grief. The ardor of her passion for Musset (and subsequently for Marie Dorval) burns some of the pages. "Return my lover to me," she prays to God, "and I shall be devout, my knees will wear out the pavement of churches!" Stern Irving Babbitt could well draw antiromantic arguments from that diary, incensed, and entertained, as he was by those feminine novels in which, whenever a woman wishes to change her lover, God conveniently stands by to facilitate the transfer. A minor romantic, Antoine Fontaney, who was also fascinated by Marie Dorval and became the lover of her daughter, kept a diary of his torment. Consumptive, both he and his mistress died in 1837. His diary records some of his doings and emotions, with no undue exaltation and with a simplicity of style uncommon in those years; but Fontaney lacked the power of insight and the vibration of style which might have assured him a niche among the *minores* of French romanticism. The scholar who published his diary in 1925, René Jasinski, assures us that as a poet, in the stories of his Spanish travels in his *Journal,* Fontaney's "perhaps unequaled interest lay in his absolute sincerity." It fails, however, to move the reader.

Vigny's *Journal d'un poète* was given that title by the poet's pious friend Louis Ratisbonne, when he first published sundry fragments from a mass of heterogeneous notebooks. It is not, however, a diary. To be sure, a number of notations on Vigny's mother, on his ailing wife, on his academic candidacy, on political events, have a personal tone. Very intimate records of his sexual prowess, often disguised in Greek characters, so frightened the heirs of those papers, who regarded them as unbecoming to the most majestically impersonal of French romantic poets, that they have never been published. Elsewhere, with as much candor as a Casanova (in the year 1835), the poet of "Eloa" jots down: "I feel powerfully organized for physical *volupté.*" It took an equal amount of frankness, from this poet of the Ivory Tower par excellence, to record for posterity, in 1832, the following item: "What often wearied me in women is that, with each mistress I had (deserving of that name), I had to educate her so that she could be in a position to talk with me."

For thirty more years apparently, even when suffering from cancer in his sixties, the Academician and haughty singer of "L'Esprit pur" resisted such weariness and raised new ladies to his level. But Vigny hardly believed that sincerity was possible in the other sex. A cruel indictment of Eva, in Letter CII, inserted in the *Journal d'un poète* in the Pléiade edition, brands her as congenitally incapable of sincerity, and of seeing it in others. "To descend into one's heart, to plunge into one's soul before speaking with those whom one loves is for her an unknown art, which she does not even need." In 1839, the poet, already over forty, confided to his journal his aesthetic credo, very close to Musset's: "When a *cri* [cry, shriek, scream of anguish hardly convey *cri du coeur* in English] comes out from a man's heart in spite of himself, that *cri* is sacred."

Maurice de Guérin, who was introduced to the British by Matthew Arnold and who has haunted the imagination of many a Frenchman of our century, notably that of Mauriac, is, along with Gérard de Nerval, the most appealing figure of French romanticism. He died at twenty-nine, consumptive, leaving behind him poetry in verse which just falls short of being invested with suggestive magic, some of the greatest poems in prose in the language, all glowing with pantheistic paganism, and the richest of personal diaries for him who would study the *mal du siècle* at its most sincerely felt. Raised in ardent Catholic faith, in the Southwest of France, while attending a Catholic institution (Collège Stanislas) in Paris, Maurice de Guérin, at eighteen, began writing down his confessions destined to a priest, indicting himself as he who confesses must do ("no one thinks more ill of me than I do myself"), feeling preyed upon by death and unable to alleviate his vague anguish except in literature. Chateaubriand was his model at first; Lamennais then fascinated him. Two souls fought in his breast, a Christian one seduced by humility and that of an indomitable Centaur, who yearned to embrace torrents and forests, to gallop over plains and rivers. Alone perhaps among the French romantics, he sought in nature a soothing education and a cure against despair, as Wordsworth, Coleridge, and John Stuart Mill had done in Britain. His pantheistic ecstasies, his mad delight in tempests and howling winds, his thirst for the ebb and flow of nature with which his heart sought to beat in sympathy would, if his mastery over verse had been greater, have made him a French Shelley.

"I am admitted by nature into its innermost and divine abode, at the starting point of universal life," he noted on December 10, 1834. He both nurtured and dreaded the power of his imagination, aware of the powerlessness of his religious faith to check his yearning for the infinite.

If his passionate communion with nature, unequaled in its intensity among the romantics of France and equaled only by Shelley or Lenau, drew Maurice de Guérin toward the world without, he was also the heir to a tradition which led him to explore the world within. Very early, in his letters to his sister Eugénie de Guérin (whose own diary, covering the years 1834 to 1840, is not unworthy of that of the brother whom she cherished), he cried out his need to confide to the white sheet of paper, "to which I never told a lie"; the overflow of life which oppressed the young man doomed to perish in his twenty-ninth year had to pour itself out thus. Other diaries strive for intellectual accuracy and for a truth about oneself reached through cold analysis; Maurice de Guérin's is the exultation of a leaping sensibility, which is sincere in rejecting the restraints of the watching intellect. "Sincere" is the adjective used by all the critics who have commented upon him, usually in the superlative. This hyper-romantic might have been judged all the more sincere perhaps in that he never laid any claim to sincerity. His sole purpose, as one of the early entries (March 15, 1833) in his *Cahier vert* notes, was to penetrate inside himself: "We live inside ourselves too little, or hardly at all. What has become of that inner eye which God gave us to watch on our soul incessantly? . . . It is closed. . . . The contact between nature and our soul has been severed." Of all those who kept a diary in France between Sénancour and Amiel, Maurice de Guérin was doubtless most free of all affectation. But his deep ambiguity, torn as he was between pantheism and Catholic orthodoxy, the vacillations of his faith, even his impatience at his sister Eugénie's engrossing devotion to him,[3] his own momentary passion for a married lady in 1837, and his unhappy marriage in 1838 (both occurred after he had ceased keeping a diary) are omitted from the *Cahier*. Perhaps such a genre of writing, if it is to be the confidant of an ardent soul, should not court repetitiousness and monotony by outliving its freshness; three years and one hundred pages were enough for Maurice de Guérin.

Delacroix's *Journal*, kept early in his career and then again late in his life, is a valuable storehouse of ideas on art, on Rubens, Poussin, Racine, Mozart, Gluck, the painter's favorite artists; but it fails to reveal much about Delacroix's own struggles, his technique, or his conversations with Bonington, Chopin, Balzac, or young Baudelaire. The most cultured of modern painters, the closest to several men of letters, the most lucid about his own goals and devices, Delacroix confides little to the three volumes of his *Journal*, and extremely little which might be regarded as an adventure in sincerity. The archromantic among painters, the master of "Liberty Guiding the People" and of "The Death of Sardanapalus," cared little for the title of "romantic" (he states somewhere that he only accepts it if romanticism is

---

3. Recently, in the *Nouvelle Revue Française* of July 1957, a strange letter of Maurice de Guérin to his friend Barbey d'Aurevilly was published. The young brother (Eugénie was five years older) made this avowal: "My sister tells me: 'Why do you forsake my prayers, my complaints, all my affection? You have enough of me, that's it.' I would gladly share with her a hundred thousand of my sad regrets, but could I confess to her that I have in my soul the whims of a much greater cruelty. I remember that at a very tender age, I experienced a bitter delight in beating the animals which I loved . . . Their shrieks gave me a heart-rending feeling, a strange *volupté* of pity for which I yearned. If I were a Roman emperor, I would perhaps inflict the rack upon my friends for the pleasure of then having pity upon them." Of Maurice de Guérin, as of tender Novalis hunting the little blue flower, and of other romantics, it may be accurate to say that somber sadism went hand in hand with tender sensibility and religious aspirations. Novalis remarks in his *Fragmente* that men should have been more attentive to the long-standing association between *Wollust*, religion, and cruelty.

taken to mean "the free manifestation of his personal impressions"); he found his romantic contemporaries uniformly distasteful. A rebel with his brush, insulted by the art critics of his day, he appears in his *Journal* contemptuous of rebelliousness, ill-humored in the presence of innovations, unmoved by Baudelaire's devotion, conservative, even more adverse in the sixties to realism than he had been to romanticism in the thirties. "The greatest genius is but a pre-eminently reasonable being," he asserts; and (October 4, 1854), "I maintain that a true great man contains not one speck that is false; falseness, bad taste, absence of true logic are all one and the same." His diary makes no pretense of sincerity to himself. In some of his letters, he was less reticent and described his melancholy, his profound solitude and the vanity of work itself, the least vain of all the Pascalian means of diversion. In his diary, he would never have dreamed of laying his heart bare. As Baudelaire remarked in the well-known appreciation of Delacroix which he gave three months after the painter's death, "because he was a man of complete genius, he had much of the dandy about him." Delacroix preferred tight-lipped Mérimée, who did not reciprocate that admiration, to Baudelaire's passionate devotion.

The poet of the *Fleurs du mal* long toyed with the idea of writing the explosive little book before which Edgar Allan Poe had recoiled, but for which he provided the title and the inspiration: *Mon Coeur mis à nu*. At the beginning of his *Marginalia*, the American writer had pronounced dramatically:

> If any ambitious man have a fancy to revolutionize, at one effort, the world of human thought, human opinion, and human sentiment, the opportunity is his own—the road to immortal renown lies straight, open, and unencumbered before him. All that he has to do

is write and publish a very little book. Its title should
be simple—a few plain words—"My Heart Laid Bare."
But this little book must be true to its title. . . . To
write it—there is the rub. No man dare write it. No
man ever will dare write it. No man *could* write it,
even if he dared. The paper would shrivel and blaze
at every touch of the fiery pen.

Baudelaire lacked the concentration upon himself, the
gift which he coveted most, to undertake the continued,
relentless, shameless exposition of his own sensibility which
his *Mon Coeur mis à nu* might have become; what he gave
us under that title is better designated by his other notebook of personal revelation which he called *Fusées*. Profound insights into the nature of love, of art, disillusioned
attacks on woman, on political chimeras, yearnings for
prayer, sketches of stories or of prose poems, recipes against
his ailings, promises to mend his ways before the inexorable
wind of "imbecility" which was to sweep his will away—
all these occur in those *Intimate Writings* of Baudelaire
which have been reprinted and prefaced a dozen times in
our century. But they are in truth heterogeneous notes and
projects for the poet's own use, rather than an attempt to
rival or to vanquish time in its unrolling, as an intimate
diary following the days and months of the calendar often
is. A dozen or so of those notations do expose Baudelaire's
contradictions and secrets as powerfully as any observations
of any diary. He was sincere, however, and even more fully
so in his pathetic letters to his mother, or rather sincere even
while playing a role, appealing for pity and for financial
help, cultivating his self-pity, humiliating himself as abjectly as any character of Dostoevsky's, a "tragic sophist"
even in his histrionic show of sincerity.[4]

4. *The Tragic Sophist* is the title of a slim English analysis of Baudelaire
by G. T. Clapton (London and Edinburgh, 1934). Albert Feuillerat has

Michelet and Amiel chose otherwise. Their journals spare no detail; implacably, they record, year after year, every event, every encounter, many of the casual as well as profound thoughts which visit them. Like Gide's *Journal* later, theirs are likely to be read only when reduced in an anthology to a mere fraction of their sprawling selves and when the "sincere" parts in them are also reduced to the significant ones. But while Amiel submitted the pages of his diary to an elaborate literary preparation and treated it as his only work, Michelet regarded his as a record of details from which to draw, as from a vessel, the surplus of his energy after he had composed volume after volume of history or of lyrical natural history. His intense feeling for nature, his visionary imagination, his style, perhaps unequaled in France, his labor as a resurrector of the past hardly appear in the haphazard and hasty jottings of his journal; they would have required a literary treatment to become communicative, and Michelet begrudged such a waste of his powers, when centuries of French history still waited for him to conjure them up to life.

The second Mme. Michelet, Athenaïs Millaret—a widow as much hated by biographers and scholars as Mme. Isabelle Rivière is by the friends of her sincerity-starved brother or Frau Forster-Nietzsche by the modern Nietzscheans who have to undo her fabrications—had truncated and falsified Michelet's diary. A few inklings of the explosive content of those hundreds of pages, not to be opened until 1950, had been offered by Michelet's historical heir, Gabriel Monod. Monod had heard his master boast of having written on his conjugal life "with a sincerity which went infinitely farther than that of Rousseau and he would have

---

analyzed the mixture of pathetic sincerity and of shrewd calculation in Baudelaire's attitude to his mother in *Baudelaire et sa mère* (1944). I have collected Baudelaire's flashes of insight into himself, and into others and life in general, in a little volume, *Pensées de Baudelaire* (José Corti, 1951).

wished to offer to the world an example of that sincerity, if the world had been pure enough to understand it." It was clear, even from Michelet's historical writings and from his passionate volume on *La Femme*, that he had been obsessed by eroticism. Woman was to him the intercessor with the earth and with religious mysteries, the fountain of tears from which he could draw exaltation and drink pity, the object of his sensual curiosity (for Michelet appears to have been a voyeur more than a possessor) which refreshed the digger into archives and the cerebral and feverish writer that he was. Alfred de Vigny, throwing his anathema on all womankind after he thought himself betrayed by his mistress, Marie Dorval, had, in "La Colère de Samson," dared allude to woman's cyclical life:

La Femme, enfant malade et douze fois impur.

Michelet was obsessed by woman's monthly crises, "that divine rhythm which, every month, measures out time for her" and humbles her. A belated surge of repressed sensuality (he was over forty-five when he married his second wife, then hardly twenty, and far from unusually attractive) drove him to his over-intimate revelations, and perhaps also the remorse of an intellectual who had neglected his first wife, who had resorted to drink, become tubercular, and died in 1839. Michelet, stung with remorse, had then had her grave reopened in order to contemplate her corpse. Except as a record of strange obsessions and as an index to his treatment of women in his history, his *Journal*, the first volume of which was published in 1959, disappointed expectations. Michelet's vaunted sincerity hardly extended to his intellectual or to his spiritual life.

Amiel was, like Rousseau, a Genevese; he was attracted and repelled by his great predecessor, who presented himself as a victim and even as a martyr in his confessions, but had failed to state the full extent of his guilt. "His ego never knew how to renounce and to mortify itself, how to crucify itself." Like Sénancour, another Swiss, Amiel adored nature and his best passages are those in which he records his joy at tramping among Alpine mountains: his style then almost becomes tolerable. He had read Maurice de Guérin's diary, but found fault with it (January 1, 1866) for not portraying his inner life in sharp enough outlines. Earlier (June 18, 1857), he had vented his impatience at Maine de Biran's journal, in terms which he must have realized were to be even more applicable to his own eighteen thousand manuscript sheets (only three thousand of which have been published, with touching piety, by another Genevese professor).

> It is the walk of the squirrel in a cage. That unvarying monotony of reflection which endlessly begins over again discourages and irritates one's nerves, like the interminable pirouette of a dervish. . . . It is the journey of an ant within limits of a field, of a mole using up its days in the digging of a modest burrow.

But if anyone, before some insignificant minds among the diarists of our own time, could have killed the genre of the intimate diary through complacency, indolence, refusal to select, through presenting a humorless and naïve record of his failures and of a monstrous bachelor's selfishness, Amiel would have done it. Maine de Biran at any rate had realized the limitations of the genre and acknowledged that "one must provide oneself with a fulcrum outside the self and higher," and he had an original philosophical sensibility. Amiel speculated on ideas and books by other people.

The practice of confiding at length to his notebooks was, with him and with others, a compensation for his inability to act. He found it easier to collect himself and to contemplate if he held a pen in hand; peace of mind descended upon him once he had thus recaptured himself. Yet his profession was not of those which lead to excessive dispersion of the self and his love life set up few obstacles to his quietude. Born in 1821, Amiel noted in 1849 that he owed his long preserved virginity to "sincerity": since he had to dispense advice to two young sisters of his, he had to be pure himself in order to recommend purity. He was, in truth, even more shy than puritanical, and selfish to a point never attained by other egotists such as Renan, who wrote ironically on Amiel in his *Feuilles détachées*, by Paul Bourget, who ranked Amiel among the ten masters of modern pessimism in his *Essais de psychologie contemporaine*, or by Tolstoi, who devoted an essay to him, published with *What Is Art?* In 1927, almost half a century after Amiel's death, the only romance of his life was revealed in a volume called *Philine;* it was received with pathos and gravity by the Swiss, with levity by the Parisians. At the age of thirty-nine, Amiel finally had agreed to allow a young and pretty widow, whom he calls Philine, to bring to him the revelation of the other sex. He came to that resolution because he felt it incumbent upon him "to pursue his study of feminine psychology." He stopped however after a single experiment, finding that over-glorified pleasure "relatively insignificant." But he allowed the young lady to serve him, to worship him for twelve years, to laud his profundity daily, and he merely noted down in his diary that "she absolutely cannot do without me; she only hides it out of generosity and for fear of diminishing my free arbitrium if she allowed all her tenderness and all her passion to be manifested."

It took courage, and a rare sincerity indeed, thus to expose himself, without a word of self-blame, and perhaps also a good deal of inability to realize the sufferings of another person. Amiel repeatedly asserts his deep idealism, his vain quest for a great cause which would have justified his utter devotion. For lack of it, he scorned the platitudinous reality around him, found those who offered their

affection to him unworthy of the reciprocity they expected,
remained aloof from the world outside, with not a word of
sympathy in 1870–71 for the French then in the throes of
the siege of their capital and of a Parisian revolution. Late
in his life, in 1876, he had the candidness to call his private
diary "a pillow for his laziness" and to blame the inevitable
complacency that goes with that search for truth to oneself. "It becomes slanted toward apology; it is an epicurean-
ism rather than a discipline." One year before his death,
on May 10, 1880, he at least offered judgment over his confidant of forty years:

> What does this monologue signify? That reverie
> turns upon itself, like the dream; that an aimless so-
> liloquy is a waste of time; these added up impressions
> do not amount to an equitable judgment, or to one
> exact thought; the private diary is a decent good fel-
> low ["bon prince"] and tolerates verbiage, reiteration,
> effusion, complaint.

It is easier, but none too charitable, to stress the narrow
limits within which the sincerity of those diarists was encompassed by the genre itself and by their temperament
than to explain them and accept them for what they are:
the representatives of a form of writing that is likely to en-
croach upon creative literature more and more in our age
of psychologists and of analysts. Many of them were men
and women doomed to solitude and prevented by some
physical limitation or psychic obsession from fulfilling
themselves in communication with other mortals. But such
a fate is hardly different from that of most creators who,
incapable of finding fruitful fulfillment in the acceptance
of the world outside, constrained to fall back upon themselves, to undertake to erect a fictitious universe of light
and warmth or to prove to "sane" readers that they too are
sick and might be, have perhaps been, monsters, haters,

lecherous lovers, misers, tyrannical husbands, and unnatural fathers.

It takes no super-acute discernment and no characterological terminology[5] to discover an impossibility to love or a refusal to love at the source of many intimate journals. "L'impuissance d'aimer" was the disease that young Paul Bourget diagnosed, and faintly hoped to cure, among the masters of the generation of 1885 in France: Alexandre Dumas the younger, Baudelaire and, naturally, Amiel. The French do not as a rule consider that inability or that impotence as their national characteristic. Bourget might have gone abroad to find even more striking instances: Count von Platen, who kept *Tagebücher,* wrote many love poems in his brief life which ended in Sicily in 1835 (he was then thirty-nine, the age at which Leopardi, also a sick man and the author of a brief *Diario d'amore* of 1817, which precedes his *Zibaldone,* died). Von Platen's most ardent poems are addressed to young men, and his bent, like Winckelmann's who also died in what is now Italy, Trieste, was that of Virgil's Corydon. Kierkegaard, whose fragments and sundry papers often take on the character of a diary, repeatedly echoed Saint Paul's boast of the humility to which he is recalled by "a thorn in his flesh and the messenger of Satan to buffet him" (II Corinthians 12:7). "I have my thorn in the flesh, too," says the Dane who recoiled before the love that devoted Regina Olsen bore him in 1855, "that is why I could not enter into general relations. . . . I was the exception. Therefore I could not marry." Kafka, who responded to Milena's love, and who could perhaps have been

5. Characterology, which the French have developed into an important province of psychology lately, owes much to René Le Senne's classical treatise, *Traité de caractérologie* (Presses Universitaires, 1945), and to Gaston Berger's *Traité pratique d'analyse du caractère* (Presses Universitaires, 1950). Along with Michèle Leleu's volume, *Les Journaux intimes* (Presses Universitaires, 1952), mentioned in the text, see Pierre Mesnard's article commenting on her study, "L'Analyse caractérologique des journaux intimes," *Psyché,* nos. 84–85, October-November 1953.

saved from his nightmare by her, chose to deny the normal consequence of mutual affection. "Sisyphus was a bachelor," he mournfully noted. And in 1922, two years before he died, he jotted down such entries as "I cannot love, I am too far, I am expelled" and "It is untrue to say that I have experienced the words 'I love you.' I have only known the silence pregnant with expectation, which should have been interrupted with 'I love you.' That is all I have known, all." Kierkegaard had confessed, in 1849, that "all love which burns in me is expressed as cruelty." Kafka needed to have in him what he calls "Evil." "Evil alone is endowed with self-knowledge. Dialogue is one of the ways of Evil." Baudelaire's pronouncements about love's being the profound urge to commit evil are well known. Léautaud enjoyed women's love, but received more than he gave, and cats mattered more to him than all women except perhaps his mother. André Gide and Julien Green, the bulkiest diarists of our age, have not been, nor have they showed their heroes to be, endangerers of feminine virtue.

Authors of intimate journals again cannot be expected to be well adapted to their age and environment and eager to exploit, like Balzac, Hugo, Zola, and impetuous nondiarists, the society whose springs they have dismantled in their novels. They feel oppressed by it, doomed to alienation from it and their private notes echo many a melancholy complaint, or a scorn which can turn to destructive hatred. Baudelaire recorded his disgust with France "where everyone resembles Voltaire," then with Belgium, and his readiness gleefully to betray every political regime. As he took refuge in himself more and more and in his last volume (his most autobiographical one) feverishly scribbled before he lost his mind, *Ecce Homo,* Nietzsche poured his contempt upon the Germans. Arrogantly, stressing his spiritual links with the Greeks and with the French alone, he explained "how I have become what I am . . . not a man, a dynamite." Jules Renard, a little man and a minor talent, whose *Journal* however is admired by many a French critic, cynically observed: "To be happy is not enough. One must also see the others unhappy." We might add: portray them as such, to convince them through literature that they are unhappy, or make them such through taxes, political defamation, or persecution and war, if one is athirst for political power. Poor Poil de Carotte (for his most famous creation came out of his flesh and bone) had had a father who had committed suicide and one day found his mother at the bottom of a well!

But both the refusal to reach out to other men and the revolt against one's surroundings may be conducive to more searching exploration of one's self. The failure of the private diary, or what is denounced as such by several students of it today, is due to other causes.

First, it can be a very adolescent and immature affair, the ready confidant of a girl in her teens, like Marie Bashkirtseff (1860–84) who amused Barrès and corresponded with Maupassant. The granddaughter of a Russian general, gifted in several arts, threatened by the consumptive disease that ravished her at twenty-four, she jotted down sweet nothings in her diary as almost any girl might do. Pierre Louÿs chose her as his model when, still in college, he also began keeping his journal, striving to be "sincere like her" and wondering whether he would ever know love, whether the woman he would marry would not be ugly (since most women are) and would not deceive him (*Journal inédit* of 1887–88, published in 1926). Even Denton Welch, incapacitated after a bicycle accident, the promising author of *Maiden Voyage* (1946), due to die in 1948 at thirty-three, evinced few signs of intellectual maturity in his *Journal*.

The reason is probably that the diary, through its very nature, is not demanding of much effort; it even precludes it. For effort would entail some attempt at transforming oneself, at seeing oneself as one wants to be, or to appear, and a betrayal of sincerity. In the terminology of some psy-

choanalysts, too self-conscious and too polished a diary
would result in the substitution of the super-ego for the
self, or of the *persona* (the social mask we parade for others)
for the ego. The *id* has scant place in that personal and
analytical kind of writing, since it eludes conscious self-
awareness and is better manifested in some of those violent
onslaughts of the unconscious on all forms of moral censorship which are expressed in imaginative literature and attributed to fictional characters (Zola, Lawrence, Joyce,
Henry Miller). In the diary, unlike the autobiography, the
writer enjoys no vantage point from which he surveys his
past as trial and error, bliss magnified by regret or emotion
recollected. He puts down the moment's happenings in
their immediacy, severed from the past and as yet wanting
any aftermath. Hence, there is a static quality in most volumes of journals, an acceptance of the present devoid of
any tension toward what is to come or toward a goal to be
pursued. The self appears as almost finished or closed in
its present dispersal; one's possibilities or mysterious di-
mensions are silenced; the privilege of unpredictability of
great characters in novels is ravished.

A third consequence is the proclivity of the diarist to include everything in himself and his life, since to select might
be also to surrender the claim to total sincerity, and selection is reserved for autobiographies or personal novels. Delicate and fastidious natures are irked by that necessity to
record much that is insignificant. Amiel went through moments (too few and far between) of scruple when he saw
his mind as "a zero perceiving itself." Léautaud himself
moaned at times against the slavery of jotting down everything, one's least ideas, facts, gestures. Virginia Woolf left
twenty-six volumes of her diary, of which only one, naturally very fragmentary and censored, was published in 1953
by her husband. Even thus truncated, it is replete with
literary chit-chat, a morbid obsession with the success or
the failure of her books and the comments of critics, and

the scruples of a deft artist who must forsake art in that kind of writing. "If one lets the mind run loose," she notes on November 18, 1924, "it becomes egotistic; personal; which I detest. At the same time the irregular must be there; and perhaps to loosen it, one must begin by being chaotic, but not appear in public like that."

The dilemma is the perennial one in which practitioners of literature are enmeshed. They want to eschew the fallacy inherent in art and reserve a notebook which will be the faithful mirror and witness of their life. The earnest passion for truth of the most touching of diarists, who are not necessarily the greatest of writers, is admirable. Eugène Dabit, a man from the people who never deserted his class even when he won some fame as a "populist" novelist, Gide's travel companion in Russia (where he died in 1936), insisted upon preferring "life" to art, emulating another portrayer of the masses, Charles-Louis Philippe, and not underlining or straining the bare truth. "This is not literature. . . . It is a heart that beats, a blood that runs" (Dabit, *Journal intime*, December 16, 1934). But does not he who expresses himself thus become the victim of literature? Jean Guéhenno, also born in poverty, the most genuine reincarnation of Rousseau in France today, published autobiographies (*Changer la vie*, 1961) as well as diaries: the *Journal d'un homme de quarante ans* and the *Journal des années noires* (those of World War II), printed in 1947. But this son of a modest laborer in a Breton shoe factory, whose gifts and will power raised him to a high academic post in France and to social action as a journalist, in the gloomiest day of the war (March 13, 1943) was clearsighted enough to record in his journal:

> Why do I keep this diary? In order to remember? to put a little order in myself and in my life. . . . But all that cannot add up to a book. A great book is a rhythm which imposes itself upon the reader, which the reader

espouses without being aware of it. . . . A journal hardly states anything but whence one came, and what matters is whither one goes and wants to go; and that can
only be expressed in books, in works meditated and
composed by our will.

Can style, that is, a transmutation of the raw material of
literature, be dispensed with altogether? Can the tension
that imagines and recreates be excluded from any kind of
writing without giving way to looseness, even to flabbiness,
and to betrayal more blatant than the style which bestows
intensity and perhaps truth? Such is the harrowing question that haunts authors and readers of intimate journals.
It will be examined in our concluding chapters. But perhaps the much vaunted genre of the private diary, so assiduously practised by the last century and a half, leads,
when all is said, to "the vaporization of the self" which
Baudelaire dreaded. Should it not remain a storehouse of
sketches, of reflections, of insights into one's innermost self,
an adjunct to the work itself which those bricks and splin-
ters and plaster should serve to erect?[6]

6. Intimate diaries, since 1750 or 1800, could be counted in the thou-
sands. We have not of course attempted to enumerate or to read them all
here. Let us merely point to four very interesting ones by women writers;
the diary, in their case, since they are seldom as "creative" as men in fiction
or drama, may be not only more amply justified but may also bring forth
revelations which women could not otherwise make: Elisabeth Lesueur
(1866–1914), whose diary is the diary of a religious conversion that in turn
converted her husband after her death when he read her journal and who
then entered the Dominican order; Marie Lenéru, (1875–1918) a dramatist
of no mean talent who, early in her life, had become dumb and deaf; Paule
Régnier (1888–1950) and Marcelle Sauvageot (1900–34), on whom I have
written in "Contemporary Feminine Literature in France," *Yale French
Studies*, 27 (1961), 47–65. In England, Katherine Mansfield and Vera Brittain
(*Testament of Experience*, London, Gollancz, 1957) might be mentioned
next to Virginia Woolf. For a wise criticism of the *journal intime* in general,
see Alexandre Arnoux, *Etudes et caprices* (Albin Michel, 1953), pp. 9–13,
and, in our bibliography, items by Maurice Blanchot, Jean Dutourd, Edmond Jaloux, and several chapters in Georges Gusdorf's monumental thesis
on *La Découverte de soi*.

CHAPTER 8

The Age of Sincerity

ALL LITERARY RULES, all conventions and traditions on
genres and their laws, on diction and nobleness or distinction in style, the stress on objectivity and the cult of art for
its own sake, even the resort to symbols which the last
decades of the nineteenth century had advocated in poetry
and the fondness for irony evinced by Anatole France and
by young Barrès were swept away at the end of the first
decade of our century. In all the arts, and in science and
psychology as well, an upheaval took place between 1908
and 1913. We are still elaborating on the innovations then
started by Stravinsky and Schoenberg, by the Fauvists and
the Cubists and the first Russian, German, and Dutch ab-
stractions, by Brancusi and Laurens, by Apollinaire, Proust,
Mann, Lawrence, and a host of other writers. For the first
time, a literary and artistic revolution was not heralded by
the battle cry of "Nature and Truth," but rather by the
determination to be more sincere and by a quest for authenticity.

In France, where the concept has been most studiously
analyzed and the word most extravagantly bandied about
(neither *"sincerità"* nor *"sinceridad,"* neither *"Ehrlichkeit"*

nor "candor," nor even less the fashionable and already meaningless "integrity" carry quite the same connotations), three influences operated in the literary realm. First was that of Baudelaire who, falling into the public domain in 1917, reprinted every year or so, discovered in his intimate writings and in his letters, appeared to whisper secrets into the ears of the young more movingly than any other poet. No less an antiromantic (after a fashion) than T. S. Eliot was to pronounce: "In his verse, Baudelaire is now less a model to be imitated or a source to be drained than a reminder of the duty, the consecrated task, of sincerity." Then Nietzsche, who was translated and passionately seized upon by the nascent century, displaced all other philosophers in his impact upon literature (Kant, Schopenhauer, positivism) and preceded Bergsonism and neo-Thomism. In *Human, All Too Human, The Dawn of Day, Morals for Moralists,* he had advocated the pursuit of *Ehrlichkeit.* In the third and the fourth parts of *Thoughts Out of Season,* concluding his celebrated onslaught on the abuse of history and lauding Schopenhauer as educator, he had urged his contemporaries to go to school, not to Rome, but to Greece, and there to learn "that everything which makes for sincerity is a further stop toward true culture, however antagonistic to our present ideals of education that sincerity may be"; and he asserted that Schopenhauer's lesson lay not in our ever hoping to become something in the future, a form of self-deception, but in acquiring "the heroism of sincerity which ceases to turn us into playthings of time." In even more striking admonitions, Zarathustra had bid us write with our blood and watch that blood become spirit.

In a cryptic and epoch-making notation, Nietzsche had proclaimed Dostoevsky "the only one from whom I learned anything in psychology." Around 1910, his novels swept many a reader of Germany, France, Britain off their feet. The Western Europeans became fascinated by those strange buffoons who suddenly laid all their shame, and ours, bare, by those practitioners of humility who indulged their un-inhibited confessions on the public square, those shrieking women and gamblers, eternal husbands and will-less waifs in whose avowals a strange saintliness seemed to dwell. Gide, Alain-Fournier, Suarès, Rivière were impressed by the candor of *The Idiot* and pondered over the grave advice of Father Zossina to Fyodor Pavlovitch, then to Madame Hohlakov: "Above all, do not lie to yourself. The man who lies to himself and listens to his own lie reaches such a pass that he can no longer distinguish the truth within him or around him. . . . Avoid falsehood of every kind, especially falsehood to yourself. Watch over your own deceitfulness and look into it every hour, every minute."

The antiromantic reaction that marked the first decades of the century in France (and to a lesser extent in Great Britain) was directed against what had often been sham in romantic emotions and the excessive or garish expression with which those emotions had been colored. Paul Bourget, in the dedication of his *Démon de midi,* in 1914 (the "daemonio meridiano" of Psalm 91, "the destruction that wasteth at noonday") vituperated against the lack of sincerity and of commitment in Chateaubriand's heroes, and demanded from the writer, especially the Catholic one, that he conform his life to his ideas. Bourget himself was ever to be torn between his inability to believe and his Balzacian conviction that Catholicism is the keystone of French society. Pierre Lasserre, Ernest Seillière, Henri Massis, a score of other critics and social interpreters or reformers of literature poured insult on the romantics—most romantically—because they had lied to themselves or refused to see soberly and lucidly into themselves. Anatole France, the skeptic, scoffed at Lamartine who loved Elvire most ardently after her death, and, in verse, made Graziella die with excess of love (for him) in the mendacious story written

around the Neapolitan fisherman's daughter. Louis Bar-
thou, a Lamartinian and a grave statesman, euphemistically
added that his poet "had his own way of loving women
which is not necessarily the one which women prefer."
Jacques Rivière, a passionate nature himself who could
worship Claudel and Gide, indicted the romantics in his
profound essay on "The Adventure Novel" (1913): "Romanticism is not only an art that is out of style. It is in truth
an inferior art, a sort of monster in the history of literature.
. . . We have nothing but a façade before us."

It is the natural course of things that inheritors to an
over-rich legacy should be overwhelmed by it and attempt
to stave off the burden from their shoulders. The new in-
flux of psychological and artistic treasures which the romantics had once added to the serene streams of former ages had
rolled much turbid confusion with it: the young men of
1910 wanted to restore clearness of outline and clarity of
vision into their own selves to a literature and an art which
they indicted for its delight in chaos. Nietzsche, again, in
La Gaya Scienza (Aphorism 173), had taught them to distinguish between being profound and appearing profound.
"He who knows that he is profound endeavors to be clear;
he who would seem profound to the crowd tries to be obscure. For the crowd holds as profound all things the bottom
of which it cannot see." Pierre Reverdy, who was twenty-
four in 1914, one of the deepest poets and moralists of his
generation, offered similar reflections in his remarkable
volume of bracing maxims, *Le Gant de crin* (1927): "We
must not mistake what is obscure with what is turbid. Tur-
bidness [*le trouble*] supposes an adulterous mixture, an
impurity"; and he maintained that the opposite of lightness and levity (the French have but one word for them, *la
légèreté*) is not depth, but heaviness, adding: "Whenever
you meet a foreigner who is intelligent, you find him as
light as a Frenchman." Jacques Rivière acknowledged as

his masters those who, in poetry, painting, and music (Racine, Ingres, Mozart) "reject the shade" and the power of blackness for its own sake.

The cherishing of their own selves by all the artists who followed Rousseau, Diderot, Goethe, and Byron had brought forth the widest range of discoveries in man's history since the Greeks. Never again would personality be immolated to the mass, to a system, to constricting rules. The lines that Suleika utters, in Goethe's *Divan,* were to be the motto of subsequent ages.

> Höchstes Glück der Erdenkinder
> Sei nur die Persönlichkeit.

But personality, that highest felicity of the children of the earth, had been pursued in its dispersal over the vast world, in its pantheistic merging into outward nature, or in its successive and contradictory manifestations. Naturalism in fiction, even symbolism in poetry, had not heeded the other advice of Goethe's "Testament": "And now take your sight inside yourself; there you find the center which no mind can doubt. . . . There alone will you experience the conviction that what is fecund alone is true. *Was fruchtbar ist, allein ist wahr" (Vermächtnis).*

The march inwards and downwards in ourselves, however, is fraught with perils, the readiest of them being narcissism and its consequent failure: the inability to locate the self in its relation to its surroundings, to observe oneself through watching oneself reflected and distorted in the eyes of others. On the moral plane, the most common assumption of the romantics, all children of the Jean-Jacques who had confessed his lies and his lapses as a boy and as a father, was that an avowal of one's mistakes, or more heinous erring ways, almost justified them and took the place of mending their evil consequences, not through a confession to the public, but through deeds. To be sure, there was no lack of exhibitionists among the pursuers of sincerity between the two world wars, and there has been none since World War II: Maurice Sachs was the most notorious of them in his *Le Sabbat,* with Marcel Jouhandeau, another devotee "utriusque amoris," not far behind him. But gravity, even a puritanical relentlessness in hunting out all that is false in each of us, was the rule in French literature. Never perhaps had its profound bent—Protestant and Jacobin and ferociously masochistic in applying the scalpel of self-analysis to what is held most dear—since the Classical Age, been manifested more clearly than in the years 1910–60. The sentence attributed to Malraux by a friend of Gide (Saint-Clair, the pseudonym of Mme. Théo van Rysselberghe) could be pinned on it as its motto: "The most effective weapon of any man is to have reduced his share of histrionics to a minimum."

The first half of the twentieth century in France applied its extraordinary seriousness to a revision of all its critical ideas and to the restoration of fervor and of inner life to religion. Since St. François de Sales, Bérulle, St. Cyran, and Pascal, France had not known an age in which Catholicism and literature were so closely interwoven as that of Péguy, Léon Bloy (dead in 1917), Claudel, Maritain, Mauriac, Rivière, Du Bos, Bernanos, Marcel, Grosjean, Cayrol, Estang, and a score of others such as Simone Weil and Malègue.

It would not be difficult, but it would certainly be tedious, to establish an anthology of the many passages in which contemporary critics have resorted to the term sincerity and to an "explanation" of genius or talent through that concept. Bergson's influence, which was doubtless more far-reaching on men of letters, and particularly on critics, than on philosophers, contributed to the spread of the notion. Bergson was far too prudent to venture into the domain of literature or to avail himself of such an unclear notion as that of sincerity; he was too modest to claim disciples, although he owned that Péguy and Thibaudet had penetrated his thought more acutely than anyone else. He lauded Thibaudet for his gift of sympathy with, or of empathy into, the creative élan of the author studied—a sympathy more akin to gentle and humorous friendship than to passionate love. Thibaudet sought in the many works on which he commented the spontaneousness that Bergsonism had taught him to cherish above all else. Ebullient and never magisterial himself, he criticized with the zest of a wine taster and the verve of an indefatigable creator of images and parallels, was repelled by the meretricious and the spurious, but was too kindly to sift the five books destined (at best) to survive out of the two hundred or so on which he wrote every year. He was entertained by the claim to sincerity of many moderns, compared it to bank deposits on which the writer will draw, but never took the notion seriously enough to come to grips with it.[1]

In contrast with Thibaudet, Charles du Bos, at his rare best (on Flaubert, Baudelaire, Proust, Goethe) the most profound of the French critics between 1920 and 1935, does not read as if he had ever relished wine, the fruits of the earth, the mischievous smile of irony, the relief of cursing. Inner life was the sole life that counted for him. Books were more real than any individuals whom he might meet on the street, if they were not authors. His inability to master the material details of living was proverbial: he never learned how to fill a fountain pen and his friends wondered how he ever managed to fill his pipe. His lack of practical sense, his reluctance to be diplomatic or even

1. See Albert Thibaudet, "De la Sincérité," *Nouvelle Revue Française* (October 1929), pp. 149–55, reprinted in *Réflexions sur la littérature* (Gallimard, 1940), Vol. 2.

tolerant (especially after religious conversion had convinced him that he was one of the elect and was invested
with the duty of summoning others to the right path) explain the harsh and sanctimonious tone of the book in
which he upbraided Gide. Du Bos had been raised in luxury and, when the family's fortunes took a turn for the
worse, he had to deliver lectures, to write occasional (but
never shallow or impersonal) criticism in order to survive—
and to keep a diary in the hope of thus emerging from the
sea of oblivion that engulfs most critics.

His bulky diary is in no way concerned with petty details
of daily life; it is free from the venom through which less
noble souls hope, in a posthumous and confidential publication, to take their revenge upon colleagues more successful than they. It deals with literature envisaged as a manifestation of "the spiritual" and, increasingly, with religion
and with piety. The authors most admired by Du Bos—
Claudel, Shelley, Proust, Baudelaire, but also and more
paradoxically Goethe, Keats, Walter Pater—all become in
his eyes exemplars of spirituality, even of mysticism. He
entered into *Marius the Epicurean* and Charles Morgan's
The Fountain and *Sparkenbroke* as into a solemn cathedral.
He annexed the dead and the living to the faith he had
recovered in 1927 through God's grace. His confessor gently
reproached him with his fondness for complexities; indeed,
his style and his critical gait became more labyrinthine
after he had answered the call of God, and divine simplicity which would make us alike to little children was denied
him. But sincerity alone mattered to Du Bos. "If innately
I am not simple," he felt bound to retort (*Journal, 5,* 86)
"nothing could be both more insincere and more vain than
to aim at simplicity." He prayed that his beloved sincerity
never be averted from him. With the strange lack of self-
consciousness which often accompanies Christian humility,
he remarked in the same volume (p. 117):

> My sincerity,—more profoundly even than in my faculty of intuition because, on the human plane, it is that very sincerity which sets the other in motion—therein lies from the start the life saving buoy of my nature. . . . The sincerity of intelligence, O, my God, grant that, wholly submitted to Thee and guided by Thee, it may never depart from me.

A singular fate afflicted that sincere man: he had to start from books in order to be brought back to his own self; he first needed to assimilate the books, through multiple coils of mental digestion, before he wrote about himself. And he dimly realized that there was a lack of robustness, an inability to see the writer as he was and to judge him on aesthetic grounds, in the transfiguration he forced upon him. His Benjamin Constant is a marvelously complex and spiritual individual, but far remote from the all-too-human real Constant. Nietzsche, the last name he invoked on his deathbed (after Bach, Botticelli, and Keats), was to him the paragon of "heroism in sincerity." He was haunted by him, perhaps jealous of him, as Nietzsche had become jealous of Christ.[2] Even the concetti of the Elizabethans brought to him the evidence of "the labor in depth which these concetti presuppose." These poets had to express themselves richly through the same scruple of sincerity which today induces us to express ourselves soberly. The objective reader is tempted to smile at all the belabored sophistry and the devious self-deception which may lurk behind a highly spiritual critic's pursuit of sincerity.

To Du Bos, the model of sincerity in his life, less impetuous and provocative than Nietzsche and more scrupulous,

2. See Jean Mouton, *Charles du Bos: sa relation avec la vie et la mort* (Desclée de Brouwer, 1954), p. 142; also two excellent articles in *The Times Literary Supplement,* April 26, 1947, and April 24, 1959, and the *Cahiers des amis de Charles du Bos,* especially no. 2.

was Jacques Rivière, younger by four years, who was mourned by all his friends when, in 1925, he died at thirty-nine, partly as a consequence of World War I. Du Bos devoted to him five essays, collected at the close of the second volume of *Approximations,* all centered around sincerity. Two books have appeared on Rivière in English since 1950, and a collection of his best essays, including part of an analysis of "Sincerity to Oneself," excellently translated and prefaced by Blanche Price, was published in 1960 as *The Ideal Reader.*

Jacques Rivière, a compatriot of Montaigne and of supple and elusive Fénelon (on whom he wrote a philosophical essay while a student at the Sorbonne), is one of the most complex literary sensibilities of the last two hundred years. Profoundly Renanian, oscillating between sentimental comfort and intellectual dissection, faith and unbelief, he came at a time when Renan's vogue had passed; dilettantism was repudiated as a betrayal of sincerity, irony rejected as out of place in the august sanctuary of self-knowledge, and science, philology, and history failed to command the unreserved devotion of the young. Gide was his master, after Rivière had reneged his early love for the Symbolists, and Laforgue and Barrès; Claudel then overwhelmed him, and he almost became Claudel's most prized conquest for Catholic faith, since Gide and Suarès had preferred the soft pillow of doubt. But other gods soon won Rivière's adoration, the most compelling one being Proust, on whom Rivière wrote essays unequaled in penetration.

Although he wrote two very earnest and searching autobiographical novels, typically French, on the powerlessness of an intellectual to love unreservedly and on the insidious fascination of unloving for him whose analysis has pierced through the delusions of love, Rivière was no imaginative creator. He was supreme as a critic who, better than Thibaudet and Du Bos, discerned the new, divined young talents, and did not neglect the observation of form and style. His plasticity, which was unusual, enabled him to lend himself totally to the painter, the musician, the writer whom he admired, to absorb him almost passively, offering no resistance and no objection; then, having assimilated him, he could, if not quite forget, at least transcend through a dialectical process which was accompanied with some ingratitude. He searched for a new facet of his own self through others.

Sincerity to him did not entail stability, a complacent satisfaction at having attained clarity in his mind, a secure haven for his heart, the peace which faith should afford. He did compose a treatise on faith; he lauded faith as more arduous and more exacting than doubt; he exposed the motives and reasons he had for believing, the inadequacy of all else including science, his craving for the truest explanation of the world, the mystical one. But throughout it is the fervent treatise of an unbeliever. "The passion of knowledge animates me, the only one which is truly impious. Science is dangerous for religion only when it is the science of oneself." Claudel had judged the young doubter well when he had advised him to wear pious medals, to kneel down at church, and to discipline what Pascal had earlier called the machine or the beast in us, through the gestures of the believer. "I lack charity toward myself" is one of Rivière's aptest phrases, too felicitous not to smack of literature. He delighted in each refined nuance of his inner life, humiliating himself and yet proud of his complexity. Extracts from the notebooks he kept when a prisoner of war in Germany have been published with *De la Sincérité envers soi-même* and *De la Foi,* and they bear the title "Chasse à l'orgueil," "Hunting out pride." But pride was never expelled and the pride taken in one's humility is the most stubborn of all. Rivière was the most scrupulous of introspectives and he noted, in October 1914, in his prisoner's camp, that "a taste for comedy is almost necessarily bound up with the taste for sincerity."

There were not two men in Rivière, as in Saint Paul, but several. Oscillating from one pole to another of his nature would have been too easy for that multifarious personality. He was in love with difficulty and, instead of indulging the natural bent of his thought or sensibility, he insisted, as Charles du Bos said of him, on "thinking against himself." He was most stern with those whom he prized most, for he felt it necessary to distinguish himself from them, and to tell them as much. Sincerity for him led not to the endeavor to become what he wanted to be and perhaps was, but to frittering his own self away or at least to dispersal. Still, he would not swerve from his pursuit of sincerity. For him, and for not a few other Frenchmen, it was his form of Puritanism.

As early as March 12, 1909, when he was but twenty-three, Jacques Rivière, eschewing the dogmatism of the young, had written to André Gide:

> Always, like you . . . I have had the feeling that sincerity is the opposite of what is customarily understood by that word. It consists in never expressing oneself candidly at one time, in a definitive manner; it is respect for the soul's complexity, the refusal of giving oneself totally within one sentence. I never say what I think, because I never think one thing, a unity. But each thought in me is a movement in several directions, a combination and a balance of forces which leans on their very contrariness.

Three years later, in 1912, he set down in a fifteen-page essay, dedicated to the founder of the Vieux-Colombier, Jacques Copeau, his analysis of sincerity. Sincerity to others designates a confession: it is easy. Sincerity to oneself is a dangerous virtue, of which only an elect few are capable.

It is opposed to yielding to the spontaneous in us; on the contrary, "it is an unceasing effort to create one's soul as it is." Second thoughts are truer than the first; they lie deeper, and a strenuous endeavor to know is needed to unearth them. Strange discoveries are made, disturbing phantasms flit before us: the sincere man accepts them; he consents to the danger.

The danger lies first in our losing faith in our feelings; every one of them is henceforth called into question. It lies also in the need to accept all the thoughts, even the most monstrous, which traverse our consciousness. We cease to be the "nice" person whose every thought could be avowable: lecherous desires, impatient hatred of those whom we normally "love" most dearly, secret wish to see them dead, even worse velleities may thus be admitted by the sincere man. To nothing will he blind himself. He spurns only the fear of what lies inside him.

A last peril lies in wait: accepting the least noble desires or greed in us may easily entail magnifying these infinitesimal particles, granting them a franchise that the less sincere man would perhaps deny, impeding any attempt we might make to alter these feelings courageously analyzed and faced unflinchingly. However, such an abdication, which banishes a moral choice, eliminates the will power which may be the most true in us. Does sincerity imply the disregard of moral censorship, the return to a premoral stage? Stern Jacques Rivière, tormented by the need to be fully sincere to himself, almost concluded against morality, or rather "moralism," in literature, when he fell under the sway of Proust's novel and, just before he died, engaged in polemics with Henri Massis on "Good and Bad Sentiments" and with Ramon Fernandez, another devotee of sincerity, in a volume entitled *Moralisme et littérature* (posthumously published in 1932).

Ramon Fernandez deserves to be bracketed with Thi-

baudet, Du Bos, and Rivière as the fourth truly significant
critic of France between the two world wars. Rivière died
in 1925, Thibaudet in 1936 when he had already begun
repeating himself (the originality of critics perishes even
earlier than that of poets). Du Bos' death came in 1939 after
several fruitless years spent on the faculty of an American
university and in envisaging literature as the vehicle of religion. Fernandez appeared to have loosened his grip on
the emerging literature of the nineteen thirties when he
fell back upon the reinterpretation of Balzac, Barrès, and
Proust in his last volumes; he died before the end of World
War II, in 1944. His early essays (on Stendhal, Meredith,
Newman, Walter Pater, T. S. Eliot), his sparkling little
book on Molière, his thoughtful treatise *De la Personnalité*
(1928) did much to influence the literary youth of France
after World War I and aroused more than casual interest
in Great Britain. He had tried his hand at the novel, like
Rivière, but he was less averse to the depiction of the concrete than Rivière, less tempted, in his analysis of the sincerest in our personality, to disintegrate the ego and sub-
ordinate the will to the delight of the dissecting intellect.
His models remained to the end Balzac, Barrès, and (he
again!) Nietzsche. Sincerity lured him only insofar as it
enlightened man on his own secrets and drove him to action; mere delight in marveling at our own complexity and
unfolding its coils for the reader struck him as a remnant
of romanticism which his sportive instinct condemned. Like
Drieu la Rochelle, Jean Prévost, and Malraux, he was made
for action more than for passive contemplation of the most
secret in him and should have found his truest self in molding others.

Friends and foes of sincerity abound among the novelists
of the two decades 1920–40—the twin hostile brothers often
struggling in the same man. The discovery of James Joyce,

naturalized by Valéry Larbaud, then of D. H. Lawrence, whose *Lady Chatterley's Lover* was commended in a dazzling preface by Malraux on the significance of a new type of eroticism,[3] powerfully emboldened French writers to comprehend the private aspects of love life, on which they are traditionally reticent, in their frank shattering of illusions. Two Italian writers, both introduced by one of the shrewdest and wisest critics of those years, Benjamin Crémieux (who was tormented by the question of sincerity as a danger to imaginative inventiveness, as will be recalled elsewhere in this study), contributed even more to the elucidation of the theme of sincerity: one was Pirandello, who stressed in his articles and plays the superiority of art over life and the unreality of life as lived unless it becomes true through being transposed into art; the other was Italo Svevo, who, isolated in Trieste, a survivor from an earlier era (*Una Vita* was published in 1892 and *Senilità* in 1898, before Gide's *L'Immoraliste*), only reached France and subsequently the Anglo-Saxon world with *La Coscienza di Zeno* (1923), five years before his death. Zeno, a precursor of Moravia's "indifferent" characters, living in comfort in Trieste, a would-be physical and psychic invalid, devoid of will power, watched himself live in idleness, stumbled into an awkward marriage, reaped ingratitude while salvaging the business enterprises of members of his family. His observation of the most elusive in his own behavior is humorous and objective. The author never comments as Proust does, never philosophizes; his hero is nowhere abnormal or out of the ordinary; he watches himself with humor and subtly convinces us that any of us might have been he; he benignly warns us that "a written confession is ever mendacious," but none appears so credible as his. Even Duhamel's Salavin, Svevo's French brother, or the hero of *L'Ecorché*,

3. That preface was translated in *Yale French Studies*, *11*, (1939), 55–58.

by the Swiss writer Robert de Traz, lack naturalness when set beside Zeno, and their sincerity is more strained.

Cocteau, Duhamel, Green, Lacretelle, Mauriac, and Montherlant appeared to the youth of the nineteen twenties in France as the most promising novelists of the generation that followed in the wake of Proust, Claudel, and Gide, with one more austere and discreet figure, that of Schlumberger, in the background. None of them could elude coming to grips with the need to bring more sincerity into their art, or avoid the force of utter candor which might smash their literary attempt to smithereens.

Many would be inclined to brand, or to glorify, Cocteau as the most brilliantly insincere man of modern French literature. "Astonish me!" Diaghilev said to him at the dawn of the Ballets Russes in Paris. Cocteau has lived up to the command. His showmanship is that of a professional illusionist; his adroitness that of an acrobat; his talent for adornment and his eye for effect have been envied by many a Parisian dressmaker; if the poet's goal is ever to surprise us, Cocteau is a poet. Indeed he is a greater poet than many in our century who have striven for pathos and concocted enigmas. His style he has defined as "a very simple way of saying very complicated things." His autobiographical fragments throw flashes into the deeper life of the writer who might well, had he cared enough, have composed the best autobiography of the age. He preferred to do what Hugo von Hofmannsthal somewhere advocates: "One must hide depth. Where? On the surface."

Cocteau is too shrewd ever to have published a continuous diary in which every pedestrian detail of his life would be jotted down. That *enfant terrible* who has shared many secrets of his contemporaries is more reticent than many a ponderously serious puritan of letters who must record every inanity uttered by one of his colleagues or rivals. A volume entitled *The Journals of Jean Cocteau,* ingeniously grouped, was published in English translation in 1959. They were drawn from varied fragments of self-analysis and confessions which he wrote, always with mockery of himself, in *Le Rappel à l'ordre*, *Le Secret professionnel*, *Opium*, *La Difficulté d'être* (mirroring the crisis of the eternally young man discovering that he had reached the fateful age of fifty-five), and in *Journal d'un inconnu*—the "inconnu" being himself, who avers he is the most misunderstood of men. He has put on more masks than Byron or Yeats ever did, and we are not altogether at fault if we have taken some to be his true face. He has never dogmatized on his sincerity and he was always too inclined to laugh at himself to boast of possessing that form of humility. Part of his undying charm is that he has never relegated intelligence to a secondary place, contending that genius (*vide* Stendhal and Nietzsche, says he in *Le Secret professionnel*) managed to do well with that maligned quality. His own way of being sincere is through paradoxes, through the cultivation of the spirit of contradiction ("in its highest form, identical with the creative spirit," says he in his *Lettre aux Américains* of 1949), and through hiding, thanks to a deeper and underlying sincerity, a straight line behind apparent contradictions *(Le Rappel à l'ordre)*.

Georges Duhamel's best volumes are not his autobiographical ones, but they are founded on the personal experience he acquired during World War I as a surgeon near the battle lines. They are among the most truthful of books written on war, or on the macabre and pitiful side of war, but the time and the place were too tragic for the author to explore his own ego in them. The *Journal de Salavin*, without claiming graphic sincerity and while being obviously a humorous "journal romancé" by one who aspired to be a saint and failed pathetically, always appealing amid the bankruptcy of all his hopes, compelling as character-creation, is one of the best personal novels of the twenties. Later, in *Cri des profondeurs* (*Cry Out of the Depths*, 1953), extracts from the diary of an imaginary businessman, Félix Tallemand, a complacent, self-deceiving character who turned into an obedient tool of the Germans when they occupied France, and in *Le Voyage de Patrice Périot* (1951), on the family trials of a well-meaning, desperately but hardly lucidly sincere, professor, as well as in reminiscences of his past, *Inventaire de l'abîme* (1944) and *Biographie de mes fantômes*, (1944), Duhamel hardly went beyond the smooth surface of his own life, or of his characters'. The resort to the first person singular or to the fictitious private diary was nothing but a thin disguise for emptiness of content and lack of intensity. The promises of an earlier and more dashing small volume by him were not kept, and the author paid the price.

That early small volume, published in 1934, was *Remarques sur les mémoires imaginaires*. The refrain, ten times reasserted, is "I shall not write my memoirs," for memoirs are either "fixed up," elaborated, striving for style and for effect, or else they are authentic but cold, negligible. The past in itself has no meaning and it must receive one to justify being presented to the reader. Truth only becomes natural through a skillful preparation which need not amplify it but must simplify it. Selectiveness is imperative. Ludicrous and mildly moving Salavin, at the close of Duhamel's *Confession de Minuit* (1920), a confession made on a bench in the Jardin des Plantes, having welcomed all the promptings of his subconscious or of his whimsical but uncontrolled mind, fell to envying the tree next to him; for the tree knew how to choose, what to draw from the soil and what to leave out. If sincerity entails telling one's own particular, topical but unpoetical and unpoetized truth, Duhamel spurns it. A kindly man, he hinted (mindful, no doubt, of Gide and of the Goncourts) that he was disinclined to contrive the clockwork of an infernal machine, his confessions or his diary, which would some day explode on his "friends."

Jules Romains, the companion of Duhamel's youth, Mauriac, his contemporary and colleague at the Academy, and the great Catholic poet whom Duhamel and Mauriac both admired in their youth, Paul Claudel, would readily assent to his belittling of a sincerity thus narrowly understood. Romains, in the eighteenth volume of his *Hommes de bonne volonté, La Douceur de vivre* (1939), ironically depicts his hero and mouthpiece, Jallez, starting to keep his diary. He rails at the genre (and, without naming him, at its most popular practitioner, Gide), which is a literature mostly suitable for the weak, the venomous, the cowardly writers, the impotents like Amiel or some spinsters; Voltaire, Goethe, Beethoven, Hugo, Jallez insinuates, would never have kept their journals. Historical truth may satisfy some minds, Duhamel, a physician, asserted; legendary truth alone satisfies the broader ones. It is regularly when reading imaginary incidents in novels that we exclaim: "This is just what happened to me." It is just as regularly when the novelist has borrowed faithfully from life that critics exclaim: "This is false and is pure invention."

François Mauriac is too authentic a novelist, too obsessed with his criminals and his would-be saints, his possessive mothers and his repulsive adolescents, to have wasted much thought and time on the problem of literary sincerity. Yet he cherished the journals of Baudelaire, of Amiel, of Maurice de Guérin, on whom he wrote in the most somber days of World War I while serving on the Salonica front (*Petits Essais de psychologie religieuse,* 1920). His most assiduous reflections on his art have centered on the dilemma of the Catholic as novelist; because their heroes must have resisted evil before they discovered their vocation for good, Catholic authors must bear in mind their responsibility. Their duty is to avoid sincerity to oneself being used as a pretext for falling down from one's higher pursuit and consenting to baseness. It lies also in avoiding the atomization of the personality of him who, fearing that he may have changed since he tentatively sketched a certain portrait of himself a few days or weeks ago, unceasingly corrects, adds, modifies in order to be "sincere." In an essay, "Danger of assuming an attitude" in the third volume of his *Journal* (1934) Mauriac asks for "demanding sincerity which may prompt a soul to become again what it was in its highest moments," implying effort and rejecting apathy. In truth, however, neither memoirs, of which he produced fragments of great literary beauty, nor journals could satisfy in him the novelist who needed fiction to become fully sincere to himself. Interrupting his *Commencements d'une vie* (1932) which, like all memoirs, tended toward unfaithfulness to the child that he actually had been (cheerful and free from care), he noted: "Fiction alone does not lie. It half opens, on a man's life, a secret door through which his unknown soul, unchecked, can steal in."[4]

It would be hard to find a single novelist of those years 1920–1939, not even Giono, who has not been singled out by critics as the most sincere of his generation. Montherlant, a master of contradictions, a doctrinaire of the alternation from one pole of his nature to another, ungratefully contemptuous of what he had previously worshiped, is regarded by his admirers as the most sincere of writers. For he confesses, not his humility, but his inordinate pride, not necessarily his tender or generous deeds, but his revolting ones. Like one of his dramatic characters, the condottiere

---

4. Charles du Bos, in the fourth volume of his *Journal* (1928), lauds Mauriac for "the wild frankness of his sincerity; if by the word we mean the condition of him who says everything about himself and about others, I would not be averse to proclaiming him the only sincere person of our time. How insincere Gide appears when compared to him." Du Bos had then broken with Gide and experienced his reconversion.

Malatesta, he would gladly allude to "my crimes." Like the character in a story about ancient but decadent Greece, who loudly announced that he would ascend a funereal pyre at the next Olympic games, and did it ("La Mort de Peregrinos"), Montherlant recoiled at nothing to keep himself in the public eye. He likes to say that the object of our affirmations hardly matters; what counts is only the arrogant sincerity with which we assert them. There is no such thing as truth, or we shall never reach it if there is; thus let us practise truth to our changing selves. The aesthetics of this admirer of Spain and of the Romans is not far remote from that of the romantics, itself closely allied to Boileau and to Horace: "Si vis me flere, . . ." "The anger which you feel comes out in cries of tenderness in your work; pain in cries of pleasure; never mind what kind of emotion yours is, it is enough that you be moved" (Montherlant, *Textes sous une occupation*).

The least inventive of the novelists of the years 1920 and following, and the first, after Mauriac, to enter the French Academy where Cocteau and Montherlant finally were admitted, is Jacques de Lacretelle. No revelation on human nature need be expected from any of his novels, not even from the earliest ones, which are the only ones endowed with some vigor. An introspective, a pursuer of sincerity, he may have been hampered in his imagination by his scruples. He confided some of them in a volume of essays which bears a felicitously ambiguous title: *Les Aveux étudiés* (1934). In it, he warns us, a novelist, that is, a professional liar, blushes at expressing a true feeling. But "any true feeling, as soon as we attempt to convey it through words, tends toward artificiality." In a mediocre collection of very fugitive pieces published much later, *Le Tiroir secret* (1959), Lacretelle recurred to the necessity for sincerity in a writer. Sincerity alone constitutes a risk for him, a touchstone for the present, a commitment for the future.

"By sincerity, I understand the wish to give the first place to certain illuminations which come from ourselves. Also the impatience to lay bare a sensibility hidden from others . . . and the will to bear a testimony which, through its nude simplicity, is unique."

Julien Green (his Christian name used to be spelled Julian, since he was born of American parents, both Southerners, his father Presbyterian and his mother Episcopalian) is, next to Kafka, the most vivid visionary and the most lurid conjurer of nightmares in the fiction of our century. His novels are very unequal, and the reiteration of his twofold obsession, with the flesh and the other-worldly, loses its force in the more recent ones. His dramas are failures, and the anxiety with which every detail concerning them is mentioned in Volumes 6 and 7 of his *Journal* palls on the impatient reader, who expects an analyst of his inner life to display sterner severity toward the weaker children of his imagination. *Adrienne Mesurat* (translated as *The Closed Garden*) and *Moira* stand out as masterpieces. In them, Green eschewed the pitfall of a desperately egocentric creator, which would be to attempt to compose autobiographical or personal novels in the tradition of *Adolphe* and of Gidian fiction. His female characters seldom strike us as true, or as compellingly credible; to his hunted-out male creations he imparted his own obsessions, magnified and driven to the point of no return which is their logical outcome: murder, suicide, spiritual self-destruction. "My true journal is in my novels," he owned (October 15, 1948) in his diary. Elsewhere, he hints that his unexpurgated *Journal*, far more revealing presumably of himself and of others than the seven volumes printed between 1938 and 1958 and covering the years 1928 to 1957, is the monument through which he expects to go down to posterity, for in it a fully sincere man will appear.

It may be doubted whether factual precisions or lurid descriptions of carnal excesses will enhance the interest many of us have found in the enigmatically discreet *Journal* of Green as we now have it. It is easy to surmise that, in the aloneness to which he seems doomed, he is a sexually obsessed man. "I hate sexual instinct," he occasionally cries out in his diary (5, 241); or claims *Moira* is a "cry of hatred against flesh." On a single half page, after he had joined the ranks of the converts to Catholicism, he confided (3, 50, Dec. 30, 1940): "Does our body never weary of craving the same thing? . . . There have always been but two types of men I have truly well understood, the mystic and the debauchee, because both, each in his own way, fly to extremes and seek the absolute." The loveliness of outward nature, the fragrance of meadows, the limpid quietude of rivers lined with trees, the observation of children, the beauty and mystery of women have no place in Julien Green's diary. His readings of fiction, of theology, Pascal, Bossuet, Calvin, his frequent conversations with visitors driven by religious anguish or forsaking their faith after wrestling with demons who defeated their chastity, his picturesque sketches of a humanity hunted by lust and by the urge to seek refuge in the invisible provide the most valuable pages of his *Journal*. Instincts and sensual craving are dreaded as forces ever ready to trample creatures under their ugly weight. "What ferocious beasts we would become if a little religious hypocrisy did not intervene to temper our evil instincts." Desire and fear alternately drive mankind.

From the very beginning, Green's reflections revolved around sincerity: confession was to him a fatality and a therapy. "The only books which count are those of which it may be claimed that the author would have been stifled, had he not written them" (7, 190). But can a man be sincere in a diary? "Sincerity is a gift like any other gift. He is not sincere who just wants to be," he notes in an entry of December 19, 1928 (*1*, 7), when the young author of *Adrienne Mesurat* was twenty-eight. Periodically, he feels compelled to record that his diary could only afford a very fragmentary, hence falsified, view of him; that his most excruciating debates are not mirrored there, nor are the ecstatic moments of pleasure through which physical delight transcends the mere body and becomes a means of knowledge (*5*, 42), for the stern preachers who assail the flesh "forget but one thing: that sexual instinct comes from God" (*4*, 32–33).

More honest than most diarists, Green warns his reader that, since decency precludes his revealing in his diary the lowest in him and in his life, he is bound not to show the very highest either, for fear of beautifying himself distortedly. He laid down as his cardinal rule not to reconcile his contradictions and not to repudiate the successive selves which had been his before reaching his present, and equally transient, ego. "Solidarity with our past is solidarity with death. I have varied, I still shall vary. . . . Baudelaire lamented that, among the Rights of Man, the right of contradicting oneself should have been omitted" (*2*, 175–76, February 5, 1939). To his many visitors who begged him to destroy the complete version of his *Journal* or not to sacrifice his novels to that prolonged confidential register with which he himself grew weary, he replied that he did not believe he was impoverishing his creative power through taking those notes daily; on the contrary.

The truth, which has been perceived most keenly by an American commentator on Green's *Journal*, John H. Meyer,[5] is that the American-born novelist, harrowed with doubts about his own talent, fearful, as artists are wont to be, that his next venture may expose the drying-up of his talent, that his dramatic excursuses are doomed to failure,

5. John H. Meyer, "Day by Day," *Renascence* (Milwaukee), *9* (1956), 49–52. See also the same author on Green's *Le Malfaiteur, Renascence, 10* (1958), 151–54.

feels reassured when he publishes volume after volume of his *Journal*. For the author of a journal cannot fail as a dramatist, a composer, or a painter can; he cannot be charged with lack of structure and order, since his work is by definition disconnected; he cannot be suspected of having nothing left in him to express, since a journal may be content with noting trivia, chance encounters, conversations overheard on the street, what the diarist ate, drank, how he suffered from insomnia or from the liver. The reader who buys the diaries of Gide, Green, Léautaud, and others no longer feels intimidated by the overwhelming talent of the creator; he is reassured that his own trivia, how he eats and talks and fails to sleep and hates his relatives and is, as Green asserts, borrowing D. H. Lawrence's phrase, "crucified by sex," are in no way different from those that are deemed worthy of note in a "great" man's diary. The author himself, when, like Green, he is haunted by his failure to emerge from his aloneness and to communicate with others *(Journal, 3,* 113), wins friends and accomplices at scant expense.

"I always distrust," wrote Green in *Le Bel Aujourd'hui*, as he ironically entitled the seventh volume of his *Journal* published in 1958, "those who talk of sincerity. In general, sincere men never whisper one word about it, just as true soldiers never speak about courage." During the years when sincerity struck most of the leading writers of Western Europe like an epidemic, a number of voices were heard in distrust or in denunciation of the vogue. None of these dissenting voices was more quietly heeded, was more sanely the expression of an earnest nature and of a thoughtful experience than that of Jean Schlumberger.

Born in 1877 in Alsace, having chosen to emigrate to France at fifteen so as to remain French, an industrialist and an organizer as well as a meditative temperament, Jean

Schlumberger, a close friend of Gide and of Copeau, assisted both men in the founding of the *Nouvelle Revue Française* in 1909 and of the Theatre of the Vieux-Colombier in 1913. His first publications were poems and dramatic dialogues of some distinction but lacking in force and a novel, *L'Inquiète paternité* (1911), which is more precisely a *récit* around a moral problem, that of a father disturbed to discover that his son is not really his but the child of his best friend, and who is thus compelled to re-examine with searching sincerity his right to educate him. The theme of the relationships between father and son, seldom treated with the care that it deserves (though touched upon diversely by Strindberg, Edmund Gosse, Turgenev, Mauriac), has hypnotized Schlumberger, whose Protestant gravity probably diverted him from the more popular subject of love and infidelity. The theme recurs, wedded to the equally neglected theme of friendship, in the novel into which Schlumberger poured some of his World War I reflections, *Le Camarade infidèle* (1922), and even more in his novel of sincerity entitled *Un Homme heureux*, published a year earlier.

Blaise, the protagonist of *Un Homme heureux*, a novel in which struggle is reduced to a minimum, is the son of a wealthy industrialist, born to an existence of security and of ease, threatened only by the lack of adventure. He marries and, to his dismay, while caring for his wife normally and being loved by her, he descries promptings of selfishness in himself. One day, after worrying about some casual delay in his wife's return, he cannot quite expel the insidious thought that his freedom has been hampered by marriage and might be recovered if something had happened to her. In a moment of sincere avowal, Blaise writes: "If the life of those who are dear to us were to depend only upon our will, assuredly we would never want them to be dead, but we sometimes would forget to want them to be alive."

His quietude henceforth is corroded by the worm of sincerity—"terrifying sincerity," he calls it, "if it is understood to be that which applies to our own thoughts. . . . It lays us bare for the rest of our lives in the presence of those who are closest to us, to whom avowals are beyond recall." He discovers that his father once had an illegitimate son; he abandons his comfortable happiness, sets out to meet his half-brother, discovers him at last in America among lumbermen on the Pacific Coast. He chooses the strenuous life himself, like Gide's prodigal son, aghast at all that a pitiless self-scrutiny reveals in him:

> You want me to be sincere and you want me at the same time not to have to blush at myself? How do you not perceive that any deep feeling has ramifications which fill us with dread? Are there, for example, any creatures whom we love and whose death we have not, at certain moments, wished? He returns home when he hears of the disease of his eldest son. But in the midst of the family comfort, the demon of adventure will survive. Once again, after his wife's death, he will yield to the lure which had sent the prodigal son away. He thus sowed desolation and ruin around him.

The reminiscences of Gide's calls to freedom and, in rebuttal of inherited security, of bourgeois and religious orthodoxy are somewhat obtrusive in that grave story. Schlumberger's Protestant gravity seems to stiffen his manner and to keep the reader at a distance. The moral problem is too disembodied in its presentation; concreteness in conjuring up faces, human persons, scenery is too easily dispensed with: the collaboration of the Devil, which Gide more perfidiously welcomed, has not been allowed. But the crisis of sincerity was one which the author had to experience, and to transcend. He emerged from it, not a more con-

vincing novelist, but a saner moralist, who clearly perceived
the symptoms of the disease from which literary France between the two world wars suffered, and warned his countrymen of the perils of the cult of sincerity.

The closest of the literary friends of Gide and of Gide's
wife, along with Roger Martin du Gard, Schlumberger survived the unhappy couple, redressed some of the distortions
Gide had imposed upon the figure of his wife in his little
volume on them, *André Gide et Madeleine*, and witnessed
many alterations of truth, and the challenge to an author's
will power, which the insistence on sincerity to oneself may
entail. While Gide was trying to emulate Dostoevsky and
repudiating Corneille as a master for the youth of France,
Schlumberger advocated a return to Corneille as a teacher
of our will to become, of resistance to passions not approved
by the intellect, and showed that genuine pleasure can be
experienced in returning to the most imaginative creator
among French dramatists; his book *Plaisir à Corneille*
(1936) was the first of a score of works devoted to rehabil-
itating the early seventeenth-century tragedian. Without
Schlumberger, it is doubtful whether Malraux and Sartre
would have aligned themselves with the tradition of Corneille against the cult of Racine. Schlumberger, in grave
but lucid and cogent articles which he collected in *Jalons*
(1942) and *Nouveaux Jalons* (1943), refusing many of the
myths that befogged the sight of French literary men after
the collapse of their country, did not go to the foolish length
of declaring: "The fault is Racine's"; but he upbraided his
countrymen for yielding to "miserabilism" under the cover
and the pretext of sincerity, for complacently exposing the
most pitiful and often the most wicked in themselves.

France, the Western country probably the most strongly
unified, where education is most highly standardized and
culture most uniformly understood and honored, is nevertheless famous for producing the most contrasting talents

at the very same time. Their passion is for stressing their differences. Gide, Claudel, and Valéry met in their twenties in Paris in Mallarméan circles; they read the same writers, among them E. A. Poe, heard the same music, encouraged each other for two decades or so. When they parted ways, as they did on the touchstone of sincerity in literature, mutual distrust and bitter sarcasm became the rule. Gide was to place the search for sincerity at the core of his inner life and of his literature. Claudel, probably mindful of his failure to convert Gide, or Gide's disciple, Rivière, scorned such an effeminate complacency toward oneself; for an ardent Christian like him, the assiduous cultivation of the self excludes the one who should, "in ourselves, be more ourself than ourselves," God. For a nefarious hypnotism with the Delphic precept, "Know thyself," Claudel would substitute "forget thyself" and "do not impede the vast music around you which is inspired by God and chants His glory." The private diary was, in his eyes, poor literature and bad hygiene. "Watching oneself is a deplorable hygiene," he declared to Frédéric Lefèvre in 1925. "We falsify ourselves through watching ourselves and fabricate a sort of artificial person which is substituted for the other. . . . What we ought to be, not what we are, alone should matter for a Catholic." For quite other reasons and in different terms, Valéry, the arch-believer whose witty nihilism used to leave Gide prostrate after an hour's conversation, would have agreed with the sturdy believer, Claudel.

Valéry's literary criticism cannot be called constructive; it offered more negations than it propounded positive precepts. A dubious service is being rendered this universal doubter with the posthumous publication of his lengthy and repetitious *Cahiers*. Among the idols he pierced with his tireless barbs were, first the superstition of sources, dear to the academic minds of his day, to whom the fortuitous and simultaneous polygenesis of ideas in several minds is a defiance to rationality; then the biographical heresy which attempts to proceed from the man to his work when it would be wiser to proceed from the work to a mask and to discern impurity and contrivance of a technical nature behind the mask; and, third, the superstition of sincerity in art as a virtue. "A poet," Valéry never wearied of reiterating—he put it best in *Variété V* (Pléiade, *I*, 1321), "Poésie et pensée abstraite"—"does not have as a function to experience the poetic state; that is a private affair. His function is to create it in others." Not "how deeply has he felt," but "how well has he communicated" is the relevant question. Poets, to be sure, speak of themselves; but exactly as musicians do: "They fuse the emotions caused by the specific events in their lives into an intimate substance of personal experience" ("Villon et Verlaine," *I*, 429). Only for a musician, Valéry might well have added, a certain form exists before the feeling is elaborated and the form conditions it; thus with "Le Cimetière marin," thus with Milton or Shelley composing a very sincere elegy on the death of a brother poet, in *Lycidas* and in *Adonais*, because they had inherited a learned poetical and symbolic tradition.[6]

Taking Racine, La Fontaine, and other enigmatic personalities as his illustrations, Valéry would repeat that criticism errs wildly when it assumes that the man is the cause of the work, as the criminal is assumed by law to be the cause of his crime. Rather is the author the effect of his work than the cause of it. The past, and his own past, hold no fascination for the foe of history and biography that he was: never would he keep a diary or even glance at any critic's attempt to relate his life. The most unfelicitous of the damned in hell would be he who would be sentenced

6. For Milton's *Lycidas*, the point has been masterfully made by Northrop Frye in "Literature as Content: Milton's *Lycidas*," *Proceedings of the Second Congress of the International Comparative Literature Association, 2* (Chapel Hill, N.C., 1959).

to see over again (which is not the same as living over again)
the happiest moments of his life; Valéry, the son of an
Italian mother, would have sided with Dante against Proust.
"Never would I be the man to try to recapture time past!"[7]
The man and the author, notwithstanding Pascal's famous
assertion, often have nothing whatever in common.

Valéry denounced Pascal as falsely sincere, since he erased
and corrected and strove to dispose of words with harmonious effects. He derided what was most romantic in the
romantics, although his admiration for Hugo as a tech-
nician was great, and he never recanted his veneration for
one of the most histrionic of poets, Poe, "perhaps the most
subtle artist of the century," as he called him in his first
letter to Mallarmé, the one who had communicated to him
(letter to Thibaudet in 1912) "the delirium of lucidity."
His few references to "sincerity," in *Choses tues* (2, 494)
are sarcastically contemptuous. Asked to write a preface to
Stendhal's *Lucien Leuwen,* attracted to a kindred spirit but
amused also by Stendhal's naïveté, he mocked his much
admired egotism and denounced the comedian in him. Trying so laboriously to be natural is turning the reader, and
oneself, into a dupe. Stendhal's intonations are three or
four times too sincere. Truth and the will to truth compose
an adulterous mixture.

> *In literature, truth is not conceivable.* We know very
> well that a man unveils himself only to produce a cer-
> tain effect. . . . All that is against the custom is against
> nature, implies effort, the consciousness of effort, an
> intention, hence an artifice. A woman who strips her-
> self nude, it is as if she made her entry upon the stage.
> . . . Whoever confesses, lies. (*Variété,* Pléiade, *1,*
> 570–71)

7. Paul Valéry, "Propos me concernant," in Berne-Jouffroy's *Présence
de Valéry* (Plon, 1944), p. 4.

Friends and foes of sincerity alike, in those years when the concept and the word were bandied about with great gusto, seldom took the time or had the patience to scrutinize its diverse meanings and to explore its implications. Several philosophers, who will be considered in our last chapter, made the attempt, often in distrust of Freud's system which, in its rejection of introspection, was hardly likely to meet with much favor among French devotees of that form of psychology. Critics could not resist using the word loosely, as they do their other favorite terms, "greatness" and "profundity," themselves equally baffling to the logician who values rigor higher than enthusiasm. Not one of them ever dared, among the French, to consider sincerity as a fault or as a mark of inferiority. Simone Weil preferred the words "purity" or "loyalty," although she went far toward excising all insincerity from herself and certainly retained nothing spurious in her Jansenist way of writing. Pierre Reverdy, the most independent and one of the truest poets of his age, never ceased denouncing the facility to which the cult of sincerity may lead, while maintaining the gift of expression as primary for any artist, that of feeling vividly often being necessary, never sufficient (*En Vrac,* 1956). Students of Marcel Proust, the most obsequious and fulsome flatterer of his correspondents, presumably half sincere in his letters and even in his life, did not hesitate to praise his art as "supremely sincere," his metaphors as admirable thereby. Subsequent readers, of whom this writer would be one, would prefer to stress his fondness for baroque ornaments and even for artifices in style. Even Maurice Blanchot, the severest of all the present-day literary judges and the least suspect ever to indulge salacious curiosity, indiscreet prying into the writers' lives, or narrating the adventures of his own soul in fiction or in criticism, has not altogether shunned the notion of sincerity when commenting on "the literature of experience" as practiced by Gide and other moderns. It would be necessary to cross the Channel to encounter lovers of paradoxes like Oscar Wilde, who lamented the decay of lying and the growth of sincerity, or that typical British product, the son of a sanctimonious and rigid clergyman in revolt against all he had been compelled to absorb: Samuel Butler. The author of *Erewhon* dared maintain that duping oneself is reprehensible but lying to others is laudable; in his *Notebooks*, under the subtitle "Hoodwinking the Public," he relegates sincerity to the most rudimentary form of virtue, found at best among the protozoa.

The French are indeed a serious nation, and it is to be regretted that they never had the advantage of some infusion of Irish blood like the inhabitants of John Bull's main island. Their Roman Catholics seldom joke about their creed, or their inner life. Bernanos, who could marshal all the devices of rhetoric when his political wrath overpowered him, praised his own *Journal d'un curé de campagne* for its "dépouillement, sincérité, sérénité," all untranslatable terms, and his country priest took pity on the poor humans who never commit their deep sincerity and live only at the surface of themselves. Maurice Barrès, a Catholic agnostic, branded as superficial all writers in whom he failed to detect "the true sincerity which is accompanied by a tremor" ("un frémissement") (*Scènes et doctrines du nationalisme, 1, 2*). Simone de Beauvoir herself, splendidly free from most of our male prejudices, aware that being sincere to others often conceals a desire to hurt, to provoke, or to manipulate one's interlocutor or mate, has not eschewed that pitfall in the second volume of her memoirs: the reader soon suspects the happiness of a woman who repeats that she is the happiest of creatures and who seems to have revealed herself otherwise under the more somber fictional veil of *The Mandarins*.

Camus has hardly touched on the notion of sincerity,

only enough to protest against the misleading deductions drawn by shallow readers who imagine that fictional or dramatic characters are the projections of the author himself. *L'Etranger* has been one of the most erroneously interpreted of novels and Camus has been many times irritated by those who would imprison him in his revelation of the absurd, which, for him, only constituted a starting point for his heroes and for him. In one of his most personal, and the most romantic, of his works, *L'Eté* (1954), he protested against that childish legacy of romanticism that deems every writer purely subjective. "Even if the author happens to portray himself, it may be held as exceptional that he says what he really is. The works of a man often sketch the history of his nostalgias or of his temptations, almost never his own history, especially when they claim to be autobiographical. No man ever dared paint himself as he is" (pp. 131–32).

Sartre has treated the theme of sincerity only passingly and often mockingly. Like Proust, whose privileged moments are derided in *La Nausée,* he is a comic writer whose tragic anguish, the most insincere myth of our contemporaries and their most complacently assumed mask, has been ridiculously overstressed. In the drama *Kean,* which he adapted from Alexandre Dumas the elder, he shows the English actor repeating on three different tones, "I suffer like a dog" and, posturing before his friends, asking them: "Which intonation do you prefer?" The same comedian cynically adds: "For us actors, when a misfortune strikes us, we have to mimic the emotion in order to experience it." The subjective sorrow has to be objectified through being expressed. But the actor becomes his mask, too. "I play at being what I am," remarks Kean.

In *L'Etre et le néant,* a long section is devoted to "bad faith" (Chapter II), in which sincerity to oneself is analyzed and defined as an ideal in direct contradiction with the structure of consciousness. "It is an exigency, not a state, an ideal to be aimed at; that of being for myself what I am. . . . The sincere man constitutes himself as what he is in order not to be it." He endlessly and complacently analyzes the motives for his actions, and concludes that he cannot be known by himself. He would like to be sincere, but believes that he cannot be and resigns himself easily. Since a man can never totally conform to his conception of his own self (a conception which implies a transcendence of that self), and since he is more than that conception, his effort toward sincerity is illusory. Man, for Sartre, is not defined by his sincerity, which freezes him in his present and in his past and turns into a conscious denial of freedom. Only the future can give a sense to the past and to the present. Real good faith is in the lucidity that projects us, through a meaningful choice, toward an undetermined future.

Among the philosophical minds of the middle of the century, the one who would have been most ready to become a martyr to sincerity is a writer of arresting originality, Michel Leiris, an ethnologist by training and profession, closer in his youth (he was born in 1901) to Surrealism than to Existentialism. No volume of self-analysis in the French language is so utterly devoid of prose, of complacency, of illusions as his *L'Age d'homme,* first published in 1935, reprinted in 1946, which several good judges, Maurice Blanchot among them, would rate as a masterpiece of lucid and pitiless sincerity. "Regards d'outre-tombe," a glance, or rather, a prolonged gaze from beyond the grave, is the title of Blanchot's essay on this book, in *Critique* (April 1947) and subsequently in *La Part du feu* (1949).

Le Havre, that mercantile harbor without a past, the city of Braque, Dufy, and Honegger, the site of Roquentin's semi-mystical experience with nausea, gave birth around the dawn of the present century to the dramatist Salacrou,

the delicate and dreamy storyteller Limbour, the ency-
clopaedist and universal mocker Queneau, and to one of
the gravest of Frenchmen, Leiris. A poet of no mean talent,
Leiris—in a strange Surrealist prose text in the tradition of
Nerval's *Aurelia* entitled *Aurora* (1928) and in verse of an
artfully and lovingly chiseled Fan for bulls, *Abanico para
los Toros* (published in Haut-Mal, 1943), which mirrors
the various rites and gestures of the bullfighter and is ap-
propriately dedicated to Picasso—has reflected assiduously
on the many pitfalls of self-knowledge and self-revelation
in literature. The subject cannot acquire the needed remoteness from the object, with which it is identical, in
order to judge it. The self-prober is uncertain which of
several goals to pursue: indict himself, beautify himself,
liberate himself, empty himself of his substance in order
to create a substitute personality that will enrich others, or
tear off all masks so as to seize his most secret ego. His
method, or rather the absence of any clear-cut method, dis-
turbs a somewhat scientific spirit: how seize the unconscious and the dreams without distorting them? how render
the moments of delight and of reckless freedom from all
worry as faithfully as those of gloom and self-pity and
sterility which usually expel other readers from a private
diary?

Leiris has rejected the form of the diary, that of memoirs
which deliberately remold the past, and that of autobiography which interprets the past as insidiously directed to the
present and preparing the future. He intersperses straight
confessions of his childhood, erotic experiences (never made
salacious or even joyful, recorded with Jansenist gravity,
and apparently attained only through a struggle with many
a psychic obstacle), concise evocations of places and people
with glimpses of dreams and clinical analyses by a man
versed in Freudianism as well as in Surrealism. Of all the
Frenchmen of the first half of our century, Leiris has come

closest to Kafka through his obsession with dreams and with death. At other times, the reader is reminded of Proust, and he longs for what Proust would have achieved with the portrayal of those inhibitions, of cowardice judging itself, of shyness, of infinite scruples. Proust would have effected a metamorphosis and invested despair with a sumptuous style.

Leiris is an admirable stylist—but one who spurns all effects and all attempt to seduce or to win. His *Age d'homme* and *La Règle du jeu*, the first volume of which, *Biffures*, followed in 1948[8] afford masterly examples of a "sincere" style, that is, an almost scientific one, detached, cold, refusing intimacy as well as ornaments, perspicuous, and exact. The reader is kept at careful distance: nothing is spared to make the achievements or the aberrations of him who records them, as an entomologist or an ethnologist might do, in any way striking or tempting. He knows what vitiates any introspection and stands on his guard to shun it: "At the source of every introspection, there lies a fondness for contemplating oneself and at the bottom of any confession lurks the desire to be absolved." This remark occurs in a significant preface to the reissue of *L'Age d'homme* in 1946, entitled "On Literature Considered as Tauromachy."

The love that Hemingway, Montherlant, Leiris, and other non-Spanish writers have experienced for bullfighting is not just a fondness for facile exoticism or a search for physical suppleness and blood-shedding vigor such as ane-

8. Leiris, who has had experience of psychoanalysis, is fond of verbal ambiguities: *La Règle du jeu* is that of the game of living and of knowing oneself, but also that of the "je"; *Biffures* means both erasures and a bifurcation or crossroad. Along with Blanchot's essay, a remarkably acute study of Leiris has appeared in *Les Temps Modernes, 11,* numbers 120 and 121, December 1955 and January 1956, by J. B. Pontalis. Leiris himself revealed some personal details on his life and his artistic aims in an interview given to Madeleine Chapsal: *L'Express,* May 4, 1961.

mic intellectuals might be expected to pursue. In a commentary on Hemingway which was reprinted in her posthumous volume, *Granite and Rainbow* (1958), Virginia Woolf declared:

> In truth, story writing has much in common with bullfighting. One may twist oneself like a corkscrew and go through every sort of contortion so that the public thinks one is running every risk and displaying superb gallantry. But the true writer stands up to the bull and lets the horns—call them life, truth, reality, whatever you like—pass him close each time.

Leiris is not alone among our fervent addicts to sincerity in suffering from a bad conscience. Whatever we write remains "literature," in the contemptuous acceptance of the word, a purely aesthetic pastime unless there is a sanction to it, the equivalent of the pointed, dreaded, and desired bull's horn for the torero. That alone can bestow on the writer's art a reality and keep it from being the idle display of the grace of a ballerina. Leiris endeavored to find in a restrained, classical portrayal of his obsessions, of his most dastardly deficiencies, of his blend of merits and failures the equivalent of the bull's horn; he, too, took the bull by the horns. In fact, this martyr to lucid sincerity nearly died in 1958 from a suicide attempt which he has only lately confessed, because he felt cured of some of his scruples through having been three days in a coma and, as sweet-tongued Richard II puts it, "led forth from that sweet way he was in to despair."

Maurice Blanchot, who admires Leiris and has been like him possessed by the utter vanity of any literature that is not sincere, is the author of a long and profound essay, "La Littérature et le droit à la mort" (*La Part du feu,* 1949, pp. 303–45). The puritanical hatred of all that is coquetry

and charm, of all that distorts or lies in the art of writing—
to those writers, not an art, but an "ascesis" and a sacerdotal
vocation—is a symptom of one of the most remarkable
phenomena of the recent decades: the hatred of literature
by the very persons who practise it, who live for it, in the
nation traditionally most infected or affected by the power
of letters.

CHAPTER 9

André Gide: Martyr and Hero of Sincerity

IT IS HARDLY IRREVERENT to hint, more than a decade after Gide's death in 1951 at the age of four-score years and two, that if a merciful god, in love with those who die in their belated prime, had ravished him in the middle 1920s, his posthumous fame would have fared better. He might be now, in the '60s, emerging from that symbolic inferno which he refused to dread and, two thirds of his too many books buried, he would speak to the youth of today which he yearned so to disturb and to win with the *Schauder* which still vibrates in his best pages. Like another didactic poet and essayist, Matthew Arnold, he resented the inevitable hardness of old age,

> The foot less prompt to meet the morning dew,
> The heart less bounding at emotion new,
> And hope, once crush'd, less quick to spring again.

The pursuit of sincerity, which was Gide's one constant amid a host of variables, was often waylaid into sterile and strained attempts to recapture his earlier self, after *La Symphonie pastorale* (1919) and *Les Faux-Monnayeurs* (1926). The feeble and often ill-advised attempts at "Littérature engagée" looked pale indeed in the decades when the voices of younger men, Céline, Bernanos, Malraux, Sartre, Camus, grew more strident. Gide's theater, except for his first two plays, is lamentable, and it was sad that he should not have admitted it. His entries in the successive supplementary pages added to his *Journal* afforded little new revelation. His posthumous confessions on his marriage could well have been dispensed with, not because we might be pharisaic enough to veil our faces in hypocritical horror at the avowals they contain, but rather because of their dubious sincerity and questionable accuracy. Gide found a safe haven and peace of mind in unbelief when at last most of his passion was spent; but he did not resign himself to the silence of convinced agnostics like Roger Martin du Gard or of E. M. Forster. Rather, like W. B. Yeats, four years his elder, did he desperately endeavor, when "a tattered coat upon a stick," to have "soul clap its hands and sing." But the siren in both of them had long become hoarse.

All his life, Gide's thinking turned around, and occasionally explored with pathetic eagerness, the notion of literary sincerity. An anthology of the passages, often contradictory, more often still repetitious, all obstinately fragmentary, in which he discussed the moral and aesthetic implications of the concept would fill a slim volume. André Walter, his earliest alter ego, Michel the immoralist, even the Nietzschean and Biblical admonisher of Nathanael, the ironical and priggish friend of Angèle in *Paludes,* Alissa and Jérome, the Swiss pastor, insupportable Edouard losing then recovering his diary and cogitating on his never-to-be-finished novel—all have been tormented by the urge to be sincere to themselves, some of them losing their souls in the process of saving what was dearer to them than life. It would be easy to adopt a superior attitude toward many a Gidian pronouncement on the subject, to detect inaccuracies in his autobiography, complacency in his confessions, coquettishness in his tricks of now displaying, now concealing the most intimate in himself, and a monstrous egotism throughout it all. Gide himself has, through his repeated revelations, provided his future critics with a whole panoply of weapons with which to pierce him. He may have at one time relished appearing like a martyr. Diabolically, he probably encouraged Francis Jammes, Paul Claudel, Henri Ghéon in their endeavors to bring him within the fold of Roman Catholicism, exposing their clumsiness and their arrogance thereby. He may well have relished the lessons in Christianity and in humility which were proffered to him, in sanctimonious and plaintive tones, by René Schwob, a converted Jew, in *Le Vrai Drame d'André Gide* (1932), or in harsher and more magisterial language by other converts such as Charles du Bos, Gabriel Marcel, Jacques Maritain, and a convert to dogmatism and "extreme rightist" politics, Henri Massis, in *André Gide et notre temps* (1933). A few typical lines in an article by Henri Massis in *La Revue Universelle* of March 15, 1935, afford a sample of his pompous aversion to the Protestant who had nearly become a Catholic and ended up as an atheist:

> As to us, Catholics, we have the sacraments and in particular that of penitence, thanks to which we can free ourselves from what weighs over us, unburden ourselves of what prevents us from living, and thereby again become more fully men. . . . It is now clear in the name of what we have attacked André Gide. The question for us is to defend what he threatens to destroy: the notion of man, on which civilization is founded.

Sincerity might well prompt the French in the second half of this century never again to parade the phrases "notion of man," "defense of man," and "human condition."

It would be more just, if not more Christian, to bear in mind that Gide's struggle to become a "sincere" man—emulating Montaigne, with whom he stressed his affinities in a small volume devoted to him, as well as Rousseau, whom *Si le Grain ne meurt* recalls, as does his attempt to borrow the latter's motto "Vitam impendere vero"—was to him as a young man a question of life or spiritual death. Sacrifices were entailed, clearly faced, and unflinchingly accepted. He refused a standard literary career of the kind that French rebels almost invariably consent to, as aging coquettes or demi-mondaines become resigned to marriage, opening a well-thinking salon and a career in good works: Valéry and Claudel (after a humiliating rebuke), both friends of his youth, Cocteau and Montherlant, *enfants terribles* and unrepentant Corydonians, all won a seat among the august Forty. There lay more than a grain of truth in Gide's sally to Edmund Gosse: "And to think that, had I not loved literature so much, I would now belong to the French Academy!"

If he was ever to survive as a man of letters, Gide had to liberate himself from his family background, from the constricting rigidity of his home solely administered by self-righteous women after his father had died, from his shyness and the solipsism it fostered, from the cult of esoteric literature and of rarefied symbols. His early conviction that he was not just like the others and that forcing or warping his nature in order to conform would amount to a spiritual mutilation, drove him to stress his difference from the hopelessly normal and conventional herd. "Sooner murder an infant in its cradle than nurse unacted desires," he was later to discover, and to translate, in Blake's *Marriage of Heaven and Hell.* The clarity that the French literary and classical legacy had bequeathed to him could not readily be his. To a greater degree than most of his countrymen who at twenty-five turn out a thin and ingenious "novel of analysis" to reassure themselves that they are the children of a safe marriage between Mme. de La Fayette and Choderlos de Laclos, Gide had to grope first into his labyrinth and find for himself the thread of salvation which a less subtle hero had received from Ariadne. Clarity could not illuminate him at the start, only at the exit from a series of tunnels. Blake again, then unread in France, had decreed: "Without contraries is no progression." Gide wanted his own progression to be a journey inwards, to the soul and not away from it, not an easy resolution of two contradictions and mental peace ever after, but a succession of ever new difficulties and of fresh solutions every time.

A writer who has been lavish of personal revelations of himself stands to be redressed on many a detail by his future biographers; but few of these biographers, even when armed with unpublished letters and with the categories of psychoanalysis, avoid being fascinated by the main lineaments of the picture of himself Gide has conveniently offered them. Only the keenest and most prudent of them, Germaine Brée, has known how to be admiring but diffident and to question the works as a more faithful portraiture of the man. Jean Hytier's equally perspicacious study of Gide concentrated on the artist in him and probed the secrets of his style. Two factors have, in perfect sincerity, been emphasized in Gide's personal declarations: the duality with which a boy like him—whose father was from Protestant Cévennes and whose mother was from luscious Normandy—was to be afflicted and which would make him a living denial of the theories of Barrès on striking roots: his pederasty which lay at the source of his estrangement. In the context of the years 1889–97, when Barrès had reneged the audacity of his youth and had prematurely become a "lost leader" (*Les Déracinés* appeared the same year, 1897, as *Les Nourritures terrestres*, which met with complete indifference), young Gide's onslaught on the Goliath that Barrès, far on the road to the Academy, was, required temerity; he was led grossly to exaggerate the import of his dual roots; his duality was far other than geographical, ethnic, or religious. Children born from two Norman or two Languedocian parents, or from two Parisian ones, mercifully, have frequently been blessed with restlessness and savage nonconformity. Likewise, in those closing years of the nineteenth century Rimbaud, Verlaine, Whitman were not yet studied in the arcana of their sexual behavior; the scandal of Oscar Wilde's trials had not yet broken out; Loti's women and later even Proustian girls were naïvely taken to be females; Lesbianism was deemed a graceful subject for Baudelaire (who consigned those sterile embraces to Inferno), for an English poetess writing in French like Renée Vivien, or for Gide's bosom friend, Pierre Louÿs; "l'amitié antique"[1] was looked upon as a peculiar deviation of the Greeks. Innumerable students of Plato, (even when they read Taine's charming essay on "Plato's young men"), of Sophocles, of Virgil's second Eclogue, docile admirers of the virile fraternity that had bound Achilles and Patrocles or Pelopidas and Epaminondas (the latter the object of Montaigne's superlative admiration) never suspected there could be anything strange in these friendships. Again Gide's perspective in making so much of his sexual difference was commanded by the mores then prevailing and, at the start, was "sincere." Later, however, in our opinion, his stress on homosexuality distorted his whole view of his career; in *Si le grain ne meurt* and in *Corydon*, which he declared (let us hope, with his tongue in his cheek and a gleam in his eye) to be the most important of his works, he

---

1. A serious and learned volume entitled *L'Amitié antique,* by the philosopher Charles Dugas, appeared in 1894. We do not know that Gide ever opened it. Its first quotation was the beautiful line uttered by the first of the pretenders who sees Ulysses led by the swineherd Eumeus to Penelope: "For always the gods lead the like to the like." *Odyssey,* 17.218.

contributed to giving a false slant to almost all biographical and critical studies of him. Even had he been "normal,"
Gide, we hold, would never have placidly submitted to the
conventionality of behavior around him or to the principles
of religious and ethical orthodoxy which had been preached
to him. Even his marriage was less amazing, to use Meredith's epithet, than he dramatically, appealing to the reader's sympathy, pictured it to be. It was, like many others and
more normal ones, founded on half-lies and on a tacit agree-
ment not to discuss, with scant purpose, what lay beyond
any remedy but required mutual forbearance. The revelations of Michel's becoming the accomplice of Mokhtir
after he stole the scissors and of his subsequent wrestling
with his farmer on his Normandy estate, those of Edouard
laboriously attempting to seduce the teenagers and boring
them with his dissertations on how to write a novel when
one has neither imagination nor sensibility, even the confessions of the author discovering in North Africa how
alluring for some natures may be "what remains of sunni-
ness on swarthy skins" (when not accompanied with feminine curves) are likely to pall on the sophisticated readers
of 1965. The audacity today would be to dare picture two
adolescents impervious to each other's charms, or a parent
and a child who have never been brushed by the slightest
temptation of incest.

André Gide's famous journey to North Africa to capture
his own Argonautic fleece took place in 1893. Two years
earlier he had attempted to write a desperately sincere little
book, *Les Cahiers d'André Walter,* and, the very last day
of that same year 1891, he had reached, in his *Journals,* his
first (provisional) definition of sincerity. The "ejaculations"
of those *Cahiers* (the scornful characterization was his, at
a later date), supposed to be those of a hyper-romantic young
novelist who died prematurely and insane, the emanation
of Gide's tense sensibility, were not poured into a form

which could endow them with any force of conviction. Werther, Joseph Delorme, even Balzac's Louis Lambert were André Walter's ancestors, and Flaubert in his early *Mémoires d'un fou.* The dying writer's chastity prevented his communicating with his beloved, as did, even more, the awareness of the inadequacy of words and of the awkwardness of looks and gestures. "Often the preoccupation [in order to convey the depth of feelings which stifles the words] of appearing to be moved takes the place of sincere emotion." Under the immaturity of the form, however, and under Gide's lachrymose sensibility, degenerating into mawkishness, the author's lifelong and most valuable weapon was unsheathed—very timidly: irony. He subsequently declared that "la morale" was the stuff of which all his books were woven, elsewhere that only in his style lay hidden and to be deciphered the secret of his works; but never was he more lucid than when he confided that, apart from *Les Nourritures terrestres* and from then on, all his writings were ironical. The best of his early treatises, along with his first attempt to delineate two characters having a semblance of reality in their dialogues and in their deportment, *La Tentative amoureuse* (1893), refreshingly mock the Symbolists. Gide laughed at himself for his sojourn among their hothouses. The theme of travel, endeared to the sensibilities of a generation which (Rimbaud and Claudel excepted) seldom ventured far away from France by Baudelaire's poems and Mallarmé's "Brise marine," is as essential to that brief work as it was to the contemporary *Voyage d'Urien* and to the *Traité du Narcisse* of 1891. Those sudden, whimsical departures for Britain, Berlin, Russia, North Africa, the Congo (but never for the New World) will periodically mark Gide's career. He was not, unlike many a modern author, seeking new subject matter or a new setting for his stories, but rather that emergence of sincerity which (he declares as much in *Les Caves du Vati-*

can) takes place in us when we break with the chain of familiar habits and effect a gap in our memories.

The earliest reflection in Gide's *Journals* on sincerity displays his moral earnestness and his scrupulousness as a stylist intent upon eschewing the delight in far-fetched verbal rarities and romantic exuberance which then affected the rank and file of Symbolism. Both concerns will coexist to the end in Gide:

> The most difficult thing, for one who has begun writing, is to be sincere. I must stir up that idea and define what artistic sincerity is. Provisionally, this is what I find: let never the word precede the idea. Or else: let the word always be made necessary by the idea; it must be irresistible, irrepressible; and the same is true for the sentence, for the whole work. And for the whole life of the artist, his vocation must be irresistible; he should not be able not to write. . . . The fear of not being sincere has tormented me these last few months and prevents me from writing. Oh, let me be perfectly sincere.

Much of Gide is already present in his early notations and in his youthful treatise; the same is true of Valéry, of Suarès, even of Proust among the men of that generation—and perhaps of nearly all others. This does not cast a doubt on Gide's maturation, which artistically led him to a greater mastery of his prose and a sedulous avoidance of too obvious mannerisms; more secret ones were later substituted for those of *Paludes* or of *Les Nourritures terrestres.* But the much abused notion of evolution does not assist substantially our understanding of Gide, or of others, as artists or as men. Gide's passion for sincerity drove him to turn away with an almost physical revulsion from the facets of himself which he had displayed in full glare in the work just completed: from *Paludes* he passed on to *Les Nourritures terrestres,* from the doleful, vibrant, almost mystical *Numquid et Tu?* to the impious and ironically antireligious *Symphonie pastorale.* The case is frequent among artists and even among critics: they do not wish to be limited to only one of their masks; the personality just delineated, sent into the public domain, at once becomes a corpse to which their vital instinct refuses to be chained. The famous Gidian, perhaps even the Goethean, evolution is half a myth. Everything coexisted in him from the start. What is expressed successively was in fact simultaneous. Gide's overcareful listing of his readings, similar to what has been termed in Yeats "misplaced intellectual loyalty," led him, to the delight of professors in search of dissertation topics for their students, to magnify the influences he might have undergone successively: Heine, Schopenhauer, Goethe, Nietzsche, Dostoevsky, Blake, Browning, to mention only a few of the foreign ones. In truth, Gide did not lie when he submitted that, had he encountered none of these men, his development would have in no way proved different.[2] His capacity to assimilate, appropriating what he needed or already subconsciously yearned for, to reject all else, was vast—as with most creators. On the central issue of sincerity, he did not evolve and reach greater depths in his middle years or in his old age than he had at thirty. He dug into one or another of his own strata, now near the surface of himself and now more deeply, according to his whims or to the promptings of chance. His standing and studious care was not to yield to conformity out of mere laziness, and to beware above all else of "that sort of wisdom

2. The point is made in Germaine Brée's *André Gide, l'insaisissable protée* (Belles-Lettres, 1953). I have treated it in "André Gide et les problèmes d'influence en littérature," *Modern Language Notes,* 57 (1942), 558–67.

which is only attained when one has grown cold and weary"
(*Journal,* January 25, 1931) and is hardly more than an
anticipated image of death.

For the writer, even the sincerest one, expression is primary and conditions all else: he must first of all love or hate
words; he must either delight in the ease with which he
finds those that convey his emotion as a woman does in the
dress which expresses best the momentary state of her
"soul," or he must be stimulated by the wrestle with a garb
which does not fit him or which paralyzes him in a strait-
jacket made for his predecessors. Things would be simple
if the epithet sincere could be pinned on one style alone.
The problem is infinitely more subtle. An artist must be
of his own age, within limits, preferably without being
aware of it: even the painter who concocts fake Vermeers
or Van Goghs or the most adroit pasticher of La Bruyère
or Balzac unwillingly incorporates into his depersonalized
imitation a curve, a nuance, a preposition, a stylistic inver-
sion which betrays his own age. Yet the genuine artist is
also he who shuns what around him is likely to become
trite, sheer mannerism, a temporary affectation and who
transcends his own period without forsaking that which in
it vibrated with life.

When he was most overpowered by his emotions or carried away by the ideas around him which he made his own,
Gide was tempted, as youth is likely to be, by glowing or
sonorous words, exclamations and interjections interrupting the sentence in its middle, harmonious repetitions and
assonances, long adjectives and present participles sinuously
tracing a sort of curve in the sentence before they allowed
it to fall back on some melancholy verb or adverb. Such a
manner of writing could not be characterized as rhetorical
in the sense that Ciceronian cadences were, or even Bossuet's majestic periods, for which Gide repeatedly declared

his admiration. It attempted to convey, and even to prolong in the ear and the sensibility of the reader, the emotion genuinely felt by the young author of *Le Voyage d'Urien* or *Les Nourritures terrestres*. Even as late as *La Porte étroite* (1909), the evocations of nature, of the changes of seasons punctuating the growing estrangement of the two protagonists, sentences curving caressingly to mold the growing desolation in two hearts once ecstatic with poetry will occur; the contrast will be all the sharper with Alissa's progressive aversion to all sensual beauty and to all art.

When Gide decided that sincerity should govern the manner of his writing as well as its substance, it appeared to him that musical fluidity and the pursuit of rare words such as the Symbolists had made fashionable should yield to more simplicity. His change was one which most French writers have undergone: from romantic exuberance to restraint, from the temptation to amplify which dilutes the emotion toward understatement; Chateaubriand, Michelet, Barrès had done likewise. "My emotion never plays with style," Gide wrote in the second preface to his *Voyage d'Urien*, "out of too great a fear that, later, style may play with it; it needs words and seeks to be on intimate terms with them. I like words as obedient confidants." Several notations in Gide's *Journals* will, at several stages in his career, vent his impatience with all rhetoric and all romanticism (March 6, 1916; February 9, 1932), his eagerness to prefer succinctness to eloquence. He will, not unreasonably, wax impatient at those disciples of his who, in the 1920s, discovering his long neglected *Nourritures terrestres*, imprisoned him in that early work which he had long ago transcended. The book was interpreted by those oversedulous disciples as a manual of sensuous exaltation, as a plea for desire set above fulfillment and for a deprivation that enhances enjoyment. Gide disavowed them, and, in 1921 in his *Journal* (p. 718), he contended that in truth only "the strict and the nude attracted him." He continued:

> When I began to write *Les Nourritures,* I understood that the very subject of my book was to banish all metaphor from it. There is not one movement of my sentence which did not correspond to a need of my mind; most often it is only a need for order. The eloquence of a writer must be that of the soul itself, of the thought.

Gide's conviction thus would seem to have been that, valuable as spontaneousness may be as perhaps the root of all sincerity, there is no such thing as a spontaneous style. Words must remain this side of the intellectual or emotional content instead of magnifying it: like Valéry, he grew to dislike *gros mots* and to affect litotes, in which he hailed the noblest achievement of classicism: to express the most through saying the least; "an art of shame [*pudeur*] and modesty": a reserve which is not coldness but incandescent glowing and long preservation of its heat rather than a deceptive blaze.[3] Far from loudly discarding all rules, sincerity in style bows in humility to artistic demands which force it to acquire greater depth; it implies a process of selection and of simplification. The passages in Gide's prose which might appear as the most heart-rending to the casual reader, such as the religious effusions and Pascalian implorations of *Numquid et Tu?* (1916) and the *Nouvelles Nourritures* (1935) with their Communist condiment and sensuous élan, are among the least sincerely felt works of Gide. The vibration, we have it from him, turned out to have been a fake one; the form of the Biblical or Rimbaldian verse had long ceased, in 1916 or in 1935, to be a natural one for the author's cultivated and somewhat stilted fervor.

3. See *Incidences* (1924), the two "Billets à Angèle" on "Classicism" translated in *Pretexts* (New York, 1959), pp. 195–99.

In a land like France where, from that of love and that of cooking to prose writing and to musical composition, most arts have long been codified into precepts and searchingly analyzed, it is inevitable that periodically rebels should arise and proclaim the value of spontaneousness. Gide confessed that Rimbaud's fascination over him had once been blinding and (in a letter dated June 4, 1911, to Rimbaud's brother-in-law) that "the *Illuminations* had been my viaticum, almost my sole nourishment, during the months of convalescence which had counted most in my life." Deliberately, a year before his own *Nourritures terrestres* appeared, and were shrouded in silence, he had plotted, he wrote to André Ruyters, "to precipitate literature into an extreme of sensualism from which it could not but emerge altogether regenerated." The admirer of Dostoevsky and of Whitman that Gide became revolted more than once against the oversedulous care with which the French tend to refine their experience and to obliterate its immediacy. The cult of Life capitalized and rhapsodically invoked raged in the first decade of the century in France, when Nietzscheism provided easy gospels of intense if not perilous living. Gide occasionally, even through Edouard's ponderous confidential notes in *Les Faux-Monnayeurs*, voiced his concern lest life and art be severed; in my best constructed sentences, Edouard intimated, I once used to feel my heart beat. But "henceforth, between what I feel and what I think, the link is broken. And I wonder if the very impediment which I feel before allowing my heart to speak is not what hurls my work down into abstraction and artificiality." Earlier in the same novel, Edouard had jotted down in his diary how a distaste for psychological analysis had grown in him when he realized that a man experiences what he imagines he is experiencing. From there to thinking that he imagines he experiences what he experiences the transition is slippery.

Such an indictment of analysis that desiccates and of
mental dissection that murders hardly represents, however, Gide's final view on the value of spontaneousness as
the way to sincerity. First because he did not have far to go
to notice—among his family, his friends and those whom
we call "the people"—for whom Gide confessed, in an early
letter to Marc Lafargue in *Prétextes*, unreserved scorn—
that allowing oneself all freedom and expressing what is
readiest in us is far remote from sincerity, and even more
from profundity; it is plain triteness, even vulgarity: platitudes, clichés, desperately ordinary feelings (*Journal*, November 24, 1928). Automatic writing dear to the Surrealists,
torrential confessions poured into the psychiatrist's ear, interior monologues however arty would bear witness to
Gide's remark. In order to reach back to what was first intensely felt and perhaps once spontaneous in us, an arduous
task of pruning, scratching, discarding has to be undertaken. The less cultured people are also the readiest to
undertake this work of selection and to strive for the perspective which places our "truest" emotions in their rightful light and disentangles them from the transfiguration
wrought by memory. They adopt not only triteness of
language but also conventionality of feeling (*Journal*,
February 10, 1929). Sincerity is a more elusive goddess: she
requires prolonged courtship, like the Précieuses of the
Hôtel de Rambouillet.

Here and there, in scattered and random notes, Gide denounced some of the obstacles that stand in the path of the
would-be sincere artist. Plasticity is one of them. A novelist
is very often a man endowed with a gift of mimicry. He
observes, probes, reproduces the features his sharp eye has
noticed, caricatures, pastiches. Gide was by nature uncommonly shy; he could be seized with girlish fits of crying;
twenty times in his diary, he records that he burst into tears
on playing Chopin, on reading a line of poetry or merely the

name of Agamemnon. Indeed his *Journal,* and the nasty digs (the French have the marvellous word *rosseries* for them) at one or another of his contemporaries acted as a revenge for his "secret malady: my humility" (March 1, 1917). He could humble himself like any Dostoevsky character; he could not bring himself to say "no" to those who sought his company, questioned him on his work, pestered him with their own confidential avowals or their professions of admiration. Reluctant to disabuse the friends who endeavored to bring him over to Catholicism or to the Royalist party, later to Communism, anxious not to rule out such a possibility in him, he repeatedly led them to believe he was one of theirs until the day when, through fleeing, or through one of the scandalous moves frequent with shy men, he would brutally disabuse them. Francis Jammes and others were not altogether guilty of imagining they had won him for the devout life.

Such pliability can be used by writers as a tactic. Gide, when reading the posthumous letters addressed by Proust to Madame de Noailles, replete with obsequious praise, noted on July 28, 1931, that the novelist could not possibly have been sincere in those hyperboles. Still the woman poet believed every word. Proust had no reason to calculate or to expect any "reward" in return; nothing could have embarrassed him more. But as a novelist he knew how to manipulate people and that almost any woman and a number of men will swell with vanity and betray the truest, if not the most clairvoyant, in themselves, under the impact of flattery. William James is supposed to have remarked: "What we love most is praise. Philosophers call it recognition." Gide never indulged such gross social comedy. But his power of sympathy was so great and so easily set in motion that, in a phrase reportedly used by Tennyson apropos of a fellow poet on the verge of death, Arthur Hugh Clough, reading out his last poem to him, "Like every true artist, he was moved by his own pathos." Vainly did he implore his heart to harden itself against that "ruinous sympathy, the counselor of all compromises" *(Numquid et Tu?)*.

But Gide knew how to turn that plasticity of his to some profit to his works. Through a process of depersonalization, he was able to become in turn, in all sincerity, each of the characters he was portraying. He is Alissa as much as he is Jérome, if not more so; he could enter into the character of Amélie, the pastor's wife, while he was seeing himself also as the pastor educating the young people (not of Gertrude's sex) whom he loved and of whom he grew jealous. Two notations in the *Journals* stand among the most penetrating remarks made by Gide on the vexing question of the role of lived experience in a creator. The first occurs on July 22, 1922. In it he discards the fallacious distinction between subjectivity and objectivity. "Each book, as soon as it is conceived, disposes of the whole of myself. . . . I have no other personality than the one which is required by that work. . . . If I happen to paint myself (and at times it appears to me that no other painting is possible), it is because I had begun by becoming the very person I wanted to portray."

On February 8, 1927, he dreamed of prefaces, never written, in which he would have elucidated further the distinction between objective novelists (those who first look at the gesture, the concrete appearance and interpret them) and the others, with whom his affinities are closer.

> The other kind first attaches itself to emotions, to thoughts, and runs the danger of remaining powerless to depict anything which had not first been experienced by the author. . . . Everything emanates from him. He is the sole guarantor of the truth which he reveals, its sole judge. All the heaven and hell of his

characters is in him. He does not portray himself; but what he portrays, he might have become it if he had not become himself. It is in order to write *Hamlet* that Shakespeare did not allow himself to become Othello. . . . Nothing is accomplished unless I have been able to become that fictional person, to the point of being taken in myself, to become so depersonalized in him that I am charged with having never been able to portray anyone but myself. . . . The embarrassing difficulty is subsequently to return to my own self for, in truth, I no longer am very clear about who I am. Or, if one prefers, I never am; I become.

It is clear that this sincerity in the creator no longer implies a rigid posture in him and a moral rejection of what might infringe on his principles. A being of dialogue, as Gide always defined himself, lost in the confusion with which the fictional characters (or the demons to be set free) befog the creator's mind, he had to create in order to grope toward some sort of clarity. Only in the work of art, with its sharp outline and its solidity similar to those which Pirandello's characters sought in a drama, fleeing the cloudiness of real life, can the novelist reach a state of equilibrium—and then hasten to stumble from that temporary security into the new confusion out of which another work will emerge. An artist who knew himself before he began writing is doomed to frigidity. "To know himself is the very last thing to which an artist should lay claim; he can only reach that goal through his works, through producing them" (February 10, 1922).

The use of the verb "to become" in a Goethean and Nietzschean sense, implying that sincerity was a dynamic process, not a state ever to be safely reached and avariciously treasured, is reminiscent of the famous motto for Gidean sincerity: "Deviens celui que tu es," Become the one thou art. This came, as is well known, out of Nietzsche's "Werde wer du bist." "How one becomes what he is" was the phrase affixed to Nietzsche's *Ecce Homo*. Nietzsche had encountered it in Pindar's second Pythian Ode (line 72), addressed to Hiero of Syracuse: Γένοι οἶος ἐσσὶ μαθών: Become what thou art, having learned [what manner of man thou art].[4] Various interpretations (see note 4) can be offered of that cryptic motto, as of Polonius' equally celebrated "To thine own self be true." The implication is that the person that we become, after having sloughed off the borrowed garb of youth, the influences of our teachers, the bastardy of assumed or unauthentic progenitors (Gide, and Sartre after him, have been haunted by the theme and symbol of bastards—probably, hinted a woman commentator, as an aftermath of the many adulterous liaisons which had filled the novels of the preceding era) is the authentic one. But who shall decide whether we reach authenticity at thirty, or at fifty, or on the brink of death and the final backward glance?

Wisely, Gide nowhere revealed to posterity where or when he had most fully become the one that he secretly was or how we could reach there ourselves. But he did scatter a few winged seeds here and there in his writings and proposed a few partial, often negative, recipes.

The first is not to fear inconsistency and not to stifle our contradictions, as uncouth young men, when they first share in the intoxication of logic, are naïvely tempted to do. The

---

4. The Index to Nietzsche's *Gesammelte Werke* (Leipzig, Alfred Kröner) and that to the *Gesammelte Werke* (Munich, Musarion Verlag), give "Werde wer du bist" as the formula summing up a famous development at the beginning of *Schopenhauer als Erzieher*, just before the famous advice: "Your educators can be nothing to you but your deliverers." In Pindar's second Pythian Ode (third epode, end) the meaning is far from unambiguous. Some have translated it as "Learn thy true self and live it"; others as "Sis, qualis es, tui recordatus," "Be ever such as thou hast been taught to be," "Sois tel que tu as appris à te connaître."

precept is not novel: from Montaigne to Rousseau, from
Novalis to Emerson, Walt Whitman, Renan, and, closer to
us, Montherlant, advocates of subtle or blatant contradiction make up an impressive company. The desire to baffle
others, to make oneself more interesting to a puzzled audience, to appear unpredictable often lurks behind coquettish
and belabored inconsistency in women, and in not a few
men who attempt to steal women's weapons. For some natures like Gide's, however, the acceptance of one's contradictions was an act of intellectual courage. It entails the
fearless and ever to be renewed journey from one pole of
our being to another—hence a wider expanse than is
covered by those who slide down their path with walls on
each side sheltering them— and the movement which maintains curiosity. Vincent, from the sanitarium where he
meditates in *Les Faux-Monnayeurs,* before he sinks into
disintegration, is one of the many Gidean characters who
maintain that to suppress dialogue in themselves would be
tantamount to stopping life. The private diary, as exasperating a device as it can become in Gide's fictional universe,
where even the gardeners, the maids, and the procurers may
be envisioned taking notes daily on the progress of their
sincerity, was for him the means of maintaining the dialogue even in solitude. As soon as an idea, an emotion, a
passing whim has been jotted down, the diarist, relieved,
joyfully bounces back to the opposite mood or view and
records it, feeling renovated by the contradiction. Better
appear fickle than to secure consistency at the cost of our
naturalness and through stubborn and morbid clinging to
what we once expressed and then believed we should remain faithfully enslaved to. A complex nature has expressed
only one aspect of itself even in the least coherent of books
and acknowledges its duty to the public to touch up that
portrait from other angles. Renan had erected that urge
into a subtle system. Gide, in the first entry of his diary for

the year 1927, was tempted to proceed likewise. What was
true for the historian or the essayist is even more relevant
to the novelist's art, for his subject is relations founded on
affinities, friendship, love. And the very essence of tenderness or of passion, Gide repeatedly noted, especially in
Edouard's journal in the eighth chapter of *Les Faux-Monnayeurs,* lies in each of the loving partners fashioning himself or herself according to what the other wants or expects:
"Whoever loves renounces sincerity." In the realm of feelings, the real and what is imaginary, assumed, pretended
are hardly distinguishable.

But even those readers who distrust logic when it might
tend to drown the *esprit de finesse* under the weight of
geometry may reject the implication that in contradictions
with oneself lies genuine sincerity. Gide, like many a man
of letters, had much of the woman in him and well knew
what a charmer a man can be when he attempts to please
and flatter young interlocutors by talking about himself
with intimacy. In his later years, he appeared like a high
priest of sincerity to his young and charmed admirers, and
in days when French writers ennobled their calling by magnifying it daily as a "Défense de l'Homme," he was hailed
as the champion of a truer notion of man. With Gide, Malraux once peremptorily averred, "a great human current
has found its modern expression, as it once had with Phid-
ias, Montaigne, Goethe: the defense of man attacked by
the Gods." The gods were not over-relentless in striking
aging Gide, surrounded with respect and with friends, with
their Nemesis. But Gide's most perilous foe was the tendency of any pursuer of sincerity to mistake complacency
and even exhibitionism for sincerity.

Some of Gide's avowals bordered on cynicism, not in his
Journal which was discreetly expurgated in consideration
of his wife, but in his autobiography. They yielded to a
peculiar desire to arouse his well-thinking friends against

himself, to play the part of a martyr at a moment in his career when he must have known he was too well established to alienate his public and had nothing to lose, not even honor. A huge element of literature lingers in *Si le grain ne meurt:* several scenes are very highly dramatized and rank among the most felicitous to occur anywhere in Gide's narrative accomplishments. The sketches of the Protestant family with which he chanced to visit as a boy in the Cévennes, of some of the literary aesthetes in Symbolist *cénacles,* of Pierre Louÿs and of Oscar Wilde are striking portraits with skillful effects of light and shade. Gide's autobiography, which is composed artfully, knowingly omits a great deal; it sifts the significant out of the mass of insignificant recordings and undramatized reflections of the *Journals* and is likely to outlive the *Journals.* But, on a criticism of his mentor, Roger Martin du Gard, who complained that he said too little, Gide was led to reflect further on the limitations to sincerity which the still higher ideal of *le naturel* proposes. At the end of Part I of *Si le grain ne meurt,* he appended the following footnote:

> But there is a degree in confidence beyond which one cannot go without artifice and without straining oneself; and naturalness is what I seek most. No doubt a need of my mind leads me to simplify to an excess, in order to delineate every feature more purely; drawing implies selectiveness; but most embarrassing is the necessity to present as successive states of dim simultaneousness. I am a being of dialogue; everything in me fights and contradicts itself. Memoirs are always only half sincere, great as the concern for truth may be; all is always more complicated than is said. It may even be that we reach closer to truth in the novel.

On the whole, Gide was too much of a Puritan, and of a Nietzschean, to consent to the facility to which sincerity

would lead if it were equated with contemplation of oneself, uncritical and complacent acceptation of all in oneself, and a boyish exhibitionism. Early in his career, he
treated contemptuously a young writer, Maurice Léon,
who, to prove his "sincerity," had put an end to his life in
1900. In December 1909, Gide poured his sarcasm on a
short-lived magazine entitled *Sincérité:* most young men
who boast of that virtue are merely pretentious, uncritical
and the very tone of their voice sounds false. "Sincerity in
art is only acceptable to me when it is 'consented' with
difficulty. Only the very commonplace souls reach without
effort the sincere expression of their personality." Far from
constituting a cheap device to win the reader's complicity,
sincerity should be rugged, even crabbed ("revêche," Gide
will repeat at the age of seventy in his *Interviews imaginaires*), and demand an unceasing search and a rare self-
mastery. The same point had been affirmed in a beautiful
passage of "Feuillets," printed with the *Journals* for 1923.
Ethics and aesthetics, in Gide, were never to part company
for long. To him, the effort to put more sincerity in literature provided the sole moral justification for literature. It
entailed a stern refusal to live only on the surface of oneself; it agreed with the Nietzschean message of hardness to
oneself, which marks real creators. Above all, in a literary
environment where it is easy to bow to social conventionalities, to yield to prevailing fashions, to subscribe to the
surrounding conception of vanity, of truth, of honor, and
even of honesty, the pursuit of sincerity led to creative dissatisfaction. Woe to those who do not even know what it
might mean to be sincere!

> There is a deeper sincerity, far more difficult to ob-
> tain from oneself than that of mere expression, and
> far more scarce. Some people go through life without
> experiencing one sincere feeling; they do not even

know what it is. They imagine that they love, hate, suffer; their very death is an imitation. . . . The true hypocrite is he who is no longer aware of the lie, he who lies sincerely. [June 21, 1931]

The noble ideal of sincerity was too lofty to be lived up to by an all-too-human and most fallible person like Gide. It proposed duties to oneself and a purely individualistic code. "What we undertake above our strength is what is called virtue," gravely pontificated wounded Philoctetes in the drama bearing his name and with the subtitle "Treatise of the Three Virtues." More virile natures than Gide's, all of one piece and brutal if need be, like that of Jean Prévost in *Faire le point,* have derided the sinuous contradictions of Gidean sincerities and, to that subtle plural, preferred, in the singular, *la franchise,* candid frankness. It must be owned that the decay of lying was proclaimed a little too early by Oscar Wilde. Between Gide's reports on those who lived close to him and the truth as others saw it, the gap was occasionally wide.

It has long been clear that, with all his heart-felt and mind-harrying torment on sincerity, Gide has not confided everything to his *Journals.* He himself had warned us (February 13, 1924) that he had not kept his diary during long periods of healthy equilibrium and happiness, but rather when he needed it in order to fight moods of melancholy. Such is the case with most literature, personal and even objective; little of it is written in the moments of intense enjoyment of life. Then, like all diarists, he was preoccupied with the way he would look to others and the figure he would cut before that posterity that mattered so much to him. Foes of intimate literature like Claudel may have exaggerated when they branded the journal as "a series of poses in front of himself by a man who is fascinated by mirrors . . . a monument of insincerity" (interview with Dominique Arban in *Gide-Claudel Correspondence*, p. 250). Jean Cocteau was equally unjust when he hinted that his rival "always confessed small things so as to avoid confessing big ones." Even so, neither Claudel in the interviews he gave prodigally in his later years nor Cocteau in his fragments of avowals proved so courageous in observing, for instance, the weakening of their senses and of their feelings, the progressive dryness which old age brings in its train: Gide did.

On two counts, however, he would not recoil, even before ridicule, even before the charge of sadistic cruelty which he must have known he would incur. In August 1942, while in Tunis, then overrun by the Germans, and amid reflections on Montaigne, on the nonexistence of God, on *Hamlet,* on the ravages or threats of age (Gide was then seventy-three), he recorded in his *Pages de Journal 1942–49* (August 3, 1942) that, two months earlier, he had been blessed with two nights of rare sensual delight. A handsome lad of fifteen had brought him, and apparently received, a rare pleasure, "a sort of joyful lyricism, of amused frenzy." Gide is careful to add that the mutual ecstasies were in no way venal or begged for, but that his young Corydon found what Aristotle terms in another connotation "the pleasure which is added to the act, as bloom is to youth." Good taste was obviously, that time, out of the question, and the *Journal* had to record such a momentous event in the career of a septuagenarian.

However, François, the young lad concerned, read the *Pages de Journal* (in which Gide had christened him Victor). While the great writer was still clinging to life and fame and his last words were collected in Paris by admirers and the thesis-subject seekers of three continents, the boy lent his notes, which contradicted what Gide had to say, to a writer, Henri Rambaud. Their book, *L'Envers du Jour-*

nal de Gide, appeared soon after Gide's death in 1951 with
a long moralizing preface by Rambaud. François asserted
that, while old Gide had showered his caressing advances
on him, he had spurned them. Their sordid quarrels
apropos of jams, sardines, and such details (food then was
scarce) did not show off the celebrated writer in a pleasant
light. Clearly, Gide might have spared us those thirty or
so allusions to "Victor" in a mediocre volume, have merely
stated as he does in the same volume (September 3, 1948)
that the urge to be liked or loved and to love had governed
his life; he would have been in no whit less sincere thereby.

Gide's posthumous revelations on his wife threw graver
doubts on his motives and on his fairness. That his love and
devotion for her, strange as they may appear to more conventional persons, were genuine and profound stands beyond question. He had implored her to alter her first determination to refuse, and to marry him; there was much
in common between them, on the spiritual and sentimental
planes at any rate. In her, young André had dimly looked
for a tender and understanding presence and for motherly
affection. She would play in his life the part of that mother
whom he had feared, resented, maligned in his memoirs,
but whom he had desperately needed. But, in the marriage
relationship, he would no longer be the one to submit and
to be dominated, as he had been by his mother after her
widowhood; he would humiliate his beloved Madeleine,
use her as a witness to some of his deviations, as a mournful
spectator of intense pleasures and joys she would not share,
but still provide the pious, restful home to which the prodigal husband returned. It is hard to believe that Gide did
not voluntarily blind himself when he maintains that she
had not read through *L'Immoraliste* and other half-veiled
avowals where she might have suspected her husband's
pederasty, or that his behavior in the course of their travels
never aroused her suspicion. In any case the urge to be as

sincere as could be in his literary works was an endeavor
to compensate for the fabric of falsehoods upon which his
married life rested. As in Gide's novels, the two partners
must have eschewed all scenes, skirted around any explanation. "Desires, I thought, are man's prerogative," wrote
Gide after her death. "It was reassuring to me not to admit
that woman could experience similar ones; or that only
evil women could."

His peculiarity, by no means unique, stemmed from his
conviction that carnal love and spiritual affection were, for
him and some other men, disassociated, and that the intimate intellectual companionship which bound them pre-
cluded physical desire, or paralyzed it. The obvious surprise in any reader, wondering why then he married at all,
appears not to have been shared by him; other men of
letters and intellectuals in the past had preferred to marry
a less spiritual mate and to have found their Egeria, Beatrice, or Clotilde de Vaux elsewhere. For nearly forty years,
Madeleine Gide accepted her role. André went about becoming the one that he was, seeking exoticism and exaltation away from her, impelled by the urge to violate not
only rules which convention and society made rigid, but
the unwritten law of order and mutual confidence of his
home. He contends that, up to *Les Faux-Monnayeurs,* the
first work he composed without taking his wife into consideration on every page, all his writings had aimed only at
convincing her. Convincing her of the legitimacy of his
impulses? of her silent guilt perhaps? Gide does not say.

Madeleine, the most constant companion of his life, perhaps the one who had instilled into him, he avers, the need
for sincerity, was hardly, and then only very discreetly, mentioned in his *Journals,* which are distorted by that absence.
Her husband's grief was deep when she died, but the man
of letters, or the martyr to sincerity, prevailed in him over
the husband and the man of feeling. He composed the

little book, *Et nunc manet in te* (1951), whose Virgilian title suggested that, Mme. Gide's religious creeds notwithstanding, she was now granted no immortality but what survived in her husband's memory, and in his works if they were to "go down to the ages." A few close friends were asked to read it. They were dismayed. The closest, most devoted one among them, Jean Schlumberger, in grieved, discreet, well-documented pages, undertook to paint the reverse of Gide's monstrously selfish portrayal in *Madeleine et André Gide* (1956). The volume, scrupulously honest and fair, rich in unpublished revelations, reads like a grave novel—the best probably that Schlumberger wrote, with more delicacy of touch in delineating Madame Gide than his own fictitious characters had evinced.

Sincerity compelled Gide, once his wife had preceded him into the grave, to add what he had excised from his *Journals,* or so he thought. There are inaccuracies, even willful distortions, however, in his account: he never was very clear on dates; he transposes incidents that occurred at a given moment on to another time and place, so as to enhance his effects; he cruelly underlines the harrowing furrows of age on her face, the weariness and loss of all charm of her body, her mental torture which at one time drew her closer to Catholicism ("I seem to be witnessing the progress of a gangrene," Gide noted in venomous terms), the sadism with which, after his escapade in England with a young man, he had the affront to tell his cherished witness and martyr, "By your side, I was rotting." What is worse is that he was offered corrections by some of his friends, who had shared the intimacy of the couple, before the publication of *Et nunc manet in te* (in English: *Madeleine*) for the general public; he heeded them not. Letters, diaries of Madeleine written before the marriage she had stubbornly and long resisted, and others written after the abnormal union which her husband imposed upon her, were available for him to use. Jean Schlumberger quotes at length from them, so as to redress the distorted view of his wife left by the (after a fashion) loving husband. Madeleine may have lacked clear-sightedness on the true sexual bent of her husband; her Protestant upbringing and the shame and repulsion she felt at the memory of her mother's irregularities and elopement (she *was* Alissa in that respect) may have caused her to accept the assumed superiority of a fraternal love and of a spiritual companionship over the vulgar satisfactions of many a marriage. But she was, or could be and could have remained, of a cheerful disposition, wisely but eagerly capable of enjoying life, uncommonly perspicacious and cultured. Her letters would have provided Gide with the elements of a fuller portrait. If sincerity implied masochism as well as sadism, turning against his married life and his wife as a means of indicting himself (for he could not but know that no book, not even *Corydon,* would harm his reputation more and alienate posterity), it should also have demanded that the martyrized heroine be presented in her own terms. Gide preferred to select and omit, occasionally to distort in order to produce artistic effects; he set the "mensonge de l'art" above scrupulous sincerity. Moral considerations excluded, and even if we must admire an author whose voice beyond the grave dared sound harsh and confess an egotism seldom equaled among men of letters, those notoriously bad husbands,[5] our conclusion must

5. Gide's portrait of his dead wife and evocation of their comic and tragic scene of 1918 when Mme. Gide made a bonfire of her husband's letters and he wept for a week, not for having grieved her, but because his letters were his supreme masterpiece (of sincere literature), called to the minds of some readers the celebrated scenes between Countess Tolstoi and her husband. But Tolstoi could retain something of a *grand seigneur's* contempt for too much sincerity—in others. Gorki, Thomas Mann recalls in his essay on Tolstoi, said he often had seen Russians undertake to pour out before Tolstoi the flood of that horrible "sincerity" which is more like the familiarity of swineherds then suddenly stop, frozen dead, having sensed his lordly scorn.

be that Gide would have enhanced his stature as a writer if, instead of a sensational volume of avowals, he had practised one of his earlier precepts: to prefer his work to himself, and force his way out of solipsism through composing a novel with the experience of his married life, creating perhaps a female character to be set beside his only living one: Alissa. Proust's counsel to Gide, recorded on May 14, 1921, might well have been heeded by Gide the sincere: "You may tell everything, on the condition that you never say 'I'."

CHAPTER 10

The Peril and the Benefits of Literary Sincerity

THE RAMBLING JOURNEY taken along the bypaths, cavernous recesses, islets, and lush pastures of sincerity through several hundred years, then opening up in our own century on a proud and royal way, should lead us to a few conclusions about what literary sincerity should be, can be, and is, and about the many fallacies to which the notion is susceptible and the genuine services which a clearer view of it may render. Many of the most worrisome problems which have engrossed contemporary theorists and practitioners of literature, in France and increasingly in other countries, have crystallized around the question: Can literature be sincere? That sincerity is to be understood on several levels: aesthetic (Does language necessarily betray? Does technique imply artifice and distortion?); psychological (Does sincerity to oneself ever penetrate into all that, in ourselves, lies hidden from us, impervious to analytical probing?); social (Is our social self to be slighted? Or do truth to others and the commitment of the author to wider groups constitute higher duties than those to ourselves? Does it really follow "as the night the day" that "to thine own self be true" assures Laertes that he cannot then be false to any

man?); finally moral (for sincerity is about the only criterion which has withstood the recent revaluation of our ethical standards undertaken by literature).

Art, at least in its plastic manifestations, and literature
are, above all, form—or so we have been told in forceful
terms in the last few decades by many a devotee of formal-
ism. The word "form," however, is a most confusing term,
since it may extend all the way from expression, superficially conceived as super-added to a content that preceded
it; to literary genres (epic, comedy, satire, etc., to which
our modern rhetoricians and literary scholastics have returned); and to forms in a nobler, Platonic, mathematical,
or Jungian sense, molding the corporeal envelope; "For
form is soul and doth the body make," writes Spenser in
his Platonic hymn "In Honor of Beauty."

Gone, however, is the day when poets such as Théophile
Gautier were content with describing their craft as that of
a chiseler, sculpting and sealing his dream in marble, or
when young Mallarmé dreamed of turning away from op-
pressive life and imitating the Chinaman painting the stalk
of a flower on a snow-white cup. The cult of formal beauty
soothed the anxiety of such Parnassians. Expression was to
them an absolute in itself which justified the world's existence. But a series of harsh jolts was dealt the religion of
form. Mallarmé, who had not been immune to metaphysical
anguish, who wrestled with God and God's absence and
replied haughtily to the scornful wind of nothingness, has
not suffered from the changed mood of the twentieth century. But the Parnassians, properly speaking—along with
Anatole France and most of the minor Symbolists, who
were hardly anything but more pretentious and effeminate
Parnassians—have fared less well at the hands of those who
had lived through the Dreyfus case, the Boer War, the
threats of revolution and of collapse in Russia and Central

Europe, and then through two world wars, with peace itself being regarded as a cold respite from hotter fighting and bombing. A new puritanism invaded the arts in the 1930s and '40s. Grace and beauty, flowers, clouds, cliffs, even women, and any suggestion that a nude could be both artistically pure and yet desirable to the normal but imaginative onlooker, were banished from painting. The women of Lipschitz, of Epstein, of Picasso and DeKooning would hardly seduce a modern Pygmalion. In literature, in a parallel fashion, tormented Jacobins have sternly called upon the art of writing to justify itself before their tribunal.

For the very fact of writing implies some endeavor to please, to surprise, or to strike the fancy of a potential reader, to convince him through beautiful reasoning or moving eloquence, to entertain him perhaps; but it can hardly lay claim to ingenuous effects or to the "unpremeditated art" of Shelley's skylark. The distressed poet finds solace in the harmonious strains in which he sings his sorrow. He wants to mourn over "the wither'd waste of life" and, like Byron in his 1815 "Stanzas for Music," he chooses a galloping rhythm which must have filled him with glee in the midst of his despair: "There's not a joy the world can give like that it takes away." Or, like Thomas Hardy, as his wife reported to Sir Sidney Cockerell, he feels elated while voicing his gloom: "He is this afternoon writing a poem with great spirit: always a sign of well-being with him. Needless to say, it is an intensely dismal poem." A writer either purifies himself of his own sorrow—like Goethe composing *Werther*—when he balances his elaborate periods, or perhaps feels invaded with pity for his own suffering or that which he imaginatively experiences—like the lovers who begin a letter to their mistresses with an indifferent yawn and, gradually inflamed with the pangs of absence and burning memories of past ecstasies, melt into tears. But an imaginative and contrived sincerity is substituted for the naked adequacy of words to the lived experience. "Such an expertly tuned sentence precludes total renouncement," Paul Valéry said ironically apropos of Pascal's sumptuous cries of fright designed to frighten the obdurate skeptics.

It is true that our literary taste has altered under the impact of the cult of sincerity. We admire in Petrarch, Ronsard, Shakespeare's sonnets, Tasso, images and figures of speech we believe to be fresh, naïve, original, when as a matter of fact they often were common coinage in their times. Tricks of virtuosity and verbal acrobatics used to elicit more admiration in contemporaries of Villon, Charles d'Orléans, even of Dante (who himself venerated some of the more artificial Troubadours) than similar feats by Joyce, Pound, Giraudoux do today, except among a few mundane or academic snobs. The immense vogue enjoyed by Stendhal as a stylist even more than as a psychological analyst (Hemingway himself acknowledged him as his master, as a score of French novelists do at present) is due to his having broken away from the sonorous rhythms and caressing epithets of the one whom he called derisively Monsieur de Castel Fulgens (the author of *Atala* and *René,* naturally).

Stendhal was among the first to distrust the patient labor of the stylist who destroys the directness of the impression he should wish to convey. To avoid the insincerity of much literary expression, he advocated, as Balzac did after him, writing quickly, thus transmitting the genuine thought or impression. After his first novel, *Armance,* he noted: "I was writing and speaking far better since I began my sentences without knowing how they would end." Gide envied him that gift and tried, vainly, to acquire it. Except for his masterpiece of poetical prose, *Le Retour de l'enfant prodigue,* Gide wrote slowly, hampered by scruples and interrupted by frequent periods of sterility. But writing quickly, for those who have not first thought slowly or steadily before rushing the flow of their sentences to the paper, may also entail a lamentable betrayal of what lies deepest within them. The automatic writing of the Surrealists has left us few striking pieces; it seldom extracted diamonds from the peat bogs of the unconscious.

The tenants of sincerity in our age have attempted to go further: to strangle style altogether, as Verlaine wanted to strangle eloquence in poetry. Every age stages its own onslaught on poetic diction and many a reformer has, like Wordsworth, attempted "to bring my language near to the language of men." In the very country of western Europe which, next to Italy, has most cherished a certain amount of care, bordering on artifice, expended on literary style, a rebellion against any forms of expression which are not those of everyday among the least educated was launched beginning in 1930 with Céline's imaginative brutality, and then later with Raymond Queneau's more diabolical as well as philological destructiveness. Neither philosophy nor literature has deemed it beneath its dignity, in our age, to meditate and experiment on language. The variegated verbal draperies of the romantics have been the butt of many an ironical barb, as constituting an impediment to the candid translation of the thought or the emotion into prose. But the Hydra of eloquence never consents meekly to its own guillotining. André Breton, Julien Gracq, Roger Caillois, Albert Camus (or, in another tongue, Henry Miller, Lawrence Durrell) in prose, Paul Claudel, Saint John Perse, Henri Michaux in poetic prose or in the most perilously rhetorical verse form, the "verset," have all upheld the claims of eloquence among us, even if they keep shy of the use of that discredited word.

Meanwhile, the puritanical diffidence of bombast, of Ciceronian cadences, of any music which caresses and lulls our inner ear, evinced by a number of champions of sin-

cerity, has scrutinized the means of literary expression trans-
mitted to the French by Pascal, Rousseau, Flaubert, Barrès,
and Proust. They have endeavored to write as if there were
to be no audience, no unknown brothers or friends to touch
or to attract. Brice Parain and Maurice Blanchot stand
foremost among those overscrupulous scrutinizers of the
pitfalls offered at every step by the use of language; Jean
Paulhan, more playfully, had sponsored their crusade. It
is true that—as Blanchot himself acknowledged in "De
l'Angoisse au langage," a series of fourteen detached brief
essays at the beginning of his *Faux Pas* (1943)—even when
he laments that he is desperately alone, the writer presupposes a public to whom he whispers that solitude is bitter,
or delectable, or becomes meaningful. No writer can ever
abstract himself totally from the effects produced by his use
of language: he may be obsessed by the silence of Rimbaud
abandoning literature altogether, by that of Mallarmé
breaking up syntax or of Joyce, forcing the reader to meet
him at four-fifths of his way and preaching the value of silence through words of twenty languages syncopated into a
new form of English. But he remains highly conscious of the
power of language, and of his own power over language,
while he acts thus. Indeed, the writer takes secret pride in
his conviction that, in severely appropriating his form to
his theme or to his mood, he remains superior to cultures
which prefer to stress the vitality of action or the deceptive
depth of thought clumsily stumbling upon abstract words.
Silence, as even severe Brice Parain concluded, may be
a worthy ideal provided we are sure of never reaching it
and dwelling in it. We cannot, like those animals Walt
Whitman envied, be "placid and self-contained." As Parain
put it, "One must learn how to speak and believe that, to
learn it is learning how to live. . . . Of the three questions of
romanticism, the Russian one, what to do?, the German
one, what to think?, the French one, what to say? It may

well be the French one, when all is said, which is the truest."[1]

The temptation of silence has perhaps not, since Rimbaud yielded to it, been more harrowingly experienced than by Simone Weil (1909–43). "To say 'I' is to lie," she asserts outright in *La Connaissance surnaturelle*. She did not take refuge in silence, since she left the substance of several volumes in her notes, and a disservice may well have been done her memory by the overzealous friends who have published posthumously six or seven books by her which she had not wished to give to the public. Pure contemplation of the divine order, purified of all desire for possession or for action, a patient and humble "waiting for God" was to her the only true religious attitude. The self has to abdicate in order that we may be granted a supernatural "knowledge" of God, obedient to some higher visitation and annihilating all lust for self-assertion or for human possessiveness implying the consummation of the object that is desired. Simone Weil had been steeped in Plato, Sophocles, and the French classics; she had been enraptured by George Herbert's poetry. She could write with artfulness and impart the *Schauder* which vibrated in her tormented heart to the reader. But she kept shy of the style that implies an attempt to please or to call attention to itself. Alone perhaps of all the French writers of the present century, she strove to reach the utmost sincerity of which she was capable through the elimination of style. Gustave Thibon, one

---

1. Brice Parain, "Lettre à Francis Ponge," *Cahiers du Sud*, *31* (1950), 115–19. Parain wrote a doctorate thesis on *Recherches sur la nature et les Fonctions du langage* (Gallimard, 1942). See also on that obsession of several modern French writers with the annihilation of language and with silence, Parain, *Sur la dialectique* (Gallimard, 1953); Maurice Blanchot, *Faux Pas* (Gallimard, 1953) and "La Litterature et le droit à la mort," *La Part du feu* (Gallimard, 1949); Jean Paulhan, *Les Fleurs de Tarbes* (Gallimard, 1941); Pierre Reverdy, *En Vrac* (Monaco, Editions du Rocher, 1956), pp. 36, 200; Vercors, *Les Mots* (Editions de Minuit, 1947).

of the two profoundly religious men whose advice she sought (often to rebel against it) related in his introduction to her *La Pesanteur et la grâce* (1948), how unforgiving she was to any trace of insincerity in Corneille, Hugo, Nietzsche. Her aim was to reduce the writer's part to that of a translator from an ancient or foreign tongue, who attempts to adhere as closely as he can to a text; she likewise wished the author to be the mere transcriber of the emotions or of the idea, which is to him like an unwritten text. "As long as nudity of expression is not attained, the thought has neither reached nor approached true greatness."

But such an arduous ascent *per angusta* toward nudity of form implies pruning, eliminating all ornaments and bombast, perhaps even desiccating the freshness of the emotion, being constantly on one's guard against excesses of language, hence destroying spontaneousness in oneself in order to reach a more striking poverty or sparseness in the style. More skill is required for such a struggle toward sincerity, and even more expert artifice, than for naïve writing. Paul Valéry, who also meditated assiduously on silence, through many prefaces, ephemeral articles, endless notebooks, remarked apropos of Swedenborg: "The sincerest man in the world, expressing what he has seen, and singularly what he has seen in a domain in which he alone was able to see, inevitably falsifies that condition of sincerity through the mere use of the common language with rules of syntax to be observed and division into words."[2] While that labor of purification, perhaps of desiccation, is undertaken by the overscrupulous writer, what becomes of the emotion sincerely experienced by the writer as a man, his laughter, his anguish, his grief, his mystical ecstasy, his burning desire? T. S. Eliot's melancholy lines in *East Coker*, when looking back upon his twenty years of "l'entre deux

2. Paul Valéry, Introduction to Martin Lamm, *Swedenborg* (Stock, 1935), p. xx.

guerres" and confessing that "every attempt / Is a wholly
new start, and a different kind of failure," most accurately
express the dilemma of the would-be sincere poet:

Because one has only learnt to get the better of words
For the thing one no longer has to say, or the way in which
One is no longer disposed to say it.[3]

The will to annihilate style implies an unflagging awareness of style itself designed to eschew its flourishes and to
sift the most genuine in our experiences or in our emotions
from what might be borrowed, assumed, feigned. It tends
to stress the author's analytical scrutiny of himself at the
expense of his free inventiveness and thus may impair his
sincerity, which might be at its greatest if he followed his
own inner necessity instead of distrusting it. It also leads
to a writer's straining of his own originality, in his anxiety
not to imitate technical devices of previous authors. In the
past, borrowing such devices had seldom detracted from
creativeness, provided the results reached through such resort to a form already polished and well refined remained
original. The fanatics of literary sincerity in the present age
have oscillated around two opposite poles. On the one hand,
the Puritans and the Jacobins, who aimed at banishing effects, superfluity, emotional intemperance from their writing: Michel Leiris, Simone Weil in France; in a different
key and intent upon the rendering of external objects, of
gestures and impressions received rather than of some inner
elaboration of such impressions, Ernest Hemingway might
be grouped among those gloomy foes of exuberance. At
the other extreme stand the Whitmanesque lovers of words

3. Nietzsche, in *Twilight of the Idols* ("Skirmishes in a War with the
Age," no. 26) had already remarked: "The things for which we find words,
we already, deep in ourselves, have transcended. In all speech, there lies
a grain of contempt."

and tenants of spontaneousness: Céline, Audiberti, Bernanos, and occasionally Jean Genet in France, Henry Miller in America and some of the unrestrained neoromantics of the Pacific Coast, Jack Kerouac and Alan Ginsberg. They conceive sincerity differently, somewhat as Thomas Wolfe might have done. Through what we must term lack of respect for their medium, they pour out deluges of words and occasionally of flamboyant images, hold their own disorder as sacred in true Rimbaldian fashion, and forget to distinguish between what is authentic in themselves and what is unconscious imitation of Rimbaud, Whitman, Céline (as is often the case with Henry Miller), and, more sadly still, imitation of themselves.

The new romantics of our century have thus striven for a more exacting truth to themselves through their rebellion against poetic diction, and through a passionate advocacy of spontaneousness and irrationality. Generalized education is liable to carry with itself a great deal of conformity; the teaching of literature in particular often consists in imposing upon countless young men and women who are destined to be businessmen, salesmen, scientists, speculators, golf or bridge addicts, or just mothers, the writing of critical essays on the authors studied in courses. It is pathetic to watch them picking their brains in order to say anything about *The Rape of the Lock,* the "Ode on Intimations of Immortality," or *The Waste Land,* which their teachers ritually and refinedly dissect at their annual conventions. They are reduced to a distrust of what they themselves feel in the presence of these texts, or even of *Oedipus Rex* and *The Tempest,* lest their true feeling horrify their teachers by its inanity or irreverence, and reap them a grade unbecoming to gentlemen. As soon as they have left college, they cease reading altogether or else they undertake to unlearn the critical processes which cramped their nascent personalities and stifled the naïve expression of their ego. They stage a return to what they take to have been more spontaneous in themselves, secretly preserved behind the crust of education. If they are writers, they proceed likewise and attempt to be sincerely themselves through being spontaneous. Like the protagonist of Gide's novel *The Immoralist,* they scratch the upper layer of the palimpsest which their mind has become through the accretions of education; they revolt against culture and revel in the tumultuous invasion of more primitive and supposedly more authentic forces into their inner citadel.

Nietzsche, through his title *Beyond Good and Evil* and many striking aphorisms in that volume and in others, stands at the source of a great many revolts against conformity and against the falsifying of ourselves which have shaken the French moderns. The history and critical appreciations of his impact upon the French since 1895 (or in the America of Huneker, Mencken, and of the "lost generation" of 1919) have not been adequately written, and the gap in our self-knowledge is thus wide. It was not Gide or Suarès or Élie Faure among the French, but Paul Valéry who wrote some curious letters on Nietzsche in his youth; and François Mauriac confessed to having been more powerfully disturbed by him than by Voltaire and other antireligious French thinkers. Charles du Bos, another Catholic, and Jacques Rivière, who was one at least for some years, were led to oppose a moral attitude to a supposedly "authentic" one by Nietzsche's provocations. In his lectures on Proust, Rivière went so far as to contrast the sincerely religious man, who dreams of redeeming and purifying what is low and unworthy in him, and thus adopts a moral attitude, to the man who, venturing beyond good and evil, seeks truth for its own sake.

The pursuit of literary sincerity thus invokes in many of our contemporaries a nostalgia for the primitive in ourselves. This is a most usual mood in weary, oversophisti-

cated, and intellectually surfeited generations, fearful of
feeling only what was felt before them, of dreaming only
dreams already dreamt, and of echoing with psittacine
monotony the teaching of their masters. In their distrust of
the nourishment overprepared and already chewed by their
predecessors, they have attempted to break away from the
passion for analysis and even from the preference granted,
in French education at any rate, to rationality and to clarity. Gide has endeavored to reach the madness in ourselves,
which prompts some of the beautiful things subsequently
made palatable through the orderliness of art. Romain
Rolland never ceased advocating passion and fervor, and
thereby communing with the people from whom musical
and dramatic inspiration should flow, instead of prostitut-
ing our artists in a market-place fair. "That art is an art
without a people," was Rolland's severest indictment of a
Parisian exhibitionist display of wit and conceit. He turned
to Tolstoi as a more sincere writer and, in 1903, in his
letters, hailed César Franck as "the most sincere of musicians since Beethoven." Henry Miller praised "the wisdom
of the heart" in his best collection of essays and stray pieces
thus entitled, and D. H. Lawrence's favorite part of our
organism was the solar plexus. An old culture must thus
periodically return to its springs and, tired of polishing
stones already extracted, and of refining devices and conventions already threadbare, proceed to a new accumula-
tion of rough materials.

The banner flamboyantly bearing the word "sincerity"
has been brandished by adversaries of moral as well as of
literary conventions. An Olympian like Goethe had once
answered that there was hardly any crime, however monstrous, of which he had not at one time felt capable. His
contemporary, the arch conservative and logical Catholic
Joseph de Maistre, stressing the need for curbs on the natural instincts of the Rousseauistic natural man, had de-

clared that, if he had never explored the conscience of a
rascal, he knew a little about that of an "honnête homme"
and was duly horrified by that alone. Modern novelists,
Catholic like Mauriac, Protestant like Schlumberger, have
laid bare the half-secret wishes of children, wives, and husbands dreaming of being freed from their parents or
spouses. "If our looks could beget progeny, with how many
illegitimate children would the world be populated!" exclaimed Paul Valéry, accustomed to the favorite pastime of
men in Latin countries, appraising fair members of the
other sex with the eye of a covetous Don Juan.

One of the purposes of literature is doubtless to bring to
light what we try to conceal or ignore in ourselves and to
explode our carefully cemented shelter of security. The
claims of sincerity have left no *terrae incognitae* in our inner labyrinths: they have rid us of much pompous Pharisa-
ism and of Victorian rectitude, taken down pathetically
deficient men like Ruskin and Carlyle from their clay
pedestals, stressed Dickens' sadism, Swinburne's peculiar
obsessions, or the earthy appetites of would-be ethereal Pre-
Raphaelites. The total picture of these men, and of man in
general, is much saner. But, under the pretext of greater
sincerity, we have also assumed that the lowest is also truest,
or the most fertile, terrain for literary exploration. One
need not be a neo-Victorian to assert the validity of our
urge toward transcendence. Freudian explanations of genius, and even of woefully average creatures, are often tinged
with childishness and throw out a challenge to common
sense, even to evidence and objectivity, which literary biographers and psychologists might well take up in a fighting
mood. The emphasis on sex urges or even on the frustration-
aggression complex, the study of rodents, of gastric secretion
in frustrated gourmets of the canine species, and of childhood as an end in itself and not as a passing phase toward
manhood, may well have misled many moderns into the

comforting belief that what is simple may explain what is very complex. In literary and artistic criticism, we have fought shy of greatness and have dissolved it as best we could into genetic or physiological components, instead of coming to grips with it.

"Ah! who will ever free my mind from the heavy shackles of logic?" cried out young Gide. The cry is typically French; logic does not constrict the brains of young people educated in a more empirical culture, where trusting one's instincts is deemed a virtue, or where surrendering, like Faust, to "der Taumel" and a vertiginous delirium is a supreme joy. With the French, the realization that the true religion of the twentieth century was that of sincerity to themselves entailed throwing a proud gauntlet to the respect for clarity, which three centuries of humanistic, Jesuit, Jansenist, and then lay education had forcibly instilled into the French. Aging Renan used to wonder with a smile at all the labor of exegesis, textual criticism, philology, and philosophical reflection which it had taken him to reach the same blissful state of religious indifference and of cheerful and tolerant pessimism which a Gavroche on the streets of Paris, even a Monsieur Homais in his Yonville pharmacy, had attained with little, if any, effort. It likewise seems to require arduous wrestling with several angels of logic and clarity for French minds to turn against consistency in order to espouse their inner sincerity with complete truthfulness.

Gide's journals are replete with the author's determinations to shun Cartesian "clear and distinct ideas" as the most perilous of all to an artist, for we dare not forsake them and, comfortably seated in them too early in life, we become the willing victims of a prefiguration of death. They also abound in involuntary contradictions and shifts of taste; like many of us, but more than most, the diarist cries out his raptures over a new book he has just opened (it may be as "unrapturing" a novel as Meredith's *The Shaving of Shagpat* or Gottfried Keller's *Der Grüne Heinrich*), to insinuate, two weeks later, that boredom prevented him from reading beyond the first half of it. Gide took issue, in his revealing volume on Dostoevsky, with the whole French classical tradition, stemming from Descartes and Corneille, which leads a Frenchman, or a character in French drama or fiction, to declare: "Faisons la lumière!", to obliterate his inconsistencies, and to mold himself according to the exemplary man he wishes to become. Far preferable, he asserted, was Dostoevsky's tumultuous display of all that rends man asunder and plunges him into gulfs unfathomable to any self-knowledge. The same dread of those abysses within the human heart and brain has imbued a number of French intellects with a distrust and fear of music as a primitive art, which shakes the physical lower depths of man, and suits negroes of Africa and America, or the Teutonic inhabitants of "the India of Europe," Germany (Victor Hugo *dixit*), but not the civilized French. The romantics of France, indeed, except for Berlioz, whom his contemporaries long refused to appreciate, were lamentably devoid of profound music, and an anthology of the statements on music uttered by Victor Hugo and by many of his successors, such as Barrès and Péguy, would not be edifying.

It took France almost a hundred years to catch up with the faith of Hegelian dialectics or of Novalis, who, in his *Disciples at Saïs,* had asserted that "to destroy the principle of contradiction is perhaps the highest duty of the highest logic." Gide, Montherlant, Green, and other tenants of sincerity formulated the need to oscillate from one pole to the opposite one ("the philosophy of alternates" as Montherlant termed it, if there lie any love of *sophia* in such an attitude), which is but another manner of being logical in illogic itself. Gide desperately wanted to be considered as a "being of dialogue," deluding himself into the belief that he had had no predecessors in the country of Montaigne, Diderot, and Renan, and even of Pascal and Rousseau, all of whom had also practised the art of opposing to each other several lobes of their brain or spasms of their heart. The surrealists, in André Breton's grave manifesto, proposed as the cardinal goal of their turbulent activity the mysterious point from which "life and death, the real and the imaginary, the past and the future, . . . the high and the low cease to be perceived as contradictory." A greater poet than any surrealist, Pierre Reverdy, who, as the most profound of the Dadaists, influenced the more quarrelsome and mystifying architects of the surrealist revolution, wrote, in one of his late volumes of reflections, *En Vrac* (1956):

> What an effort it is to be logical and consistent! And yet man becomes keenly conscious of himself only through contradiction. He is essentially contradictory; when he is not helped to be thus by others, he finds in himself the resources he needs in order to be; and therein lies what makes him another animal than beasts. The being of beasts is a one way track; that of man is a dual or a multiple highway; it always stands at a crossroad.[4]

The search for illogic, the acceptance of one's contradictions and oscillations, the refusal to make once and for all a choice among our different potentialities have certainly brought the writers of the twentieth century closer to a greater sincerity to themselves, and to the acceptance of their own truth, than their predecessors who had believed

---

4. "En vrac" means "loose," "in bulk," "piled up indiscriminately." The word comes from the Dutch and originally applied to mediocre herring piled up at random. A painter who is as serious as a painter as Reverdy was as a poet, George Braque, also advocated contradiction, or a dialectical process. He wrote in his *Notebooks*: "One should always have two ideas: one to destroy the other."

in the ultimate victory of reason over error, of rationalism over all that defied it, of wisdom over folly. Still, it is doubtful whether the gain has not been offset by severe losses. Morally as well as psychologically, the passive acceptance of our contradictions and the laying bare of them in self-analyzing fictional characters who watch for every symptom of disunity in themselves and record all that is ignoble in their desires or in their dreams may not be distinctly superior to establishing a hierarchy, an order of priority, among all the promptings which solicit our attention. To state one's complexities may make us interesting to a portion of our public; to confess our impotence at choosing among the all-too-rich possibilities in ourselves sets us on a different plane from that of businessmen, politicians, and audacious heroes of action whom we like to imagine as expert in decision-making and reluctant to lend the shelter of their skulls to several ideas at the same time. But much of the disunity in ourselves could be transcended if we agreed to mature; a certain impulse toward finding our own unity is no less fundamental in man than the contemplation of our variety. In many of the specialists of sincerity the assimilation of sincerity with inconsistency often entailed a lack of the mental discipline which might have explored the one or two main channels of their inner lives in greater depth, and, more regrettable still, it entailed an absence of humor.

Perhaps the most common interpretation of sincerity when applied to a writer or to an artist is that which demands that the creator have lived the events, have experienced the feelings, have felt the ideas or the themes which make up the substance of his work. Such an exorbitant demand may not appear to be too preposterous for autobiographical literature: we naturally distrust Cellini or Casa-

nova or other authors of mendacious manuals of self-glorifi-
cation. We check the facts and the dates of Rousseau's *Confessions* and gravely condemn his inaccuracies or distortions. We come to suspect a diarist who, having asserted his
intention to prove more truthful to himself than ordinary
mortals, willfully omits essential events of his life and otherwise fabricates a bust of himself more handsome or more
fascinatingly repulsive than reality. Many of the authors
of private journals discussed in our previous chapters,
among them Gide and Green, have thus seemed to deserve
our reprobation. The conscious pursuit of sincerity easily
leads to narcissism. Narcissus was alone when he gazed at
the reflection of his own loveliness;[5] he neither wrote nor
sang. But a man of letters has to impart his experience to
others; and his narcissism soon becomes tinged with exhibitionism. The motives he has, or invents, for loving himself do not necessarily coincide with the reasons for which
he wants others to love him. W. H. Auden expressed it
pungently in a reflection published in April 1956 in *Encounter:* "The image of myself which I try to create in my
own mind in order that I may love myself is different from
the image which I try to create in the minds of others in
order that they may love me."

No aspect of the myth of sincerity has led to as many
rash assertions, even on the part of thoughtful creators or
of prudent critics. We want Michelangelo to have been disturbed by the violent passions he painted and to have ex-

---

5. It is hardly surprising that ever since, in the last eighty years, sincerity has become an obsession with French writers, the myth of Narcissus
has also become a favorite with a number of them: Gide, Valéry, Gasquet.
No literary historian has yet treated the subject as it deserves. A moral con-
demnation of narcissism, done with subtlety and acumen, which led the
author to offer many valuable remarks on sincerity in art, has been presented by the philosopher Louis Lavelle in *L'Erreur de Narcisse* (Grasset,
1939).

perienced the feelings, both of "normal" and homosexual love, expressed in his sonnets. We insist upon da Vinci having been attracted by Mona Lisa or by his ambiguous St. John the Baptist. We even venture to contend that Perugino, Andrea del Sarto, Ghirlandaio, Carpaccio, Canova, are inferior to the greatest artists because they do not impress us with the same force of sincerity to themselves or to their art. Yet the remark attributed to Stendhal would apply to his contemporary, Canova: "In bombastic natures [*les natures emphatiques*], bombast is natural." Dufy is probably less great an artist than Rouault, at least for many of the contemporaries of Rouault who forget what is literary in his painting and relish his tragic sentiment of life: it is tempting to jump to the conclusion that Rouault is superior because more ardently committed than Dufy, who portrayed few Christs, judges, and prostitutes. But Fragonard, who once also took life playfully, has outlived Greuze, who endowed his painted scenes of family life with high, at times tragic, seriousness. Which of the two was more sincere? Rembrandt moves many of us more profoundly than does Rubens, and Bach than Haydn, and Delacroix than Ingres: is it because a more ardent sincerity lay in the depth of their art and because they had lived their works more truly?

The answer must clearly be a negative one. Bach's first Prelude in C major, with its ascending arpeggios, the recurrences of its structural devices, is admirably pure. But does it reveal anything of Bach the man, or merely display his extraordinary control over his art? Delacroix was a Voltairian skeptic in matters of faith; yet he painted several Passions of Christ, several crucifixions, and the grandiose fresco of Jacob wrestling with the Angel in the Church of Saint Sulpice in Paris. One of his biographers remarked that he, a spiritual son of the Encyclopaedists, probably an atheist, had also been the greatest, perhaps the only, religious painter of the last century.[6] The process of creation is infinitely too subtle to be reduced to any Procrustes' bed, not even that of sincerity.

First, a writer often recaptures, while he composes, a grief or a delight experienced months or years previously. It has been pointed out that Victor Hugo, in this hardly an exception, wrote his poems describing the winter during the summer months, those which conjured up vernal raptures during the autumnal season, and that his most heart-rending pieces on the death of his daughter Léopoldine alternated, in their dates of composition, with songs of sensual love. Palestrina composed his funeral laments, supposed to have been inspired by his wife's death, not as he was afflicted by his bereavement, but just as, eight months after her death, he had arranged to marry a widow, enriched by the fur trade, at substantial benefit to himself.

An author, as soon as he has given expression to one side of his nature, ceases to be engrossed by it, even ceases to be the person he was and whom he portrayed; Molière ceases to be Arnolphe after *L'Ecole des femmes* (if he ever was), as Goethe ceases to be Werther and Thomas Mann, Aschenbach. With the plasticity of creators, those writers, like painters or musicians, then become the new character they are impersonalizing, portraying, or endowing with life. Like any performer, orator, or lecturer, they live the new part they must portray. Irreligious teachers can well be at their best when teaching Pascal or Newman, and feel unmoved by Voltaire and Aldous Huxley and interpret those men, whose unbelief they may share, with listlessness and a yawn.

There is, moreover, a vast amount of voluntary illusion, or self-delusion, in many an imaginative artist, which it would be very rash to equate with insincerity. Rather

6. The remark is by Joubin. We borrow it, from *Les Grandes Evasions esthétiques* by Charles Lalo (Vrin, 1947).

should it be assimilated to one of those lies that produce the impression of truth and succeed in reaching a higher truth. We are not alluding only to those small details that the reader feels bound to admit as unmistakably authentic and which the expert storyteller adroitly scatters here and there, as Diderot advised him to do. "In every poetical production," said he in one of his weaker tales, *Les Deux Amis de Bourbonne,* "there is always a little lying, the limit of which is not, and will never be, determined." The writer who proceeds thus is not the victim of his own guileless deceit; he resorts to the means necessary to him to communicate his imaginative truth.

Many a creator carries within his own heart impossible dreams of an ideal woman, a Beatrice or a Laura, which are the sincerest part of himself, jealously concealed in life from those closest to him, mocked by his family and his friends. Stendhal and Proust have made us familiar with that mechanism of the total subjectivity of love, persisting in the imagination of the person—more usually a man, at least in literature—who crystallizes all his dreams around it. But poets and musicians are still greater adepts at idealistic self-deception than Julien Sorel, Lucien Leuwen, or Robert de Saint-Loup. They must worship a muse who, revered from afar, transfigured by them, will receive their semireligious tribute of adoration and embody their pursuit of the impossible, "the desire of the moth for the star." The philosopher Etienne Gilson has, with uncommon penetration and tact, studied general examples of that amorous fervor, purified and sincerely self-deceptive, in a volume translated as *Choir of Muses* (1953). Artists in love, he shows from the examples of Dante and Beatrice, Petrarch and Laura, Baudelaire and Madame Sabatier, Wagner and Mathilda, Auguste Comte and Clotilde (and he could have added Shelley, Novalis, Hoelderlin, and a score of romantic temperaments), annihilate their ego in their beloved, but both their ego and that of the loved woman become devoured in turn by the muse herself. "The muse is what is needed of the woman in order to mold the being of dream, and yet real, at one and the same time desirable and inaccessible, like the perfect beauty which the artist wishes to create. . . . All that is sincere in those love stories is so in terms of art, not of love." Like Goethe's artist in "Kuenstlers Erdewallen" (1774), the poet can declare to his work:

> Du bist ich, bist mehr als ich, ich bin dein.

Baudelaire, in "L'Amour du mensonge," a poem probably inspired by a woman other than the "White Venus" who had disappointed him when she decided to reward his worship with a night of "real" love, lucidly if ungallantly cried out his craving for self-deception:

> Mais ne suffit-il pas que tu sois l'apparence,
> Pour réjouir un coeur qui fuit la vérité?
> Qu'importe ta bêtise ou ton indifférence?
> Masque ou décor, salut! J'adore ta beauté!

Finally, if sincerity can take refuge in an imaginative and vicarious experience as well as in an actual one, it should be supplemented by a second degree of sincerity, which has also been called honesty, integrity, respect of the artist for his medium and effort on his part not to belie or betray the demands of the literary or artistic genre he has selected.

Karl Shapiro, in a series of lectures, *Beyond Criticism* (1953), offered the following remark apropos of "the true artificer," as his second lecture is entitled:

> The poet has a dual obligation to sincerity, one to himself and one to the poem. . . . Sincerity to self in art means the power of accepting the reality of one's milieu in terms of oneself. . . . It is the essence of humility before actuality. . . . Sincerity to the poem fol-

lows naturally from acceptance of the scene. Sincerity
to the poem is the expression of the other deeper sincerity.

In less imperiously cryptic terms, a French poet of some
distinction, Luc Estang, publishing in 1943 an *Invitation
à la poésie,* also noted that there are two phases in the process of being a sincere writer, synchronized when the writing actually takes place: that of the man and that of the
author. "Sincerity is to itself its own mirror. In literature,
we only find reflected sincerities." With more charming
levity, and in an age where literary genres were more playfully honored, one of Shakespeare's characters, Touchstone,
in the third scene of Act III of *As You Like It,* jested with
Audrey: "I wish the gods had made thee poetical!" When
the naïve girl asked whether poetical meant "honest in
deed and word, a true thing," Touchstone vehemently retorted: "No, truly, for the truest poetry is the most feign-
ing."
    Critics have long suffered from twinges of conscience
when they dared assert that a poem could reach greatness
while being the game of an artificer and a mere variation
on a much used but still fresh lyre or flute. It may be easier
to concede it in music, and we forbear to question whether
Vivaldi, Scarlatti, Bach, or even Mozart was sincerely moved
when composing, for the fiftieth time, the same piece with
only slight variations. It pains us more to admit that Shakespeare's Sonnet XX, which is one of the most poetical love
declarations made by a male poet to a young man, may be
simply an exercise upon an ambiguous theme and not cor-
respond to a homosexual ardor experienced or imagined.
Students of Milton have been disturbed by Milton's *Lycidas,*
mourning the death of the poet Edward King, whom Milton hardly knew and whose accidental drowning cannot
have filled him with torrential tears; nor was Shelley close-

ly acquainted with Keats when he mourned Adonais. Northrop Frye does not suffer from the sentimental qualms of his predecessors. In an essay published in 1959, he bluntly declared: "Personal sincerity has no place in literature, because personal sincerity as such is inarticulate. One may burst into tears at the news of a friend's death, but one can never spontaneously burst into song, however doleful a lay." Milton's impulse to write, after he had experienced some surprise and emotion at the death of a friend, came, contends Frye, from his previous familiarity with funeral elegies.[7] In the eyes of some of us, however, and not necessarily of those who dislike Milton, the awareness of Milton's practising an exercise, almost as he might have done a Latin or an Italian poem at Cambridge, detracts from the force of communication of *Lycidas* to the reader. The structure, the symbolism, and the skillful utilization of the devices of the ancients win our admiration. But if literature is a mere game to that extent, it must remain the privilege of a few learned students in graduate schools and cut itself off from broader audiences.

An English critic, Arthur Melville Clark, offered shrewd reflections on the subject apropos of the least sentimental of literary genres, satire, in "The Art of Satire and the Satiric Spectrum," included in his *Studies in Literary Modes*, (1946). A satirist, he contends, must be sincere if he is to reach excellence; but he may also and at the same time be rancorous, spiteful, mean, indignant, without cause, coarse.

7. Northrop Frye, "Literature as Content: Milton's *Lycidas*," *Proceedings of the Second Congress of the International Comparative Literature Association*, 2 (Chapel Hill, University of North Carolina Press, 1959), 51. Swinburne knew Baudelaire even less than Milton did Edward King and than Shelley knew Keats when, hearing the news (premature) of his death, he wrote "Ave atque Vale." But he and Shelley in Adonais, and Mallarmé in his "Toast Funèbre" for Théophile Gautier, wrote in truth about themselves and, in this reader's opinion at least, reached greater depths and moved us more lastingly.

Juvenal and Martial, after all, were, and the moderns lag
only a little behind them. Satire is dying today because we
have become softer and take our literary quarrels less to
heart. But, Clark goes on, sincerity in a satirist means "his
fidelity to the medium in which he writes, an acceptance
of its conditions, and a genuine attempt to extract from its
exigencies the maximum effect . . . the poet in general must
feel what he writes; he need not feel what he writes about."

But "sincerity to one's art" and integrity in the practice
of it hardly provide us with a better standard of literary
evaluation than our predecessors had. Indeed, skilled practitioners of the sonnet, virtuoso neo-Latin poets like San-
nazaro, Jean Second, Marullus, Du Bellay, Milton himself,
honest and convinced, but unmoved, composers of Pindaric
odes like Ronsard, Malherbe, or Akenside evinced those
virtues of sincerity to their art. But something more fundamental is missed in their stillborn art.

Is the notion of sincerity to be banished altogether from
our critical vocabulary? The attempt at such banishment
would be at least as arduous as it would be to do away with
terms like "romanticism," "myth," "greatness," and "profundity"—and doomed to failure. Many uses of the word
"sincere" would long ago have ridiculed the term if ridicule could ever kill criticism. Those uses would be found
among the most respected judges of art and letters, and not
alone among journalists hastily commenting upon an ex-
hibition, a recent novel, a lecture, or a piece of clothing.
For even clothing can be sincere, without being transparent
or even tailor-cut. Frederic Wakeman in *The Hucksters*
(1946) ironically portrays a character, Victor Norman, se-
lecting the right attire to apply for a job in advertising. He
first stops at a "temple devoted to the cravat" and picks the
most sincere tie he can find. "It was hand-painted, rich, and
very, very sincere, being priced at thirty-five dollars." On a

higher plane, Matisse, as quoted by Father Coutourier in a booklet on the chapel at Vence (1955) denied that his work stemmed from his intelligence. "All I have done, I have done out of passion . . . in my whole life, my sole strength has lain in sincerity." A severe specialist of architecture, J. A. Brutails, a member of the Institut de France, in a useful volume, *Pour Comprendre les Monuments de la France* (1922) began by the assertion that "During all great ages, architecture had drawn near to sincerity. Greek art is true; Romanesque and Gothic art is even truer." But Roman architecture was not sincere (and Brutails buttresses his statement with a declaration of Gounod's, of all musicians, on the need for art to be sincere), while concrete is not conducive to good architectural creation. It is poor, has to be covered up; "It will never produce anything but an art devoid of sincerity." Renan, with more subtlety, had, in the pages preceding his celebrated *Prayer on the Acropolis,* seen the superiority of Greek temples over Christian cathedrals to lie in their absolute honesty; and he was ready to agree with an architect who had traveled with him, who used to contend that the truth of gods was proportionate to the solid beauty of the temples that had been erected to them. Pirandello, as ingenious and as volatile a mind as Sicily ever produced, did not hesitate to lay down the criterion of sincerity as the only valid one in art.[8] Charles Mauron, respected among modern French critics and the author of exegetic and psychoanalytic analyses of Racine and Mallarmé, likewise declared in 1942 in *Fusées,* a volume by several authors devoted to sincerity: "Other things being equal, a lack of sincerity in art automatically carries

---

8. Luigi Pirandello, *Saggi, 1* (Milan, Mondadori, 1939), 203–04. "Whichever feeling and thought we select, it is sufficient that they be sincere . . . if sincerity in art has any meaning, those will *not* be sincere who let extraneous reflections intrude into their work, instead of allowing the work to be born spontaneously in their mind?"

with it a fall to a secondary rank." An English critic who
perished in World War I and whose thought influenced
British neoclassicism strongly, T. E. Hulme, avid for safe
standards of literary excellence, likewise and more oracu-
larly decreed in *Speculations* (1924) that the author should
possess "the concentrated state of mind, the grip over oneself" and added: "wherever you get this sincerity, you get
the fundamental quality of good art without dragging in
the infinite or the serious."⁹ Even Henry James, who did
not underrate the role of technique in the craft of fiction,
and who could be diffident of romantic facility in art, pronounced in "The Art of Fiction" (*Partial Portraits*, 1888)
that "the only condition that I can think of attaching to the
composition of the novel is that it be sincere."

In truth, sincerity as a criterion of value in fiction is
neither worse nor better than the mind of the person who
makes use of it. We would readily submit that, at some
time or other, every critic of note has resorted to it to damn
an author whom he found inferior or to praise one whom
he admired. Chateaubriand, whose hypocrisy was as blatant as any French prose writer—and who adored posing
in the forests of the New World, by the ruins of ancient
temples in the Roman campagna, while building his grave
on a rock beaten by the waves, and even for his readers
beyond the grave—has nevertheless been praised by his lat-

9. Another neohumanist, born in the Middle West, who influenced
T. S. Eliot as much as Hulme did, showed more sarcastic defiance of a
sincerity which no Emersonian "inner check" would correct. He is Irving
Babbitt, who, in *Democracy and Leadership* (Boston, Houghton Mifflin,
1924), p. 84, wrote: "It seems to be assured in certain quarters that almost
any opinion is justified, provided it be held with sufficient emotional vehemence. One cannot help reflecting that perhaps the best examples of sincerity in this sense are to be found in insane asylums." Still another Middle
Western American, Marianne Moore, declared in *Predilections* (New York,
Viking, 1955), p. 11: "Originality is in any case a by-product of sincerity;
that is to say, of feeling that is honest and accordingly rejects anything that
might cloud the impression."

est biographer, a German, Friedrich Sieburg, in a book translated in 1961, in the following terms: "His partiality for visiting famous graves and deserted ruins . . . imbues his literary style with the most admirable purity and sincerity." A British defender of Sir Philip Sidney's sincerity ingeniously argued that the poet aimed, in his whole life as Astrophel, at Stella, who would take him at his word when he protested his truthful passion, and that his other audience, the public at large, mostly appreciated the conceits of his sonnets and lyrics. Stella would then be more gullible than the author himself; for, in his *Apologie*, Sidney had confessed that, if he were someone's mistress, he would never have been persuaded by declarations in verse and "fiery" speeches which remain of ice.

An enumeration of many more uses of the laudatory adjective "sincere" by critics of several nations would soon grow tedious. Its usefulness would lie in enabling us to clear away some of the confusion which has been the besetting sin of the critic's trade. The eruption of the concept of sincerity in modern criticism has carried with it a looseness of terminology and of thought which we deplore. Even if absolute precision can never be hoped for in matters of taste and of enjoyment, from which the exclusion of subjectivity is neither desirable nor possible, some progress toward sharpening our blades (the critic is, after all, etymologically, he who, decisively, slices) may be effected. First of all, the word carries with it a moral connotation in many minds: for better or for worse, since we have come to distrust rhetoric, to shun flamboyance, to hunt out adjectives and metaphors, sincerity in style has been lauded as a virtue. Smiling and shrewdly naïve Izaak Walton, in the seventeenth century, declared: "Though I cannot adorn it with eloquence, yet I will do it with sincerity." Since the debauchery of confessions of the last hundred and fifty years, undressing for one's reader has become, if not virtuous, at least a moral justification *per se*. The romantics claimed that sincere passion justified all, even if that passion flitted from one object to another; even a courtesan, as in a famous line in *Marion Delorme,* could, through sincere love, refurbish a "new virginity." The characters, and presumably some at least of the contemporaries of Françoise Sagan and of Christiane Rochefort, consider that "sincere," i.e. "ardent," desire, justifies itself and that the person at whom the desire is directed (presumably a man, in an age where the initiative has shifted to the females) may without any qualms yield to the contagion thus imparted. Prudence, compromise, reticence, even discretion are branded as a form of bad faith, as in the famous example of the frigid woman analyzed in Sartre's *L'Etre et le néant.*[10]

The cult of sincerity, as we have had occasion to point out several times, led to a large number of works containing no subject, referring to nothing (and sincerity should refer to something behind and beyond itself), involving little constraint over a rebellious material or little restraint, and banishing even style from many works of literature. If the grand style of some romantics palls upon us, there is much charm in the adorned, playful way of writing which aims at pleasing with engaging urbanity, as practised by Goethe, De Quincey, and Renan in their reminiscences. The bald dryness of a diary, with no organization but that of the dates of a calendar, can reach a monotony which, as in the volumes of Léautaud, and in Gide's *Journals,* will some day astonish our successors as a monument to the incapacity for boredom of the twentieth century. And they were not yet written, as the works of tomorrow may be,

---

10. J. P. Sartre, *L'Etre et le néant* (Gallimard, 1943), pp. 93–96. Several moralists have attempted to warn us against that view of sincerity as justifying amorous adventures and consisting primarily of spontaneity: for example, Jean Rimaud, in "Les Illusions de la sincérité," in the Jesuit monthly review *Etudes* (January 1951), pp. 60–72.

with a view to the long hours we are likely to spend in shelters, reading and yawning, waiting for the atomic fall-out to become innocuous on the scorched earth!

The direst predicament into which the worship of sincerity (conceived as a factual record of our doings and as an introspective analysis of the author's self) has plunged literature is the consequent loss of irony, and, even more, of imagination. Keen spirits had long ago warned us that no man knows himself who knows only himself and that the Delphic motto adopted by Socrates presupposes first observing the outside world and knowing other men. Novalis noted in one of his fragments that "no man knows himself as long as he is but himself and not at the same time another man." Nietzsche, in his anti-Socratic wrath, echoed that saying. In the twentieth century, a dearth of imaginative inventiveness has afflicted literature. We have, over and over again, poured wine, which temporarily tasted like new, into the very old, at times porous, goatskin containers bequeathed by the Jews, the Greeks, and the medieval singers of the Grail and of Tristan. Critics have proudly philosophized about the impoverishment of our imagination and discoursed at length on myths and archetypes. But we have lost sight of the higher truth, even of the deeper sincerity, which lie in imagination; we have become obsessed with the more prosaic and narrow truth of a sincere record of ourselves.

"All that we invent is true," declared Flaubert in one of his letters. Before him, another novelist whom Flaubert failed to appreciate, Stendhal, had, after many attempts at autobiography and self-analysis, acknowledged that we can only reach truth in novels, through re-inventing it. Mauriac, in his *Journal II* (1937), submitted that "There is no great fictional work that is not a fictionalized inner life [*une vie intérieure romancée*]." Aphorisms of creators could be quoted in large numbers, which point to the same respect for the higher sincerity, as well as truth of what is invented. Max Jacob, in his *Art poétique,* hints that "Sincere is a word endowed with sufficient force to make the illusion real." His friend Picasso proclaimed the same conviction: "Art is a lie that shows us the truth." And Anouilh, well aware, as a dramatist and a theatrical director are bound to be, that truth on the stage is far from being "natural," defined his playwright's craft thus: "through every possible artifice, do truer than truth." The critic who has most acutely discerned the perils lurking in that kind of sincerity which desiccates and reduces the work of literature to remembering the past and jotting down the present is Benjamin Crémieux, who perished in a German extermination camp during World War II. He had been one of the three or four earliest and most discerning appraisers of Proust. But in Proust he had hailed, not just a psychologist who might have been fascinated with the discontinuity of the self and the intermittences of the heart, but also a creator who, far from leading us to the brink of a huge void at the end of his saga-novel, discovered the higher value of imagination. In a brief but suggestive article on "Sincerity and Imagination," in the 1924 *Nouvelle Revue Française,* Crémieux foresaw the yielding to facility which literary sincerity, conceived as reliance on memory and resort to interior monologue and to diaries, might entail, and did entail, for the writers between the two wars. He concluded: "Is not the greatest artist also the greatest impostor, the most capable of giving a form to whatever imaginary reality, of bestowing upon it, through expressing it, a soul and an appearance of truth which others than the creator will accept?"

If given free rein, the puritanical tenants of sincerity in art and letters today would prove to be nothing less than the gravediggers of literature itself. They would substitute volumes of travel diaries by journalists and reports on Burma, Guinea, Russia—adorned with a few interviews of the rulers of these countries and with an occasional taxi driver or coffee waitress—for the imaginative but also the far deeper and truer picture of life in Burma or Guinea or Russia that a novelist might give us. Sincerity, surrounded as it has lately been with a halo of sanctity,[11] might well play the part of a nuclear fission applied to literature in order to disintegrate it. We would all be the poorer for it.

When a soldier sees his comrade die in a foxhole while he himself must implacably push onward to an attack; when an airplane team loses an engine or runs short of fuel and knows itself to be doomed; when a workman on a scaffolding feels himself losing his balance and reels down a hundred feet to his death—the cry uttered through these lips might be moving in its sobriety: an oath, a prayer, a call to their mother or to the Virgin, a curse. But it moves us, onlookers or readers of the four lines devoted to the accident in the daily paper, infinitely less than the story that might be made out of it by a writer of talent. That writer would lie in the literal sense—"lie in order the better to express a certain truth."[12] But he would possess the gift of conveying forcefully, elliptically, colorfully, the feeling the real character must have felt. Cambronne probably never pronounced his famous five-letter word at Waterloo, nor Bonaparte his eloquent declaration in the shadow of the Pyramids, nor another hero the sentence praising the Lord and requesting the ammunition in the same breath; surgeons report that they never heard their dying patients whisper any of the impressive "last words" posterity generously

11. As late as September 1 to 6, 1961, the cinema critic in the best French weekly, *Le Monde Hebdomadaire,* praising the winner of the Venice festival *L'Année dernière à Marienbad,* lauded it as a "sincere document" and inevitably used the word which is the twin brother of sincerity, "authenticity."

12. Louis Aragon, in an interview with Claude Sarraute *Le Monde Hebdomadaire,* October 13–19, 1961.

so-called masses on the part of orchestras, theater producers, movie magnates, and book publishers, the plea for sincerity in literature came as a protest on the part of those who refuse to surrender to conformity and hypocrisy. The revolt of our grandfathers, between 1875 and 1900, against the so-called Victorian cant had to be supplemented with more revolts against the social cant that has replaced the moral and sexual ones: that which business, wealth, the apathy of nations ready to abdicate their freedom of judgment into the hands of paternalistic or demagogic leaders insidiously offer to us. It will remain to the credit of France that, whatever perishable elements remain in their work, Gide, Giraudoux, Céline, Green, Bernanos, Mauriac, Malraux, Camus, Anouilh, Sartre, Simone Weil, Simone de Beauvoir, and a score of other writers between 1920 and 1960 have all been passionate advocates of constructive revolt—often under the banner of sincerity.[13]

Existentialism was a vogue which, like many others, will prove ephemeral. But, like Surrealism before it, for ten or fifteen years, it constituted the marching wing of the literary forces in continental Western Europe. As our perspective becomes more serene toward it, and as the leaders of the movement are nearing the age of that reason which is also resignation and the preparation to confront nothingness, we must concede that it was far more than an accident or a fad. It taught us that there must be in us an existential perception of "our truth" and a relentless insistence on experiencing it. The phrase "ma vérité," which Hermann von Keyserling, in 1938, considered as typically French, does not seem to befit the compatriots of Descartes, of Montesquieu, and of the universal lawgivers of the "Declaration

---

13. The point was made with vehemence in 1949 in a volume of eloquent essays by a then young professor of talent, René Marill Albérès, *La Révolte des écrivains d'aujourd'hui* (Corrêa).

of the Rights of Man."[14] But it concealed less sham and
self-deception than more pretentious formulas coined by
existentialist, or merely rationalist, ages. The existentialist
insistence on good faith as the first rule of ethics prolonged
the teaching of many a moralist, religious thinker (Pascal,
Bossuet), or layman (La Rochefoucauld, Vauvenargues) of
earlier centuries. "We deceive ourselves in order to deceive others," noted Vauvenargues, the infantry captain
who died in 1747 at thirty-two years of age, and elsewhere
he said: "We persuade ourselves of our own lies in order
not to have them denied." The value of commitment has
been misunderstood and exaggerated. The espousal of a
cause (which may, in good faith, be a practical or a narrow
or a criminal one) cannot in itself be a mark or a guarantee
of talent. But our age had to be reminded, after the smiling
skepticism of Anatole France (who ended by subscribing to
a cause but failed to let his books be ignited by it), or Paul
Valéry or Aldous Huxley, that literature may also care
deeply about ends and means. George Orwell is closer to
the readers of 1960 than Huxley—as is Lawrence and also
Camus—and his best writing does not suffer from being
honestly committed, and "sincere." He himself declared:
"Talent . . . is a matter of being able to *care*, of really believing in your beliefs, whether they are true or false. . . .
For a creative writer, possession of the 'truth' is less important than emotional sincerity."[15]

14. The volume by Hermann von Keyserling alluded to was written
partly in French by the Baltic Count; it has a fifty-page first chapter on
"sincerity." Its title is *De la Souffrance à la plénitude* (Paris, Stock, 1938),
and it is among the least admirable by that thinker.

15. George Orwell, "Inside the Whale" in *Selected Essays* (London, Pen-
guin, 1957), p. 45. Lionel Trilling, in his introduction to Orwell's *Homage
to Catalonia* (New York, Harcourt, Brace, 1952) p. viii, praised Orwell
as "a figure" rather than a genius. Figures are, in his view, "Men who live
their visions as well as write them, who *are* what they write, whom we
think of as standing for something as men because of what they have written in their books."

We may be grateful to the champions of sincerity in modern literature, even when we reject some of their assertions or refuse, as the statement by Orwell dangerously implies, to sacrifice truth on the altar of sincerity. They have recalled to us that craft and artifice and technique are important, but secondary. Literature also should create in us what Hegel calls "Unruhe" and singles out as the privilege and nobleness of man. It is an art, but one which should never become divorced from life or be refined over in critical disquisitions, as was its woeful lot with the poets and grammarians of Alexandria and, sixteen or eighteen centuries later, by the humanists of Italy. It has a content, and that content should be ambitiously audacious, rich, and lived by writers with intensity, as the eloquent author of *Democratic Vistas* proclaimed a few years after the Civil War:

> Viewed, today, from a point of view sufficiently
> overarching, the problem of humanity all over the
> civilized world is social and religious, and is to be
> finally met and treated by literature.

Selected Bibliography

(When no city is mentioned before the publisher's name of a French book, Paris is understood.)

Albérès, R. M., *Portrait de notre héros,* Le Portulan, 1945.

———, *La Révolte des écrivains d'aujourd'hui,* Corrêa, 1949.

———, "L'homme divisé," *Revue de Paris, 59* (1952), 146–54.

———, *Bilan littéraire du vingtième siècle,* Aubier, 1956. (In those four essays, the author treats the obsession with Promethean revolt in the name of purity and sincerity in modern French writers and in Kafka, Pirandello, Alvaro, Moravia.)

Allen, Archibald W., "Sincerity and the Roman Elegists," *Classical Philology, 45* (1950), 145–60.

Arnoux, Alexandre, *Etudes et caprices,* Albin Michel, 1953. (See pp. 9–13.)

Bazaillas, Albert, *La Vie personnelle,* Alcan, 1905.

———, *Musique et inconscience,* Alcan, 1908.

Béguin, Albert, "Baudelaire et l'autobiographie," *Poésie 45, 28* (1945), 51–57.

Belaval, Yvon, *Le Souci de sincérité,* Gallimard, 1944.

Belot, Gustave, "La Véracité," *Revue de Métaphysique et de Morale, 11* (1903), 430–54.

Berger, Gaston, *Traité pratique d'analyse du caractère,* Presses Universitaires, 1950.

Blanchot, Maurice, "Gide et la littérature d'expérience," *L'Arche, 4* (1947), 23, 87–98, reprinted in *La Part du feu* (Gallimard, 1949), pp. 216–28.

———, "De L'Angoisse au langage," in *Faux Pas,* Gallimard, 1953.

———, "Sur le Journal intime," *Nouvelle Revue Française* (April 1955), 682–91.

Blin, Gorges, *Stendhal et les problèmes de la personnalité,* J. Corti, 1958. (Part I, Chapter 6, "De la Contrefaçon de soi"; Part II, Chapter 11, "L'Autobiographie.")

Bourget, Paul, "Benjamin Constant," *Le Livre du Centenaire du Journal des Débats,* Plon, 1889.

———, *Nouvelles Pages de critique et de doctrine,* 2, Plon, 1922.

Brooks, Van Wyck, *The Malady of the Ideal: Obermann, Maurice de Guérin, Amiel,* Philadelphia, University of Pennsylvania Press, 1947. (The essay was written in 1913.)

Brunschvicg, Léon, edition of Pascal's *Pensées et opuscules,* Hachette, 1914. (p. 289: "The transparency of style is, in Pascal, the immediate effect, the reflection of that absolute sincerity." p. 292: "Pascal is not concerned with style [as other moralists are]. . . . All is sincere in Pascal.")

———, *De la Connaissance de soi,* Alcan, 1931.

Burgelin, Pierre, *La Philosophie de l'existence de J. J. Rousseau,* Presses Universitaires, 1952.

Butor, Michel, *Histoire extraordinaire: Essai sur un rêve de Baudelaire,* Gallimard, 1961. (On the multiplicity of levels of sincerity in an author, pp. 22–23.)

Claudel, Paul, *Entretiens avec Frédéric Lefèvre,* Lemercier, 1927. (p. 160, on sincerity.)

Collignon, Jean, "Gide's Sincerity," *Yale French Studies,* 7 (1951), 44–50.

Cordle, Thomas, "Gide and the Novel of the Egoist," *Yale French Studies,* 7 (1951), 91–97.

Crémieux, Benjamin, "Sincérité et imagination," *Nouvelle Revue Française, 12* (1924), 528–48.

Dabit, Eugène, *Journal intime, 1928–36,* Gallimard, 1939.

Dobie, Frank, "The Unveiling of a Self-Portrait," *The New York Times Book Review* (September 1, 1957), p. 1.

Drïjkoningen, Ferdinand Frans, *Temps et Journal intime: essai sur l'oeuvre de Maurice de Guérin,* Leiden, Van Gorcum and Co., 1959.

Dromard, Gabriel, *Essai sur la sincérité*, Alcan, 1910.

———, *Les Mensonges et la vie intérieure*, Alcan, 1910.

———, *Sur la sincérité en amour*, Picard, 1920.

Du Bos, Charles, *Approximations*, Crès, 1927. (Vol. 2 on Rivière and sincerity.)

———, *Extraits d'un journal*, Schiffrin, 1928.

———, *Journal*, 8 volumes; Corrêa, Vols. 1–4; La Colombe, Vols. 5–8.

Duhamel, Georges, *La Confession de minuit*, Mercure de France, 1920.

———, *Journal de Salavin*, Mercure de France, 1927.

———, *Le Notaire du Havre*, Mercure de France, 1933. (Long preface by the imaginary hero, mocking the "debaucheries of intimate literature.")

Dutourd, Jean, "Du Journal en général," *Nouvelle Revue Française, 9* (1961), 1050–63.

Edel, Leon, *The Psychological Novel, 1900–1950*, London, Rupert Hart-Davis, and New York, Lippincott, 1955.

Fernandez, Ramon, "L'Autobiographie et le roman" or "L'Exemple de Stendhal," in *Messages*, Gallimard, 1926.

———, *De la Personnalité*, Au Sans-Pareil, 1928.

Frye, Northrop, "Literature as Content: Milton's *Lycidas*," in *Comparative Literature: Proceedings of the Second Congress of the International Comparative Literature Association, 2*, Chapel Hill, 1959.

Fusées, Nos. 4–5 (August-September 1942) on "Sincerity," Marseille, Robert Laffont. (230 pages of essays on the subject by Charles Mauron, Hubert Larcher, Christian Marrel-Courtois, Emile Arrighi, De Casanova, Philippe Baer, Pierre Klossowski, Pierre Raymond, Michel Mohrt.)

Gilson, Etienne, *Choir of Muses (L'Ecole des muses)*, New York, Sheed and Ward, 1953.

Giraudoux, Jean, *Littérature*, Grasset, 1941. (On Laclos, Nerval.)

Green, Julien, *Journal 1928–58*, 7 vols. Plon, 1938–58.

Grillparzer, Franz, *Sämmtliche Werke*, Stuttgart, Cotta, 1872, Vol. 10 (Selbstbiographie-Tagebuch aus dem Jahre 1836 —Beiträge zur Selbstbiographie).

Groethuysen, Bernard, *Jean-Jacques Rousseau,* Gallimard, 1949.

Guéhenno, Jean, *Journal d'un homme de quarante ans,* Grasset, 1937.

————, *Journal des années noires, 1940–1944,* Gallimard, 1947.

————, *Jean-Jacques Rousseau,* 3 vols. Grasset, 1948.

————, *Changer la vie,* Gallimard, 1961.

Guggenhein, Michel, "Des *Essais* aux *Confessions: deux écrivains devant leur moi,*" *The French Review, 34* (1961), 517–24.

Gusdorf, Georges, *La Découverte de soi,* Presses Universitaires, 1948.

————, *Mémoire et personne,* 2 vols. Presses Universitaires, 1951.

————, "Conditions et limites de l'autobiographie," in *Festgabe für Fritz Neubert: Formen der Selbstdarstellung* (Berlin, Duncker und Humblot, 1956), pp. 105–23.

Hebbel, Friedrich, *Sämmtliche Werke,* ed. Richard Maria Werner, Berlin, 1911–14. (Vols. 13 and 14 contain Hebbel's *Tagebücher* for 1835–54.)

Hubert, Judd, *L'Esthétique des Fleurs du Mal: Essai sur l'ambiguité poétique,* Geneva, Cailler, 1953.

Hytier, Jean, *Les Romans de l'individu,* Les Arts et le Livre, 1928.

Jaloux, Edmond, "Journaux intimes," *Le Temps,* May 28, 1937.

Jankélévitch, Vladimir, *Du Mensonge,* Confluences, 1942.

Jeanson, Francis, "Gide contre Gide," *Les Temps Modernes, 4* (1948), 656–83.

Jolivet, Régis, *Essai sur le problème et les conditions de la sincérité,* Lyon, Vitte, 1951.

Jones, P. Mansell, *French Introspectives, from Montaigne to André Gide,* Cambridge University Press, 1937.

Lacretelle, Jacques de, *Les Aveux étudiés,* Gallimard, 1934.

————, *Le Tiroir secret,* Paris and Naumur, Wesmael-Charlier, 1959.

Lalo, Charles, *L'Expression de la vie dans l'art,* Alcan, 1933.

————, *L'Art près de la vie,* Vrin, 1946.

————, *Les Grandes Evasions esthétiques,* Vrin, 1947.

————, *L'Economie des passions,* Vrin, 1947.

La Rochefoucauld, *Maximes* (on sincerity, nos. 62, 114, 115, 116, 119, 135, 316, 366, 377—*Traité du faux* in *Réflections diverses,* XIII).

Laumonier, Paul, *Ronsard, poète lyrique,* Hachette, 1908. (Part I, Section II, Chapters 1 and 2 on the sincerity of Ronsard in his imitations.)

Lavelle, Louis, *La Conscience de soi,* Grasset, 1933. (Chapter IX on "Amour-propre et sincérité.")

——, *L'Erreur de Narcisse,* Grasset, 1939.

Léautaud, Paul, *Journal,* Mercure de France, 1954–61. (Ten volumes up to 1961. See article by Seymour S. Weiner on "Sincerity and Variants: Paul Léautaud's *Petit Ami,*" *Symposium,* Fall 1960, 165–87.)

Leiris, Michel, *L'Age d'homme,* 2d ed. Gallimard, 1946.

——, *La Règle du jeu, 1. Biffures,* Gallimard, 1948.

Leleu, Michèle, *Les Journaux intimes,* Presses Universitaires, 1952.

Lemonnier, Léon, *Les Poètes romantiques anglais,* Boivin, 1943. (Chapter III, pp. 113–20, on sincerity and pose in Byron.)

Le Senne, René, *Le Mensonge et le caractère,* Alcan, 1930.

——, *Traité de caractérologie,* Presses Universitaires, 1945.

Lewes, George Henry, "The Principle of Sincerity," in *The Principles of Success in Literature* (new ed. University of California, Students Cooperative Association, 1901), pp. 103–33. ("Whatever is sincerely felt or believed . . . will always maintain an infinite superiority over imitative splendor.")

Marcel, Gabriel, "André Gide d'après son *Journal,*" *La Vie Intellectuelle* (January 25, 1940), pp. 125–39.

Martin-Chauffier, Louis, *André Gide et la sincérité,* Studio franco-russe, Cahiers de la Quinzaine, 20th series, No. 6, April 5, 1930.

——, "Proust and the Double I," *The Partisan Review* (October 1949), pp. 1011–26.

Martin du Gard, Roger, *Notes sur André Gide: 1913–1951,* Gallimard, 1951.

Merlant, Joachim, *Senancour (1770–1846),* Fishbacher, 1907.

——, *Le Roman personnel de Rousseau à Fromentin,* Hachette, 1905.

————, *De Montaigne à Vauvenargues: Essais sur la vie intérieure et la culture du moi,* Société Française d'Imprimerie et de Librairie, 1914.

Merton, Thomas, *No Man Is an Island,* New York, Harcourt, Brace, 1955. (Chapter x on sincerity.)

Mesnard, Pierre, "L'Analyse caractérologique des journaux intimes," *Psyché,* Nos. 84–85, October-November 1953, 16 pp.

Meyer, R. "Zur Entwicklungsgeschichte des Tagebuchs," *Gestalte und Probleme* (Berlin, 1905), pp. 281–98.

Michelet, Jules, *Journal, 1, 1828–1848,* Gallimard, 1959.

Misch, G., *Geschichte der Autobiographie, 1, Das Alterum; 2, Das Mittelalter,* Bern, A. Francke, new ed., 1949 and 1955; translated as *A History of Autobiography in Antiquity,* Cambridge, Harvard University Press, 1951.

Monglond, André, *Vies préromantiques,* Belles Lettres, 1925. (On Rousseau, Senancour, Constant.)

————, *Histoire intérieure du préromantisme français,* 2 vols. Grenoble, Arthaud, 1929. (Vol. 2, Chapter 5 on "Confessions and Interior Lyricism.")

Montherlant, Henri de, *Montherlant par lui-même,* Par Pierre Spiriot, Editions du Seuil, 1953.

Moreau, Pierre, *Autour du Culte du moi: Essai sur les origines de l'égotisme français,* Archives des Lettres romanes, December 1957, No. 7.

Neubert, Fritz, *Festgabe für, Formen der Selbstdarstellung,* Analekten zu einer Geschichte des literarischen Selbstportrait, Berlin, Duncker und Humblot, 1956. (See in particular the essays on Gide's autobiography by Friedrich Schürr, on Renan's by René Pintard, on Julien Green by Julius Wilhelm, on Maine de Biran by Henri Gouhier; on the subject in general by Gusdorf.)

Osborn, James M. *The Beginnings of Autobiography in England,* Los Angeles, University of California Press, 1959.

Parain, Brice, *Recherches sur la nature et les fonctions du langage,* Gallimard, 1942.

————, *Sur la Dialectique,* Gallimard, 1953.

Pascal, Roy, *Design and Truth in Autobiography,* Cambridge, Massachusetts, Harvard University Press, 1960. (Chapters previously appeared in *The Yale Review* and in *Essays in Criticism*, 1959–60. See also "Truth to Life" in *The Times Literary Supplement*, September 8, 1961.)

Paulhan, Fréderic, *Le Mensonge de l'art*, Alcan, 1907.

Picard, Raymond, *La Carrière de Jean Racine*, Gallimard, 1956. (See section IV, Chapter 1: "Racine devant sa carrière: le problème de la sincérité.")

Pichon, Jean Charles, *L'Autobiographie*, Grasset, 1956. (A few reflections on the inadequacies of autobiography, pp. 53 ff.)

Picon, Gaëtan, "Remarks on Gide's Ethics," *Yale French Studies, 1* (1951), 3–11.

Pirandello, Luigi, *Saggi*, A cura di Manlio lo Vecchio Musti, Milan, Mondadori, 1939; in Vol. 1, "Soggettivismo e oggettivismo nell'arte narrativa," pp. 199 ff.)

Platen, von, Count, *Tagebücher: 1814–34*, Stuttgart, Cotta, 1896–1900.

Polles, Henri, *Journal d'un raté*, Gallimard, 1956.

Prévost, Jean, *Essai sur l'introspection*, Au Sans-Pareil, 1927.

———, *Faire le point*, Albin Michel, 1930 (new ed., 1948).

———, *La Création chez Stendhal*, Mercure de France, 1951. (See pp. 38–39, 92–98 on Stendhal's sincerity.)

Rambaud, Henri, and François Derais, *L'Envers du Journal de Gide*, Le Nouveau Portique, 1951.

Raymond, Marcel, "Deux Aspects de la vie intérieure de J. J. Rousseau," *Annales Jean-Jacques Rousseau, 29* (1941–42), 1–57.

Renard, Jules, *Journal (1887–1909)*, Gallimard, 1935.

Reverdy, Pierre, *Le Gant de crin*, Plon, 1927.

———, *En Vrac*, Monaco, Editions du Rocher, 1956.

Rey, Etienne, *Eloge du mensonge*, Hachette, 1925.

Rimaud, Jean, "Les Illusions de la sincérité," *Etudes* (January 1951), pp. 60–72.

Rivière, Jacques, *De la Sincérité envers soi-même* (1912), Edition des Cahiers de Paris, 1925; new ed. Chronique des lettres françaises, 1927; new ed., Gallimard, 1943 (includes *De la Foi*).

———, *The Ideal Reader*, New York, Meridian Books, 1960.

(Translation of the essay on sincerity by Blanche A. Price, with an introduction.)

Rougemont, Denis de, *Les Personnages du drame,* New York, Pantheon Books, 1944. (Contains an essay on Gide's *Journal.*)

Salvan, Albert, "Private Journals in French Literature," *American Society of the Legion of Honor Magazine,* 25 (1954), 201–14.

Schlumberger, Jean, *Un Homme heureux,* Gallimard, 1921.

———, *Jalons,* Sagittaire, 1942.

———, *Madeleine et André Gide,* Gallimard, 1956.

Scudéry, Madeleine de, *Conversations upon Several Subjects,* English translation, London, Rhodes, 1683. (Ch. III on sincerity.)

Shumaker, Wayne, *English Autobiography, Its Emergence, Materials and Form,* Berkeley, California, University of California Press, 1954.

Starobinski, Jean, *Jean-Jacques Rousseau: la transparence et l'obstacle,* Plon, 1957.

———, "Stendhal pseudonyme," *L'Oeil vivant,* Gallimard, 1961.

Table Ronde, La, Number 89 (May 1955) on "La Connaissance de soi et les lettres," pp. 66–118. (Essays by Pierre Spiriot, Alain, Marguerite Yourcenar, Charles du Bos. B. Berenson, sketching his own portrait, remarks that "total sincerity is not within our reach and the gods, who have known how to make the paths leading to it inextricable, are probably the only ones who know what it is.")

Thibaudet, Albert, *Gustave Flaubert,* Plon, 1922. (Chapter IV, on "Flaubert's Laboratory," p. 87.)

Valéry, Paul, "Stendhal," *Variété II,* Gallimard, 1930.

Vercors, "Suis-je sincère?" (a short story) in *Les Mots,* Editions de Minuit, 1947.

Weinberg, Kurt, "Gide romancier: la sincérité truquée," *Romanische Forschungen,* 67 (1956), 274–87.

Woolf, Virginia, *A Writer's Diary,* New York, Harcourt, Brace, 1953.

Index

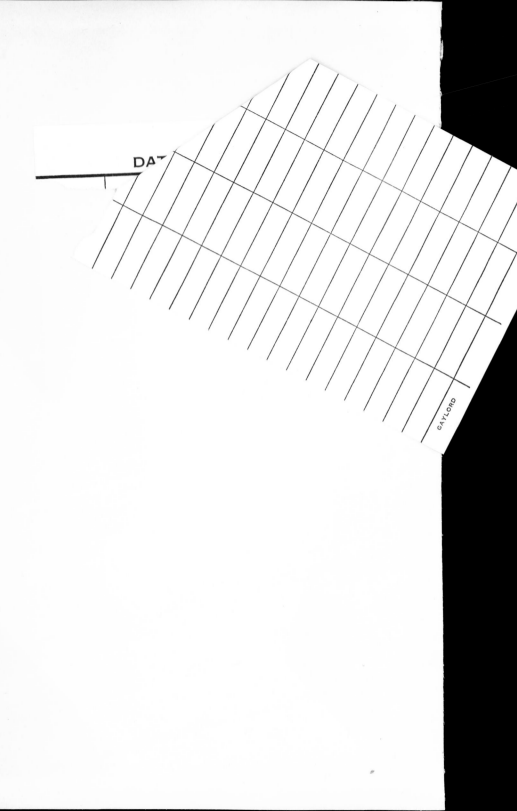

DAT

GAYLORD   PRINTED IN U.S.A.